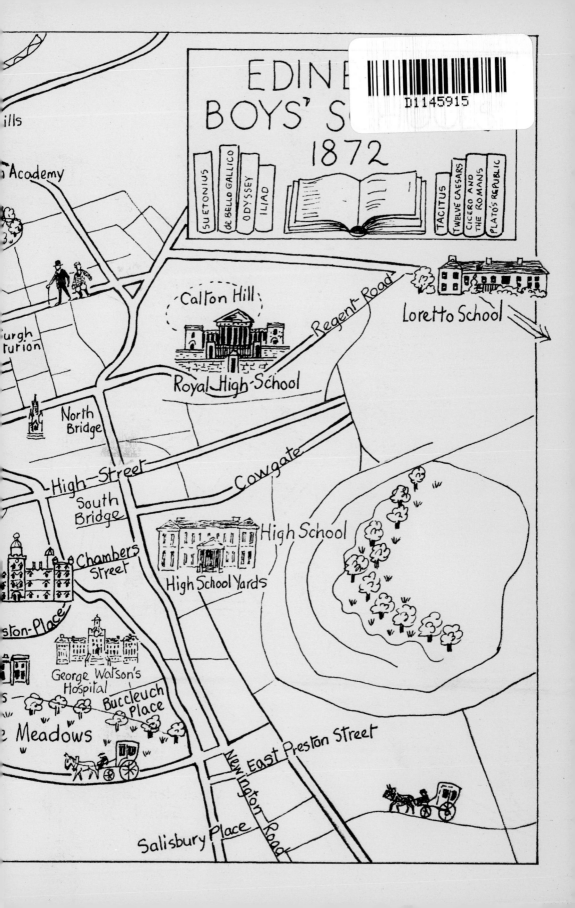

Ties that Bind

By the same author

Out to Play: the Middle Years of Childhood
Tales of the Braes of Glenlivet (ed.)
Midges
Tales of the Morar Highlands
Crème de la Crème: Girls' Schools of Edinburgh

Ties that Bind

Boys' Schools of Edinburgh

Alasdair Roberts

Steve Savage
LONDON AND EDINBURGH

Steve Savage Publishers Ltd
The Old Truman Brewery
91 Brick Lane
LONDON
E1 6QL

www.savagepublishers.com

Published in Great Britain by Steve Savage Publishers Ltd 2009

ISBN: 978-1-904246-29-9

Endpaper maps by Ann Dean

Typeset by Steve Savage Publishers
Printed and bound by The Cromwell Press Group

Acknowledgements

An aspect of the book which the author finds particularly pleasing is the pair of the endpaper maps by Ann Dean. When our collaboration on this kind of thing began, we shared the idea of a 'Milly-Molly-Mandy' map from the stories told and illustrated by Joyce Lankester Brisley. That concept may not appeal to a largely male audience of solemn maturity, but Ann's animated street-pictures are worth a thousand words. Once again thanks are due to my publisher Steve Savage for his input, both editorial and otherwise.

In the interests of accuracy, a group of readers (as in scrutineers) was recruited to keep me right, chapter by chapter, and offer suggestions. Such errors as remain are mine, but in case enraged FPs out there are reaching for their pens I will not link the reading team to schools. They are, in alphabetical order, Calder Benzies, James Rainy Brown, Alan Fyfe, June Dunford, Fraser Simm, Elizabeth Tracey. Les Howie, Brian Lockhart and Robert Philp have also written about the schools they know so well. Thanks are due to all of them, and such errors as remain are mine.

Tribute is paid in the Introduction to the large number of volumes dedicated to Edinburgh boys' schools: their authors and titles appear throughout the text. Frank Stewart's *Loretto One-Fifty: The Story of Loretto School from 1827 to 1977* may be taken as a case in point since it built on what had gone before. Most recent was the fourth *Loretto Register*, its 416 pages packed with entries on pupils. Beyond that was *Loretto's Hundred Years, 1827-1927*, beautifully illustrated by Hely Smith as shown on p.152. Still further back, just after the death of the artist's cousin, Magnus Magnusson's favourite Academy Rector R. J. Mackenzie wrote *Almond of Loretto* from the great man's papers and letters. These included manuscripts for six publications including *Sermons of a Lay Head-Master*. Loretto and its head were exceptional, but all this shows why it was not necessary to go round with a tape-recorder.

Lydia Skinner's Mary Erskine history, *A Family Unbroken*, has again proved its value in explaining how three threatened institutions came together into a form of co-education. The index of people and places is not so full as the last, being more focused on schools. Only two women appear, both involved in the move to that now generally accepted arrangement. Finally on people, help was received from Christine Allan, Robert Botcherby, David Brown, John Brown, John Davidson, Neal Clark, David McDowell, Sandy Macfarlane (again), Bruce Ritson, Dick Scott, David

Standley, Ann Thomson and Bob Young. Particular thanks are due to my brother Martin for bringing schooldays back to mind in a recent birthday tribute. The book is dedicated to him.

Acknowledgement is made of permission given to use numbered illustrations where copyright is held by existing schools: Daniel Stewart's and Melville College – 14, 17, 25, 31, 44, 53, 54, 59, 61, 68, 85, 94, 95, 96, 97, 104, 107, 112, 115, 121, 123, 128; the Edinburgh Academy – 12, 22, 47, 52, 57, 58, 69, 71, 72, 78, 86, 92, 101, 116, 124: Fettes College – 6, 7, 18, 23, 24, 29, 35, 38, 45, 46, 73, 83, 98, 100, 106, 108, 114, 129; George Heriot's School – 4, 5, 9, 39, 40, 50, 51, 56, 70, 109, 127; George Watson's College – 1, 2, 3, 10, 19, 20, 26, 27, 33, 36, 41, 42, 49, 62, 66, 75, 77, 80, 81, 82, 84, 87, 99, 105, 113, 117, 122, 126; Loretto School – 16, 21, 30, 32, 67, 74, 79, 89, 119, 120; Merchiston Castle School – 15, 48, 63, 76, 93, 102, 103; the Royal High School – 8, 13, 28, 34, 37, 43, 55, 90, 110, 111, 118. Nos. 11 and 125 were in *John Watson's School: A History* by Isobel C. Wallis, published in 1982, and thanks are due to the publisher. Every effort has been made to identify copyright for any illustration where this might apply.

Contents

To my brother Martin
who also attended that school in Edinburgh

Introduction

At the start of *Crème de la Crème: Girls' Schools of Edinburgh*, along with a certain focus on Muriel Spark and Miss Brodie there was discussion of what drew a retired teacher-trainer to the subject. It began with recollections of the 1960s, when students from northern Scotland were inclined to dismiss fee-paying schools as an 'English' thing. In fact there was no great difference between the two countries overall, but the absence of these institutions from Aberdeenshire and Orkney was offset by Edinburgh. There, in the days of my early college lecturing, no fewer than twenty-four per cent of pupils went to schools for which parents paid fees.

There were private schools in other Scottish cities (and in the country, particularly Perthshire) but Edinburgh was unique 'in Scotland, Britain, the world.' Since then I have learned that Surrey comes close. In these days the grander Edinburgh institutions were independent and expensive. The majority were grant-aided (equivalent to England's direct grant schools) with central government money putting them in reach of middle-class families. There were also local authority fee-paying schools, subsidised out of rates as well as taxes. The fees were low and pupils were selected from aspiring families where the householder (in very many cases) worked with his hands.

Since then government and local authority money has been withdrawn by stages and the number of primary school children being privately educated in what is now more evidently Scotland's capital (we have a parliament) has dropped sharply. But at secondary level the fee-paying phenomenon is much the same. The figure of very nearly twenty-four per cent persists, although fees for day pupils approach £3,000 per term. Boarding fees are almost twice as high but plenty of pupils still come to Edinburgh from elsewhere – which partly explains the high attendance. Since the great majority of boarders were boys in the Sixties, as I have recently come to realise, fee-paying was more of a male than female thing. Even now, with the financial community under pressure, one out of four teenage pupils attends a fee-paying school. Yet the subject is hardly ever discussed. The last book to be written about fee-paying in Scotland is John Highet's *A School of One's Choice*, published in 1969.

When the project began to take shape, friends advised that Edinburgh's fee-paying schools were too familiar to be of much interest; others, 'educationists' more expert in the field, warned that it was a hot potato to be avoided at all costs. It certainly has been. Ignoring both forms of advice, I became a collector of school histories and frequenter of second-hand bookshops. School magazines were used to bring things up to date. So much interesting material came to hand that what started out as a single project divided itself into girls' and boys' schools – though nowadays co-educational fee-paying schools are very much part of the story.

Something should perhaps be said about why one centre of learning and creativity does not form part of the story. The Rudolf Steiner School in Merchiston has always been co-educational, so not strictly relevant, but John Watson's School (also for both sexes) features in the buildings chapter and again at the end in 'Boys and Girls at School'. John Watson's in its last phase made strenuous and largely successful efforts to become like the boys' schools of Edinburgh, whereas the Steiner school has always been self-consciously different: the time when they thought about taking up rugby is still recalled ironically. Crushed strawberry dungarees rather than maroon blazers sums up the difference: Alexander McCall Smith has made a running joke by contrasting his non-uniform-wearing neighbourhood school with George Watson's College on the other side of Colinton Road.

The experience of bringing the youthful days of old girls back to mind was an agreeable one, but the 'yardage' of my bulging bookshelves reveals a contrast: there is much more in print about boys' schools. Boarding schools are well to the fore, with several volumes for each to celebrate formative years in residence. Former pupil memories (including auto-biographies) are not the only source. The Royal High School has produced at least four histories of Edinburgh's oldest academic institution for boys, three of them with the semi-official stamp of having been written by senior masters.

Information kept accumulating but there were gaps, so I thought of borrowing. Where better than Moray House, Edinburgh's college of education where I received my own preparation for the classroom? Moray

House is now part of Edinburgh University and the library is well equipped, but no gaps were filled. There were scarcely half a dozen books on Edinburgh's fee-paying schools at that old campus on the Royal Mile. Was that why no one had attempted an overview? Perhaps scholarship was keener elsewhere, among those academics who assisted post-graduates like myself to gain the Diploma in Education. The high university library on the south side of George Square looks across the gardens at what used to be George Watson's Ladies' College, but once again the shelves were almost bare of books on schools like that.

Links do exist between teacher education and the city's independent schools, of course. Students spend weeks at a time in them (or in those run by the local authority) for the sake of teaching practice or 'school experience'. It would be wrong to assume from the absence of books on library shelves that teacher-trainers in Edinburgh take no interest in the private sector. And in any case schools themselves must take some of the responsibility for being ignored. The history of a given institution, often produced to mark a significant date, is distributed in-house and through former pupil clubs. It does not appear in book shops. A short account of the *Schola Regia* was given to every High School leaver for a third of a century, and naturally a copy can be found in the public library's Edinburgh Room. Other school histories are missing even there, however.

School magazines now take the form of multi-coloured display, in contrast to the grey chronicles of former times. Like school histories, they are not intended as organs of self-criticism. In *Crème de la Crème* the question of objectivity was explored at the personal level, with the process of recall tending to be positive – hence the adage 'schooldays are the happiest days of your life'. Unhappy days are rarer in recollection, except among literary folk – as Frank McCourt in *Angela's Ashes* with 'Your happy childhood's hardly worth the while.' Irish-American best-sellers apart, I was thinking of a more obscure book called *Jock Tamson's Bairns: Essays on a Scots Childhood* where happy days were rare. By contrast *A Scottish Childhood*, drawing on the experience of seventy famous Scots, offered more variety than the *angst* of intellectuals.

At any rate there was a gap to be filled. Some may judge my approach too positive, based on the schools' perceptions of themselves. In fact there is plenty of negative comment in school histories, particularly boys' ones.

If anyone wishes to write a critique of these bastions of educational privilege the field is still wide open, and now there are two books to be savaged. Perhaps the old school tie evoked in this one's title will provide the necessary stimulus. Half a century has passed since I left my *alma mater* of distant recollection: author's privilege to side-step the inevitable question when Edinburgh people meet, 'Which school did you go to?' Most of that time has been spent in other places, helping to provide a certain perspective. Now I find I am neither 'for' fee-paying schools nor against them, just fascinated by a key feature of Scotland's capital city.

The presentation of *Ties that Bind* bears more than a passing resemblance to *Crème de la Crème*, not least in the endpaper maps of Ann Dean which show Edinburgh schools in 1872 (when Scotland's modern education system was legislated into being) and a hundred years later when prime time was giving way to problems. Edinburgh boys' schools have a longer history than girls' ones and the first two chapters reflect that. This book is more historical than the last, but an early focus on the Victorian base leads on to the middle third of last century as a more significant period. And some of the subject matter is thoroughly up to date.

Chapter 1 considers the question of how boarding 'Hospitals' for a few needy children were turned into enormous day schools. This happened at the expense of small private schools – long gone but interesting to know about for anyone walking these streets. Chapter 2's account of buildings places some emphasis on the High School emerging from the Old Town to a new site below the Calton Hill – the Edinburgh Academy having arisen as a classical rival in the New Town. The contribution which other boys' schools have made to the appearance of a beautiful city, Heriot's and Fettes in particular, is celebrated. Again the theme is pursued of charitable intentions for the few benefiting a remarkably broad swathe of families in Edinburgh.

Chapter 3 continues the idea of external appearances through the clothing worn to school. Uniforms originally carried an element of 'charity' stigma, so that Victorian day boys and boarders wore clothes of their parents' choice. Then uniforms became associated with school spirit, compulsory to the last detail, and formed a highly visual part of the Edinburgh streetscape. As in the girls' book the fourth chapter is about 'ethos', but with more emphasis on strictness and authority. Physical punishment was such a characteristic feature of boys' schools that in some of them prefects were licensed to beat.

The liberal education represented by classical subjects (Latin and Greek) was a strong feature of boys' schools. This gives the chapter on schoolboys at work – in the classroom and eventually the laboratory – a sense of dedication to one ideal or another, as new subjects struggled for a place. Schoolgirls 'at play' featured boyish behaviour with hockey sticks and liberation from earlier corseted times. Boys' schools which led the way into team games and competitive sport require ampler consideration. Rugby football came to distinguish the fee-paying sector, and cricket to a lesser extent. Twice as much attention to games is paid here as in the first book.

The effect of two world wars on boys' schools was very considerable but more so the first. The Great War of 1914–18 came at a time when officers' training corps were being introduced to the boys' schools of Edinburgh, and many young men died within months of leaving school. The memorials and honour lists of those killed were influential enough for entire upper schools to be attending in khaki once a week even after National Service came to an end.

As in *Crème de la Crème*, the former pupil phenomenon is discussed partly through school magazines, and it leads on to Chapter 11 which samples old boys' memories. This time the final chapter is not elegiac in the way of the last book, which kept spirits up by pointing out that – despite the loss of famous names – girls' schools still flourish in Edinburgh. Here there is hardly any cause for sadness, but something to think about in the fact that all but one of the boys' schools have become co-educational.

Chapter 1

Which School did You Go to?

Cameron Cochrane, a product of the Edinburgh Academy, became headmaster of Fettes College at a time when the school was in process of becoming fully co-educational. His sister was headmistress of St Denis, one of the city's leading girls' schools. Robert Philp's Fettes history, *A Keen Wind Blows*, presents him as a sounding-board: 'Cameron Cochrane was suffering from a severe case of "dinner table blight". The citizens of Edinburgh, with its high proportion of fee-paying schools, had long been obsessed with education… To simplify the complexities and guide one another through the maze of school choice, middle-class parents who gathered at the soirées of the New Town or the coffee mornings of the Grange exchanged stories of schools and their heads for a pastime. These crystallized into word pictures of schools which, once sanctioned by repetition, fed upon themselves.'

In *A School of One's Choice* John Highet was able to demonstrate higher demand for places at fee-paying schools after the last war than in the Twenties and Thirties. He went so far to sketch out a sociology of coffee-mornings in which the anxiety of mothers about selection (very often at age five) was a prominent feature: 'The girls are always talking about it round the coffee table. "Has … not passed his test yet?" is one of the commonest questions you hear. Tremendous tension. As for … [mentioning a girls' school], they really lose their heads and go high-hatted when their daughters get in there.' Arnold Kemp, one of Scotland's leading journalists, addressed the matter in *The Hollow Drum: Scotland Since the War*.

In the mainly industrial city of Glasgow the question 'Which school did you go to?' was about religious allegiance so that Catholics could be kept out of the better paid jobs in shipyards and elsewhere. In Edinburgh when Arnold Kemp was a boy (and hardly less so in the years that followed) the question carried even more significance because it concerned social status. Even a child knew that there was a pecking-order which reflected the level of fees charged, although the Royal High School provided very good education at very low cost. Like James Gillespie's School for Girls it was a selective local authority school. Most of the pupils came from ordinary unprivileged homes and their education was mainly financed out of rates and taxes. George Heriot's was similar in social status, but this schoolboy scrum-half (putting snobbery aside) mainly associated the school with skilful rugby players. Looking back as an adult, Kemp could not resist presenting George Watson's College in terms of the Morningside accent which expressed a somewhat prim respectability. The other Merchant Company boys' school, Daniel Stewart's, he paired in memory with Melville College as playing-field weaklings compared with Heriot's and Watson's.

Kemp's own school the Edinburgh Academy occupied a place above them all in social terms but somewhere below Fettes, Merchiston and Loretto. Most Academy pupils were day-boys, and there was a sense of not quite matching up to these three boarding-schools. His ideas on this in relation to 'Scottishness' are reserved for the second last chapter, but something may be said here about Scots Law as a major destination for Academicals. When the question arose in the swinging Sixties of placing a legal ban on an article about drug-taking, almost a dozen judges had to be rejected before one was found who had not attended the Academy.

Arnold Kemp went so far as to claim that there was an 'Academy voice' – surely no more than received pronunciation Scots, otherwise the lightly accented BBC Scottish which has found favour south of the border. At any rate he was clear that this voice was not the Morningside accent dramatised by Maggie Smith in the film of Muriel Spark's best known novel. A knock-knock joke makes the point:

Knock knock, who's there?

(In a *Prime of Miss Jean Brodie* voice):
Emma Watsonian. Who're you?

(In gruffer demotic tones):
Humphrey Heriot's.

Joking apart, the boys' schools known as Watson's and Heriot's provide a suitable entry into a serious subject. In *Crème de la Crème* one answer to the question of why Edinburgh has so many fee-paying pupils was offered in a phrase: the Merchant Company. In describing the formation

1. *The first Merchants' Hall in the Cowgate.*

of the large Merchant Company girls' schools which became familiar – from their locations – as Queen Street and George Square, I ignored the educational politics which lay behind a remarkable change of use. I wanted to press forward into the twentieth century, but here it is appropriate to dwell for a while in the past.

The High School and George Heriot's both have a longer history, but the Merchant Company story deserves to be given priority. Edinburgh's merchants sought to maintain a monopoly of local trade, but also took a broad interest in civic affairs which they largely controlled. A charter of Charles II recognising the Merchant Company's rights was ratified by the Scottish Parliament in 1693. Times were hard, and in the following year a widow called Mary Erskine donated 10,000 merks for 'burges children of the female sex', stipulating that the Merchant Maiden Hospital should be administered by the Merchant Company. Burgess children of the male sex were already being given charitable support through George Heriot's Hospital, and more was to be provided by the opening of George Watson's Hospital in 1741 – again as a Merchant Company institution.

Other hospitals followed, notably John Watson's and Daniel Stewart's in the nineteenth century. Buildings were generally of high quality, and the circumstances of those boys and girls who benefited were not always as impoverished as seemed to be required by the founder's bequest. Class distinction arose in Scotland's major city, although there had long been rural and small town schools (as envisaged by John Knox) which enabled the poor but clever 'lad o' pairts' to go to university. Hospitals were different: boarding institutions set up for the children of struggling merchants and craftsmen (sometimes orphans) in which the number of pupils rarely reached three figures. In the Victorian age opinion turned against a charitable hospital system which was believed to make its pupils lethargic and sly. A visitor to the different version which was Daniel Stewart's, ten years after it opened in 1855, made the point by contrast: 'I was struck today by again observing distinctly the frank, open look of the boys here – so unlike the old, well-known "smorrl" or *scowl* of the Hospital boys.'

There was also the question of value for money at a time when the Westminster Parliament was seeking to provide elementary schools for all children on both sides of the border. The Merchant Company had an annual income of £20,000 when the Argyll Commission on Scottish Education revealed in 1868 that Stewart's spent an annual £47 5s. per boy, Watson's £64 and the Merchant Maiden Hospital £47 per girl. *The Scotsman* newspaper offered a wider comparison: 'The sum annually expended in the Hospitals of Edinburgh is larger than the total assessment for the maintenance of the parochial schools of Scotland.'

2. Hospital 'smorrl'.

George Heriot's Hospital developed outside the Merchant Company scheme of things, and the Heriot Trust additionally set up free 'outdoor' schools in each of Edinburgh's thirteen parishes for 5,456 pupils, a fifth of whom had fathers unemployed. A link with the architectural wonder which is George Heriot's School can still be seen in a turreted building on the corner of Holyrood Road and the Pleasance. It was once the Cowgate Port School. Free schools were popular institutions (town councillors among the Heriot's governors drew support through them) but no longer necessary when the Edinburgh School Board was set up following the Education (Scotland) Act of 1872. Rates and taxes now provided elementary schools for all, but free education was not yet on offer throughout Scotland – except to the very poorest in industrial or 'ragged' schools. Thirteen years later, when the Heriot outdoor schools were on the point of being closed by Act of Parliament, 42,000 people signed a petition 'to prevent the poor of the City from being robbed and the free schools closed for the purpose of providing scholarships and bursaries for the middle and upper classes.'

The Merchant Company's response to the threat to their funds represented by the Argyll Commission was to request Simon Laurie, Secretary to the Education Committee of the Church of Scotland and an influential figure, to inspect their schools. He commented favourably on the teaching, emphasised that 'the opinion which prevails in many quarters, that they are Institutions characterised by inefficient work and filled with half-idle loafers is without foundation.' However he went on to condemn the hospital system as 'monastic' (a common charge) and recommended that there should be more free time and holidays. Senior pupils aiming at university should attend classes at the High School.

Laurie's report was used by the Merchant Company to show its willingness to reform at a time when the very considerable hospital endowments seemed likely to be redirected to wider educational ends. In France and Germany state secondary schools offered a contrast to Britain's lack of system. Faced with an Endowed Hospitals (Scotland) Bill in February 1869, an energetic group of Merchant Company members went south to lobby government ministers. By means of a redrafted 'permissive' clause, allowing them to act independently, they were able to make it different from England's Endowed Schools Bill. There was very little debate, most MPs apparently thinking this was a minor piece of legislation about Scottish medical provision.

The Merchant Company moved swiftly when its emissaries returned, and in February 1870 a meeting of its Education Committee resolved that the hospitals should be turned into day schools – provided government approval could be obtained. The George Watson's Hospital building was to be sold to the Royal Infirmary and its boarders moved into that of the Merchant Maidens off Lauriston Place – the girls to go elsewhere. The foundationers would then become fellow-pupils with day boys in a new George Watson's College. The Merchant Maidens were also to be reconstituted as a girls' day school, location un-known – nor was there any sign at this stage of premises being purch-ased out of Watson's funds for a second girls' school in George Square. The Company was eager to have the scheme in place by September, but permission still had to be sought. Much was made – through further

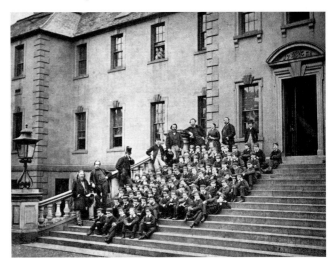

3. *George Watson's Hospital.*

lobbying in London – of the moderate fees, scholarships, bursaries and allowances which would be on offer for poor pupils 'of merit and promise' and new schools would be opened 'where they were most needed' – presumably in working-class districts. The detail of all this has been clearly presented by Les Howie in *George Watson's College: An Illustrated History*:

'They met the right people once again including Lord Advocate George Young, Henry Bruce (Home Secretary) and William Forster (Vice-President of the Committee of Council on Education). Being economical with the truth was one strategy when, for example, the politicians were assured that all the other Edinburgh institutions agreed with the Company reforms when, in fact, there was no such agreement. Buttering up the Lord Advocate by wining and dining his son was another, as was paying the Lord Advocate's Secretary £20 for his "trouble"! But the politicians were mostly impressed by the charm, knowledge, preparedness, thoroughness and determination of the Company leadership. There was no public enquiry and the Provisional Orders became law in July 1870.'

Little attention had been paid locally to what was afoot, but parents were quick to spot an opportunity when prospectuses were circulated. By the end of September 3,300 pupils were crammed into the hospital buildings, but there was no sign of the other proposed changes which had helped to persuade Westminster: 'Where was the public benefit? A storm of protest hit the Company, the press and the Government. Edinburgh's small army of private schools was the hardest hit as fees for the new Company schools were not "moderate", as promised, but downright low. To be more exact, they were high enough to exclude working-class people, but low enough to entice middle-class customers. As good businessmen the Company had simply undercut its competitors… Private schools in the southern districts, above all Newington, were devastated, schools on the north side suffered considerably and the Royal High by 1872 had lost about 100 pupils.' The High School roll now stood at 284. Three hundred teachers petitioned the Lord Advocate, but it was too late to reverse a *fait accompli*.

The 1820s interaction between the old High School and the new Edinburgh Academy which led to the erection of two fine buildings will be considered in the next chapter; likewise the Edinburgh Institution which completed a powerful trio of boys' schools on the north side of town. Here the residential/day school question which prompted the

Merchant Company to action is taken further. How did things stand with George Heriot's Hospital, on the other side of Lauriston Place from Watson's? It was the first such institution in Edinburgh and the leading one. As a show-piece building it received many visitors: Hans Andersen was delighted to find that Heriot's boys, persuaded by a porter, had been reading the books of 'Denmark's Walter Scott'. Americans were favourably impressed by the range of modern subjects. Most boys completed their four-year residence at fourteen before beginning a trade apprenticeship supported by the Heriot Trust, but there were also a few 'hopeful scholars' who stayed on longer so as to reach university.

As elsewhere, however, residence in Heriot's Hospital had come to be seen in negative terms. With 180 inmates (compared to eighty-six at Watson's and seventy-two at Stewart's) the 'dingy, low-roofed dormitories' were more crowded than elsewhere, although the health of Heriot's boys was good. Several inspections took place around this time, including one by Simon Laurie. He came down on both sides of the fence: no better hospital could be imagined but the system was fatally flawed. Daniel Fearon was less positive on behalf of the Schools Enquiry Commission when he found that attainments were below that of boys in 'a good burgh day school' – despite longer hours in

4. *Heriot's Hospital from the Castle.*

class. Fearon also reported that the pupils were 'less full of life and vigour in their studies'.

Encouraged by Merchant Company success, the Heriot governors attempted to imitate it by turning their hospital into a day school, although in the struggle which ensued there was always a commitment to poorer boys. Unfortunately for them the governors' reform proposals coincided with outrage by petitioning Edinburgh teachers, and elected representatives were already having second thoughts at Westminster. In his history of George Heriot's Hospital and School Brian Lockhart has observed that the

Merchant Company acted more promptly than the Heriot directors, but the delay which occurred was largely due to government. It took nine months for word to come back from London that it would be unlawful for Heriot's to reduce the number of residents and create a day school – this despite the fact that George Watson's had just been transformed in precisely that way.

Fifteen years of argument and delaying tactics (in what some regarded as the 'siege' of Heriot's) passed before the Hospital finally became a day school. The early argument took place before a government commission set up to investigate Scottish endowed institutions under the chairmanship of Sir Edward Colebrooke, Liberal MP for North Lanarkshire. Simon Laurie acted as secretary, and under his influence Colebrooke recommended that Heriot's should become a secondary school entered by competitive examination. The artisan emphasis, on the model of Germany's *Realschule*, would be on mathematical, scientific and practical subjects.

5. *Heriot's and the Old Town.*

The Commission conceded sixty orphan boarders but caused offence by suggesting that they might come from any part of Scotland: there seems to have been a shortage of suitable orphans in Edinburgh. Only a third of Heriot's foundationers had lost even one parent, although nearly all came from poor households living on about a pound a week.

A Heriot's Trust Defence Committee pointed out that High School fees had trebled to £12 per annum at the same time as support for the long-established 'tounis scule' from burgh funds rose from £200 to £900. The great majority of citizens, many of them poor, were subsidising the education of the better off. Against this it was claimed that the nineteenth-century occupants of the old building represented a class lower than that which George Heriot had intended to benefit. There were no longer any sons of indigent merchants whereas those of 'hammermen' were prominent. Social distinctions were constantly under debate. As the High School's rector informed the commissioners, 'there is no place on earth where to a greater extent caste prevails than in Edinburgh.'

A scheme similar to the Colebrooke proposals was finally introduced in December 1885. George Heriot's School enrolled seven hundred day boys, after two years of adapting the building while preserving its appearance. With the nearby Heriot Bridge outdoor school modified to provide technical classrooms, and foundationers boarded out or returned to their families, there was almost enough space for the new entrants. Six additional teachers were appointed to join the seven Hospital ones. Technical drawing had good facilities from the start, with laboratories and workshops added. Strong links developed with the Watt Institute and School of Arts in Chambers Street when it was taken into the control of the same governors to become Heriot-Watt College.

In this search for origins a word is due on the eighteenth-century Scottish Enlightenment. Voltaire, familiar with the *philosophes* of France and the English whose open society he admired, nevertheless said: 'We look to Scotland for all our ideas on civilization.' Although no longer enjoying the status of a capital since the 1707 Union of Parliaments, Edinburgh became a focus of intellectual endeavour. Adam Smith returned regularly from Glasgow University to talk with David Hume, James Boswell, Adam Ferguson and William Robertson. They met in High Street taverns, an English visitor observing: 'Here I stand at what is called the Cross of Edinburgh and can, in a few minutes, take fifty men of genius by the hand.' Magnus Magnusson, chronicler of the Edinburgh Academy, developed the point: 'They were a closely knit group... All were politically conservative but intellectually radical (Unionists and progressives to a man), courteous, friendly and accessible. They were stimulated by enormous curiosity, optimism about human progress and dissatisfaction with age-old theological disputes. Together they created a cultural golden age.'

In this climate the university became a power-house, its medical faculty in particular gaining worldwide renown, and from that old college there also emerged men who were well able to pass on knowledge to the young. From all over Scotland those who could afford it sent their sons to school in Edinburgh. As Alexander Law pointed out in his *Education in Edinburgh in the Eighteenth Century*, historians have tended to concentrate on schools which were in one way or another official. Statutory parish schools created by acts of the Scottish parliament led to high levels of literacy and sometimes scholarship. Burgh schools made Latin available to boys who were clever enough to benefit from the liberal education provided by four universities. Edinburgh, however, presented a much more varied range of schools than elsewhere. It increased when the New Town was built, street by geometric street, after the erection of the North Bridge in the 1760s.

A century later, at the point when the new Merchant Company day schools were about to change everything, the Edinburgh Directory of 1867–68 listed forty-two boarding and day schools and thirty-eight private schools. Some prepared boys for Latin by teaching them how to read and write in English. George Fulton conducted one of the best-known private schools in the New Town at 21 North Hanover Street. There he emphasised the sounds of letters, and many copies of his *Pronouncing Spelling Book* were bought by Edinburgh parents. George Paton opened a private academy on South Bridge after being dismissed from his post as writing-master at the old High School. It was advertised as having apartments 'more comfortable, dry and airy than the room which is there allotted to the same purpose.' Paton taught writing, arithmetic, book-keeping, geography and several branches of mathematics. Part of each day was reserved for 'Young Gentlemen of the High School'.

A forgotten curiosity known as the Scottish Naval and Military Academy was advertised at 67 South Bridge in July 1823 as 'a seminary where young gentlemen intended for the Navy, Army and the East India Company's civil and military service might obtain a systematic course of education necessary for them to qualify them for any of these departments, upon moderate terms.' In fact the fees were high at £40 a year, but parents were saved the expense of sending their sons to England. Fortification and military drawing were only two of the subjects which made this school different. Modern European languages ranked above Latin, with Persian and Hindustani also available. The school, which prepared more than a thousand boys for army careers over a 35-year period, moved to 85 George Street before taking over the Riding School in Lothian Road which became the Caledonian Station.

Canonmills House Academy has been forgotten because even the United Presbyterian Church which was built on its site in Fettes Row (at some distance from mills on the Water of Leith) is lost to modern development. It was acquired for educational purposes on the death of

Dr Patrick Neill, a noted horticulturalist who designed much of Princes Street Gardens. His own garden was renowned for exotic plants and also for a collection of 'cats, parrots, cockatoos and animals of rare stamp which were allowed full liberty in his establishment.' Canonmills House took up rugby football, and also joined with Merchiston Castle and Dreghorn College (outside Edinburgh) in a curious indoor competition called the Annual Assault which is described in Chapter 7.

The Edinburgh Collegiate School at 27–28 Charlotte Square flourished for quarter of a century at a time when the major schools were turning to sport. Collegiate teams played rugby and cricket against Merchiston and Loretto at a field next to Daniel Stewart's. Good academic standards were achieved, Dr Archibald Hamilton Bryce having been a master at the High School. Class sizes were held at thirty with promotion by ability rather than age – unlike the Edinburgh Academy. Boys who entered at age nine embarked on a course which was either classical or commercial. Book-keeping and shorthand supported a strong emphasis on English and mathematics, with a nod in the direction of modern languages. As Alexander Law put it, 'The school had very much in mind the after-school careers of its pupils.'

Circus Place School (in the north-east quadrant) was founded in the 1820s. It received boys and girls into a beginners' department of eighty pupils with 120 in more advanced classes. Essentially a preparatory school, Circus Place flourished until the major institutions began adding their own junior departments. Another enterprise lasted longer than most, a father and son taking Oliphant's School into the twentieth century. It was also in Charlotte Square at No. 23. Thomas Oliphant senior was rector of the Church of Scotland's teacher training centre in Johnston Terrace and then of the breakaway Free Church version which became Moray House. He then opened what was formally called the Charlotte Square Institution. Unusually for the time, he always tried to employ trained teachers. Once again the Institution was co-educational, at least until boys went on to higher things at eleven.

The impression of boys proceeding from one centre of learning to another is well caught in Clement Gunn's memoir *A Country Doctor*: 'At the age of five I entered on school life. St Stephen's School was the arena. This school, yet in existence, a large substantial building in St Stephen's Street (then called Brunswick Street), was surmounted by a huge open Bible wrought in stone… In 1869, when a little over the age of eight, I entered Heriot's Hospital as a boarding scholar. Two of my elder brothers had been educated there… My new schoolfellows were strong and rough; I was delicate and gently nurtured. I was homesick continually. All the masters, save one, were severe; some were brutal. The visiting masters (for writing, singing, drawing, French, and dancing) were all unmercifully teased by the boys, and suffered much. Their sufferings were, however, amply revenged upon the boys by the resident staff… Later, when a spell of ill-health supervened and I was sent home, a physician of the cold-blooded school handled me like a dying kitten and sneered: "However did *you* get into Heriot's?"'

During the fifteen-year period when the 'monastic' hospital system still represented by Heriot's was approaching its end, the Gothic pile of Fettes College stood as a new landmark on the north-west edge of the city. Destined to become a prestigious boarding-school, it might have been opened as yet another hospital like the one erected from Daniel Stewart's bequest. Sir William Fettes (a former provost) had left money for 'the maintenance, education and outfit of young people whose parents have either died without leaving sufficient funds for that purpose, or who, from innocent misfortune during their lives, are unable to give sufficient

6. *Fettes Foundation stone.*

education to their children.' The trustees nevertheless managed to devise something distinctly different from Stewart's, and within ten years twice as many fee-paying boarders were in residence as the fifty foundationers. Even these 'necessitous' boys were the sons of distressed gentry or professional men and quite different from their hospital equivalents.

Duncan McLaren, a former provost and Liberal MP for Edinburgh, had been involved in initiating the Heriot's free outdoor schools and was a long-term defender of the hospital. With specific reference to Watson's, Stewart's and Fettes, he asked: 'When is this transfer from poor to rich to stop?' McLaren went on to lead a campaign for the legality of Fettes procedures to be investigated. The House of Commons was told by him that a 'hospital was really nothing more than a public school for the poorer classes.' Hospital boys spent 140 days a year out of Heriot's, mixing regularly with non-residents and day scholars so that, in the reformed style of these latter days, it was actually less of a boarding-school than Fettes. Pressure to change direction at what became the grandest of the Edinburgh boys' schools was successfully resisted, however, and a monastic regime – truly ascetic in winter – for sons of the rich was accepted by the Educational Endowments Commission in 1885.

A common objection to Fettes arose from the fact that it was based on an English model. A member of the Edinburgh Chamber of Commerce expressed it: 'As to the education the boys in Fettes College obtained, he must say that it seemed very desirable that any education given in Edinburgh should be of a distinctly Scotch character, and that it appeared to many of them that education given on the lines of Eton or Harrow was entirely out of place…' Rugby School would have been more to the point. The reforms of Thomas Arnold there were brought to Scotland by Alexander Potts, Rugby's Sixth Form Master who became the first head of Fettes College. Eton was among England's nine leading schools subjected to the scrutiny of the Clarendon Commission, before the Taunton Commission looked at eight hundred lesser English schools supported by charitable bequests. Despite Taunton's radical proposals for using old money to create a new educational system on continental lines, the Endowed Schools Act of 1869 left the Headmaster's Conference in a position to resist further attempts at government control.

Robert Philp (on behalf of Fettes, having been a classics teacher and housemaster) shows how Edinburgh was affected: 'The English public school system was finally cleaning up its act under pressure from Clarendon and Taunton. With the rapid growth of the middle classes and the spread of

7. Edinburgh from Fettes.

railways and evangelical religion, boarding public schools were proliferating. Boys from Scotland, even, were starting to travel south to attend them. This, thought the Fettes Trustees, was where the need lay in Edinburgh. Edinburgh's golden age between 1820 and 1835 had brought new schools in the shape of the Edinburgh Academy, Merchiston Castle and (at Musselburgh) Loretto, but the Academy was a day school and Loretto was a preparatory school until it was bought by H. H. Almond in 1862. Merchiston was a small private school until it expanded in 1863… The [Fettes] Trustees now decided that the professional classes were under-catered for, and arrived at the concept of "a public school with a charitable foundation as its basis, but with a large superstructure of education and pupils, in which there is nothing either of charity or gratuity". Fettes foundationers were expected to bring their own 'outfit' of clothing and other necessities. Meanwhile Merchiston and Loretto (to be approached through their buildings in the next chapter) contrived to flourish as private schools without income from endowment. Most pupils at all three boarding-schools remained Scottish, but common policies of recruiting staff from Oxford and Cambridge represented a clear anglicising tendency – for better or worse – in those schools which charged the highest fees.

The struggle over Heriot's was matched by the uproar over Fettes. Both are featured in Robert Anderson's widely-praised *Education and Opportunity in Victorian Scotland*. As with Highet there is value in having these matters placed within a wider Scottish context, and Anderson was well placed to recognise what was distinctive about Edinburgh. The range of schools was remarkable as the city had long been a focus for pupils who arrived from all parts of Britain and beyond. All Scotland's towns had a burgh school offering more than one kind of course, but in the case of Edinburgh it became possible for the High School to concentrate on classical studies. Civic pride was taken in the fact the scholars represented a broad spectrum of social classes. *Schola Regia* receives its due in the next chapter, where a rivalry of buildings is associated with wider social concerns.

Anderson added analysis to the issues touched on here. The Merchant Company boys' schools were deliberately put on an unequal footing, with Watson's fees higher than those of Stewart's, but they soon became indistinguishable except as to size (Watson's much the larger institution) with classical and commercial sides at both and parents charged the same moderate fees. Anderson observed that whereas Watson's had long been recognised as a school for the sons of merchants, so that the day school which emerged was more or less in line with the founder's intentions, Daniel Stewart's bequest to families in real need was recent enough for the post-hospital development to represent 'a very clear diversion of resources towards the middle class'. Inspired as it was by George Davies' account of Scotland's Victorian universities, *The Democratic Intellect*, Anderson's book is interesting about entry to Edinburgh University where, unlike elsewhere, schools attended were on record. Fully a third of the students came from city schools. In 1870 the names of these were various, but by the turn of the century a clear majority of boys for whom fees were still being paid (free education to the leaving age having been introduced a decade earlier) attended large day schools created out of former hospitals – Watson's, Stewart's and Heriot's.

Chapter 2

Boys' School Buildings

In *A School of One's Choice*, John Highet drew attention to 'the relative opulence of the city's fee-paying accommodation' in comparison with the ordinary schools of Edinburgh. Part of that was about playing-fields, laboratories and other marks of more generous funding, but opulent accommodation also had an architectural aspect. Returning to the subject of school buildings after *Crème de la Crème*, I realized that girls were the poor relations. No school was built with their education specifically in mind until 1890, at which point – as if to make up for lost time – two identical ones were opened in Newington and Morningside, both called St Margaret's although one became St Hilary's. Linked to this lack of purposeful building, a major theme for the girls was mobility. During Queen Victoria's reign 'dining-room table' schools moved from house to house in the New Town; much later the 'Great Trek' took Mary Erskine's from Queen Street out to Ravelston. By contrast the boys' schools of Edinburgh tended to stay put for long periods, and they did so in fine buildings which still enhance the city's appearance.

The High School provides an obvious starting-point. For centuries, coming out of medieval times, it was the principal place for serious learning below the level of the town's college, although lesser Latin grammar schools catered for the Canongate and Leith. There was a 'waist and falled down' building at Kirk o' Field which gave way to something better off the Cowgate in 1578. Raised in the grounds of the former Blackfriars monastery, it was solid enough to survive two hundred years in the High School Yards. Twenty years after the erection of this 'Tounis Scule' the Council decreed that 'ilk ane of the four regentis sall teach their class in several howssis [separate classrooms] and to this effect the Hie Scole sall be devydit in four howssis by three parpennis [partitions].' The school had previously accommodated everybody in one large schoolroom, as happened elsewhere, and the masters known as regents represented a new system.

Following the 1707 Act of Union the number of boys in attendance fell, and the Rector was soon noting that among his pupils there were 'scarce any of the nobility and very few of the gentry of the country residing in Edinburgh, and the youth who attend my instruction are almost altogether the children of burgesses.' Later in the century prosperity had the effect of increasing the number of landed families with town houses, and well-known Scottish names appeared again in High School records. Of course burgesses – merchants and craftsmen organised into guilds – considered themselves a cut above their fellow citizens. Sometimes the resentment of the majority found expression in riots, for Edinburgh had the reputation of being a violent city.

The High School premises continued in use for longer than might have been expected, but the rising population of Auld Reekie eventually led to overcrowding in a worn out building. By 1775 the need for a new one was

8. *Building again at High School Yards.*

apparent, and public subscription (along with annual Shakespeare performances) raised money well beyond the level of the Council's grant. A new school was raised on the old site by pulling down two class-rooms and creating extra space at right angles. The ground floor contained a Great Hall with library and writing-room off it, and above there were five classrooms reached by outside staircases. The portico added dignity to a building which is still in use, most recently by Edinburgh University's Department of Archaeology. Two years later the *Caledonian Mercury* enthused over these 'spacious lofty apartments for the accommodation of so very promising a race of young gentlemen.' There were 350 of them, comfortably assembled, when the Earl of Buchan delivered a Latin oration in the new hall.

It was James VI who first described the High School as *Schola Regia*, hence the Royal High School it later became. But the jewel in Edinburgh's scholastic crown lay elsewhere. It resulted from Jamie the Saxt's departure to London in 1603, where he became King James I of England, Wales and Ireland. George Heriot's School was closely associated with royalty, the goldsmith who founded it growing rich through the Queen's love of jewellery. 'Jinglin' Geordie' became even wealthier in London, where costly commissions were sent to his house in the Strand. He died a childless widower in 1624 leaving the vast sum of £50,000 – sterling, not Scots pounds. As a resident in the English capital George Heriot was impressed by Christ's Hospital for orphans, known as the Bluecoat School, and planned a Scottish version of this charitable institution 'for the public weill and ornament of the said burgh of Edinburgh'.

The building did become a civic ornament, but many years went by before pupils were admitted. Forty masons at a time carried the work forward with the help of wrights, barrowmen and labourers. The site was an open one beyond Greyfriars kirk yard, and the new structure faced the town with its back to the Meadows. The royal master-mason William Wallace, who designed it, died while the 'wark' was in progress. After several decades of the seventeenth century – the invading Oliver Cromwell housed his sick and wounded there – the school opened in 1659. Anne of Denmark (James's jewel-loving consort) comes into the Heriot's story again since the plans were partly based on the palaces of her native land. Other cosmopolitan influences derived from the sixteenth-century pattern-books of Sebastiano Serlio, an Italian painter and architect whose designs were followed at Fontainebleau in France. Heriot's historian Brian Lockhart has all this at his fingertips. He describes how four ranges of building were created to enclose a central quadrangle in what was the first fully regular design in the country. Square towers at each corner took it a storey higher with spiral staircases in the manner of an old Scottish keep or towerhouse. The two-storey classical entrance facing the town across the Grassmarket was and remains the building's finest feature.

The interior has also been lovingly charted with its through-going rooms in traditional style, but here it is enough to say that George Heriot's Hospital was

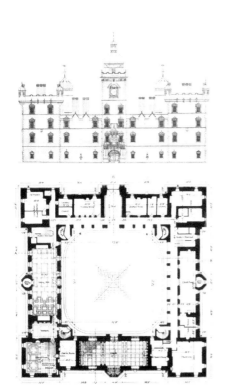

9. *Heriot's – a planned hospital.*

Scotland's finest architectural achievement of the seventeenth century. As such it influenced buildings to come and encouraged the spread of 'hospitals' (in the Scottish sense) as a feature of Edinburgh life. The Adams brothers paid tribute to it during the Age of Enlightenment, when a high standard of building was maintained in the New Town. As to management, Heriot's Hospital came under the control of the Town Council almost as fully as the High School and some pupils went from one to the other. Ministers of the city kirks were also involved.

What kind of boys were accepted for George Heriot's 'pauper palace', as critics dubbed it? The intended roll of twenty-four boys rose quickly to forty-three, making selection necessary. The doors were originally opened to 'poor fatherless boys, friemen's sons', as well as others from burgess families lacking a mother or merely hard-pressed by the number of mouths to feed. The Blue Coat example was being followed – more or less – according to the founder's intentions. But a Town Councillor's son was admitted early and soon the majority of foundationers had fathers in life. Whatever their home circumstances, however, all pupils looked up to the statue of George Heriot which was garlanded with flowers on Founder's Day.

George Watson lost his father as a child and was brought up by an aunt. Of merchant stock, he proceeded from apprenticeship to work in Holland where he learned the best book-keeping practices of the day: Watson was an accountant before that occupation became common in Edinburgh. He also lent money and invested it with care, preferring the new Bank of Scotland to the Darien Scheme for trading through a colony in Panama which brought many Scots to ruin. George Watson was never a member of the Merchant Company but he admired Mary Erskine – who followed Jinglin' Geordie's example by offering funds to the Merchant Company for the daughters of its financially embarrassed members. Intending the same for their sons, Watson bequeathed most of 'the great wealth which he had not inherited from his parents but had won, though the grace of God, by his own integrity and perseverance ... for the benefit of the needy sons of the aforesaid Merchant Company whom he, a bachelor and without offspring, wished to be adopted as his own.' When Watson died in 1723 his bequest was in excess of £12,000 sterling. As the school's latest historian has observed, 'he was buying a kind of immortality.'

The rivalry between the boys of George Heriot's and George Watson's has been a marked feature of Edinburgh school life, and its origins lay in a time when the buildings were on opposite sides of the road. A closer rivalry might have developed with the High School, for the original site of Watson's (with land purchased) was intended to be at neighbouring Thomson's Yards. Years passed, with George Watson's money gathering interest, before a decision was reached to build outside the city walls at Heriot's Croft. One of the reasons for buying this piece of land on the edge of the Meadows was to avoid the bad example of university students – to which High School boys were inevitably exposed.

Part of the George Watson's Hospital building survived into the twenty-first century in the western block of what was until recently the Royal Infirmary on Lauriston Place. Railings there evoke a time when those of Heriot's Hospital replaced the city wall. In these days 'the universal architect of his country' was William Adam whose sons Robert and James

10. *Watson's – Queen of the Meadows.*

were to achieve still wider fame. Despite the distinction of this architect there were difficulties over the roof, and the interior was reported as damp when the Hospital opened in 1741. An incompetent craftsman had nailed down slates which did not overlap, so that twelve years later they had to be stripped and put to rights.

Eleven boys aged between nine and ten were the first to be admitted. Those fortunate enough to be accepted became the Merchant Company's responsibility until the age of twenty-five, having been apprenticed to some occupation in most cases. Numbers rose until a peak of eighty-six foundationers were receiving these benefits in the 1840s. Extensions to the rear of what was mainly a three-storey building – the central section with its stone stairway to the main entrance rose one storey higher – became necessary. Always a humble building compared with Heriot's, George Watson's Hospital was recognised by its own governors as less than ideal: 'Dining and School Rooms … are finished in the very plainest manner and in winter more especially exhibit a most cold and comfortless appearance.' But prudent financial considerations always prevented a change to anything better.

John Watson's Hospital deserves a place among the boys' schools of Edinburgh although it was always run on co-educational lines. In William Burn it shared an architect with the Merchant Maiden Hospital (occupied for many years by George Watson's) and the Edinburgh Academy. John Watson who died in 1762 was an Edinburgh lawyer, which explains why his bequest and the school which eventually resulted from it were managed by Writers to the Signet. As elsewhere, it was soon catering for children well above the social level of the founder's intentions. What he actually had in mind was the prevention of 'child-murder': John Watson may have been affected by the trial out of which Scott created Effie Deans in *Heart of Midlothian*. By the time practical decisions were being made half a century after his death, however, public opinion had turned against the idea of a 'Hospital within the City of Edinburgh for receiving secretly infant Children … and Women big with Child and assisting them in their delivery so as to conceal their shame and take care of their Children as Foundlings.'

11. *John Watson's Hospital.*

An 1822 Act of Parliament was required to redirect the bequest – which had increased fiftyfold from John Watson's original £2,000 – to a Hospital for Destitute Children. Despite increase through investment over many years, the money was barely sufficient for all that had to be done. A site on the Dean estate was acquired at reasonable cost but William Burn had to fight for his wide three-storey building and compromise on the size of classrooms. Burn's Greek revival design with pillared portico out front was accepted at last, and his achievement (now a gallery of modern art) has stood the test of time:

'The exterior of the main building, although weathered by wind and rain and sun, remained otherwise as it had been on the day that the first foundationers clambered up its steps, walked across its porch and stepped into the Entrance Hall. Austere and grey even in sunlight, its classically symmetrical façade looked uncompromisingly across the park, across the road to that more elaborate building that had been the Orphan Hospital.' This almost-matching institution was built soon after John Watson's received its first pupils in 1828 and continued as a charitable hospital until the reform of endowments described in the previous chapter. Fee-paying boarders were admitted in the following century, and then day boys and girls who came to outnumber the rest. Two more Edinburgh hospital schools remain to be considered, but here it is appropriate to follow architect William Burn to his other site at Canonmills.

The 'Academy Scheme' for a classical school in the New Town, put together by interested citizens who lived there, prompted the Town Council to act. Everyone agreed that something had to be done about the situation at High School Yards, when in 1820 the Rector's pre-university class reached a peak of 257. The 890-pupil roll was swollen by scholars from England and overseas, so great was the school's reputation. Some boys walked daily across the North Bridge from homes beyond Princes Street, but others attended private schools more convenient to their homes. In negotiations between the Council and lobbyists for a new 'academy' the decision came down to either providing one larger High School at the foot of the Mound or creating a second one further north. Cost was a key consideration, with £8,000 the limit envisaged. Once again the architect was persuaded to lower his sights. For a while it looked as if public money would be provided for a new classical school, but the Council reversed its decision in April 1823. In response Sir Walter Scott chaired an Academy Scheme meeting in the Waterloo Hotel. It approved the building of a major private school, funded by shareholders and managed by directors.

The site chosen was beyond the northern limits of the city and had already been criticised. The Water of Leith might prove dangerous to pupils, and busy streets would have to be crossed going to and from the school. There were industrial smells from a tannery and a brewery (although red-tiled cottages suggested a country district) but meanwhile Saxe-Coburg Street was advancing in splendour. Matters went ahead with remarkable speed and efficiency. Records survive of the detailed attention paid to every piece of stone and slate, the thickness of every window frame and wooden privy seat being determined in advance. A dry summer allowed the interior plaster to dry in classrooms and hall in time for the opening day. Difficulty in obtaining hard enough stone from Fife meant that the portico was not erected until midway through the first session to complete William Burn's design. On 1 October 1824, 372 boys entered

12. *The Edinburgh Academy.*

the new building in what had still to be named Henderson Row. Fees, though kept as low as possible, exceeded those of the High School by forty per cent.

Enrolment at the Academy was hotly debated, and 'A Plebeian' expressed the feelings of many in a letter to *The Scotsman*: 'However manly and liberal may be the opinion of many encouragers of the novel scheme, I am sufficiently uncharitable to suspect that it derives a very powerful support from the aristocratic feelings of the papas and the mamas whose hearts sicken at the thought of Master Tommy being obliged to trudge through dirty streets jostled by all sorts of low and crude people; triumphed over in school by the son of the shoemaker and beaten when out of it by the son of the butcher, and associating with vulgar companions.' Others argued by contrast for a new kind of education which would match that of the leading English schools, giving access to a wider range of careers. Taking both sides of the argument into consideration, Academy chronicler Magnus Magnusson conceded that the Edinburgh Academy was distinctly different from the relatively classless High School and socially divisive from the start.

Controversy also raged over the Town Council's decision to build a new school away from High School Yards for fear of the Academy's effect on the old one. High School masters who lost income from pupils' fees might sue them. The Calton Hill site (following the rejection of a relatively cramped one at St Andrew Square which became the headquarters of the Royal Bank of Scotland) was regarded as too exposed to the elements and dangerous to boys. But the Council owned it, and on 25 June 1825 the Lord Provost led a procession of civic dignitaries and leading citizens to lay a foundation stone 'with Masonic honours'. The architect Thomas Hamilton was the son of a New Town builder and a former pupil of the school. Despite the Council having balked at much smaller sums,

13. *The High School at Regent Road.*

costs rose from the £16,590 estimate to £33,970 3s. 9d. during the four years it took to carry through the project. Some of the criticism was diverted by selling the old school and taking in public subscriptions which included one from George IV.

The ground had to be flattened and hard stone from the Craigleith quarry polished (softer Arbroath stone at the entrance was replaced after twelve years of trudging feet) but gradually the new High School took shape. From Magnusson's perspective, its classical lines were specifically intended to put the Academy in the shade. When a copy of the Parthenon was attempted on the hill above, picturesque though incomplete, it became natural to describe Edinburgh as the Athens of the North. Smaller temples or lodges at the east and west ends of the High School completed the effect. Hamilton's achievement was linked, in the opinion of Alexander 'Greek' Thomson of Glasgow, with St George's Hall in Liverpool as 'unquestionably the two finest buildings in the kingdom'. A second procession from old to new, this time including the masters and pupils, was led by a military band. Fewer than sixty pupils were lost to the Academy, which recruited rather from 'private seminaries'.

Some of these have been discussed. In general private schools were in premises designed for different purposes though often grand enough. When the High School Yards ceased to echo to the sound of boys at play, a new school promptly opened at 1 Buccleuch Place: 'It was a peculiarity of the Southern Academy that it was the first seminary in which private teachers combined, on their own responsibility, and without the aid of any proprietary board, to afford under one roof instruction in all the branches of a liberal education. This formed a new epoch in the educational history of the city.' It offered a mainly classical curriculum and flourished for quarter of a century. Other schools came and went on the same side of town. Newington Academy educated older boys in adjoining houses at 41 and 43 Newington Road, and girls – along with small boys – were round the corner in Salisbury Place. The Longacre Hospital for Incurables moved in later. Robertson's Academy in East Preston Street was also a striking edifice with Gothic windows and a belfry.

Hamilton Place Academy was accommodated at Numbers 10 and 11, 'three-storeyed houses with areas' (or basements with windows on to the street) round the corner from Henderson Row in Stockbridge. It was owned by James McLaren who not only taught his classical pupils Latin but also Greek. Girls were present throughout the school, though not for ancient languages. The fourth English class consisted of boys and girls who included geography in their studies, 'one young lady, in particular, showing a most marvellous acquaintance with the last mentioned department by taking a voyage round the world and enumerating all the British possessions in little over five minutes.' Thus a press report on the annual prize-giving which was used for public display and advertising.

'The Edinburgh Institution of Languages, Mathematics, etc.' became a serious rival to the classical schools because of its emphasis on modern subjects, especially science. It was aimed at twelve-year-olds (often

14. *Inside the Edinburgh Institution.*

attending the High School or Academy) whose parents saw them as destined for business rather than university. When Robert Cunningham gave up his post at George Watson's Hospital he leased rooms at 3 Hill Street, below George Street, and prospered. Four years later in 1836 he had 241 boys, including some as young as seven, and No. 5 was added as the school continued to grow. In 1853 the Institution took over 8 Queen Street with its three storeys and a basement. A fourth storey and gym extension were added later. This Adam building was dignified by a wide hall. On the first floor what is now the council room for the College of Physicians has had its stuccoed ceiling restored in fine style, but 'each room had an atmosphere of its own... Upstairs there was the long Writing Room, presided over by the pleasant and ingenious Mr Happer; next door there was "Geordie" Whyte of upright mien, and above were the Lecture Room and the Top Room... If one secured a certain coveted seat a scene was visible out of the window the like of which may not be equalled the length and breadth of the Lothians.' Institution boys climbed ninety steps to a laboratory which was Edinburgh's first for school use. Looking down, they might see 'a black gown swirl round a corner, far below, and a mortarboard on the head of "The Beak".'

The end of the Great War brought a move to Melville Street, where suitable accommodation became available when St George's girls left their four linked houses for pastures new. 'Stution pupils had come from all directions to Queen Street, and confidence was now placed in electric trams and steam trains converging on the West End. One head contrasted the premises with modern ones: 'In his opinion, the spirit of a school hung about the old building, and was apt to disappear with the advent of germ-proof, white-tiled corridors. In the Institution, although they were continually making alterations to the buildings, they had tried to give the

School a very definite character, so that the boys would remember the place throughout their lives.' They had every opportunity to do so. Uniquely among Edinburgh boys' schools the junior and senior departments were housed together and some pupils entered the same Melville Street door (porch added, since removed) from five to eighteen. Institutions having lost their former prestige, the name Melville College was adopted in 1936.

Merchiston Castle Academy, as it was first called in 1833, was unusual in receiving its mainly boarding pupils into an ancient Scottish tower-house. John Napier, the inventor of logarithms, lived there in the seventeenth century and the rural setting had hardly changed: 'At that time the southern boundary of the city of Edinburgh lay no farther out than Tollcross, and Merchiston Tower stood in open country. To the north were farm fields running down to the canal half a mile distant; to the south an uninterrupted view of the Braids; and to the west, a few hundred yards away, two farms called the Grange and Myreside...' Shortly after the Napier family's house became a school an extension consisting of basement and two storeys (still castellated) was added to the south front.

15. *Merchiston Castle.*

A negative verdict was returned by Lord Cockburn, High School boy and one of the Academy founders: 'Merchiston Castle has been greatly injured by a recent and discordant front.' Its former appearance is now restored within Napier University. The building accommodated about eighty boys, and other houses were acquired as the roll rose gradually to 180 by the time the city was abandoned in 1930. Colinton House, built for an Edinburgh banker near the ruins of another castle, still serves (mainly for science) alongside the rest of Merchiston Castle School which looks out on to broad acres given over to sport.

In 1827 the Rev. Thomas Langhorne leased Loretto House, 'a fine example of eighteenth century architecture' six miles from the city centre at Musselburgh. The first pupils included the sons of Episcopalian gentry from as far away as Ross-shire and Argyll, numbers limited to fifty by the size of the house. The school spread physically (rather than merely growing) under fitness fanatic Hely Hutchinson Almond, starting appropriately with the 'Gymmy'. Godliness was next to healthiness, with a 'Tin Tabernacle' or chapel added: 'When it came to building, Arnold was never con-

16. *School House, Loretto.*

cerned with architectural finesse. All he was interested in was the practical use to which the building could be put, and if this could be achieved simply – and cheaply – so much the better… He walked outside and drew a line in the gravel with the toe of his shoe. "I want it here," he said, and there it was built. He allowed one concession to artistic sentiment, however; it was rough-cast to match the rest of the building.' The school presents an interestingly scattered appearance unified by yellow walls: 'To some it is an attractive colour which enhances the buildings, especially when after rain it assumes the rich orange hue employed throughout the fine buildings of Rome… The original yellow-wash mixture has proved to be ineradicable.' Shortly after Almond's death the distinguished architect Robert Lorimer began to be engaged on a regular basis to improve the design of several buildings. Grandeur was added in mid-twentieth century when Pinkie House (of the painted ceiling) became part of Loretto across the A1. A tunnel under the road safeguards young lives, and at the other end of the policies there is a footbridge across the River Esk to the Junior School known as the Nippers.

Daniel Stewart, who died a bachelor in 1814, held the not especially lucrative post of Macer to the Court of Exchequer. His wealth, carefully invested over the years, came rather from going to India in his twenties as valet to a master who died there. Typical

17. *Daniel Stewart's Hospital.*

of other Scottish hospital projects, there was a 41-year interval between the benefactor's death and the admission of pupils. The instruction in Daniel Stewart's will had been that his generosity towards 'needy' boys should not be put into effect until the money available reached £40,000. The hospital was destined to pass into the care of the Merchant Company five years after it opened. As the time for action approached, however, it came to be felt that there were not enough boys in Edinburgh from needy – but respectable – homes to justify another hospital. It was only the veto of the Lord Advocate in London which prevented Daniel Stewart's bequest going instead to a home for incurables. Of the first fifty foundationers at least thirty-four had lost their fathers. Most of these were labourers or artisans, but inevitably when Daniel Stewart's renamed Institution grew larger as a day school after the reform of endowments (and with leaflets circulated to ten-pound householders) the fathers were usually found in white collar occupations as merchants, clerks and commercial travellers.

On the question of architectural influence, William Playfair's neo-classical pre-eminence had found expression four years before in 1851 across the hill in Donaldson's Hospital for the Deaf, which Queen Victoria is said to have resented for outclassing some of her palaces. The architect chosen for Daniel Stewart's Hospital was David Rhind whose reputation was based on the Commercial Bank in George Street. When the trustees asked for a choice of designs in three styles, Rhind offered Gothic, Italian and Elizabethan. The third of these (otherwise 'flamboyant Scottish Jacobean') won approval. It was a reduced version of what had come second in a competition for the Houses of Parliament. Two gatehouses shielded the entrance to what was then an unroofed courtyard, and the effect of its *fouillis de tours et de tourelles* was enough to inspire verse from château-loving Henri Meslier on a visit to Edinburgh.

The erection of one more nineteenth-century school remains to be discussed. Fettes College was built from the fortune of a wholesale grocer who obtained the contract for provisioning Scottish army camps just as the Napoleonic Wars were beginning in earnest. William Fettes prospered further through banking, properties and estates, including one to the north of Comely Bank where the school which bears his name arose. Master of the Merchant Company and Lord Provost on two occasions, he was knighted for public services which included the opening of soup kitchens when there were food riots in other cities. Sir William's wife died three weeks before him in 1836, and there were no surviving children. The £166,000 left for the education of children in needy circumstances had increased threefold by the time it was put to work. With the hospital system now generally discredited, a compromise was suggested of matching fifty boarding foundationers with fifty day boys. However the

18. *Fettes College.*

site was too far out for many to walk to it and the decision was made to accept an unspecified number of fee-paying boarders.

The architect should have been Playfair, but when he died the appointment went to his rival David Bryce. In the words of Robert Philp, 'Bryce, designer of many Edinburgh banks, the Royal Infirmary and around 150 country houses, was a very different prospect from Playfair. To choose him was to choose intricacy, flamboyance, prodigality. He built to be noticed, and the site offered him by the Trustees was wonderfully conspicuous, dominating the north-western vista from the New Town… Synthesising the Scottish Baronial style with the French Gothic of the Loire valley, he created his masterpiece on this site. It was to be a unique and astonishing building, but the extravagance of the external ornament, the gargoyles, the bartizans, the gilded ironwork and the crockets and pinnacles of the traceried gablets helped to drain the Fettes coffers.' That was partly why there was to be such a heavy dependence on fees which, even at the start, were higher than intended. A fashionable crowd of Edinburgh citizens gathered when the foundation stone was laid in the summer of 1864, and Fettes College was six years in the making. Architectural historian Charles McKean regards it as 'undeniably one of Scotland's greatest buildings.' It should be noted that there was plenty of room on the considerable Fettes estate for large residential houses to be built as soon as the first fee-paying pupils were enrolled, foundationers being accommodated in the main building otherwise School House.

George Watson's College carries the construction story into the twentieth century. After the Watson's Hospital premises were exchanged for those vacated by the Merchant Maidens at Archibald Place, Thomas Hamilton's building of 1818 was expanded to provide for eight hundred day boys. Behind the main block which looked on to the Meadows a hall was soon added, but twenty years went by before new wings arose surmounted by ornamental towers. The college acquired a gymnasium and the crumbling main entrance stair was rebuilt in granite. Meanwhile 'a gaunt, unlovely building of four storeys high' served as an elementary school which boys entered at the age of five. Aesthetically speaking the Archibald Place premises of George Watson's College once again offered no sort of challenge to Heriot's, but former pupils mourned its passing when, after purchasing the site, the Royal Infirmary razed every stone to the ground.

That took place after a new George Watson's College was inaugurated in 1932. Before ending the chapter with that major project, it is worth noting that other day schools added elementary departments about this time – to say nothing of preparatory boarding institutions like Cargilfield House in Trinity. The New School for Heriot's youngsters, though dignified by a pillared entrance, was otherwise a plain building of the thirties. The same could be said of the Royal High although its new Preparatory School acquired a clock tower as well as a portico. From his High School classroom at Regent Road William Ross wrote: 'It is the painful duty of the historian to record that during the years 1921–30 the playground was defaced by wooden huts in which some of the Preparatory and Junior School classes were housed, to the manifest discomfort of themselves and their teachers... We suffered, by no means in silence, while the quest for a site went on. The ultimate choice was exceedingly happy. The authorities acquired the portion of ground lying to the east of our Memorial Field at Jock's Lodge, and there erected a building on the most modern lines.'

The departure of George Watson's from Archibald Place arose partly from a wish to be closer to the college's playing field at Myreside. Merchiston Castle School were looking for a move, and it was on their playing-field that the new George Watson's College took shape. Money was in short supply during a period of recession ('economy' the watchword) but architect James Dunn's plan was in a 'simple, direct and masterly style'. He died soon after work began, to be succeeded by his son and a partner. There had been some resistance to the move among older Watsonians and the recently erected war memorial was transported from Archibald Place with their sensibilities in mind. The main building at Colinton Road took the form of long corridors on two floors with classrooms facing south to the sun. An entrance hall and assembly hall gave added dignity, although no attempt was made 'to imitate a temple or Gothic cathedral.' Instead everything was self-consciously modern, from automatic period bells to filtered swimming pool. The new College represented 'a revolution in architectural method and purpose'.

Chapter 3

Caps, Blazers and Shorts

A chapter on school uniforms in Edinburgh should perhaps begin with the London Bluecoat School which was the inspiration for George Heriot's Hospital. Dark blue cassocks were worn with a white clerical stock at the neck when these boys walked out in the neighbourhood of Newgate – the charity at Christ's Hospital being directed largely to the orphaned sons of Protestant clergymen. Unbuttoned up to the waist, however, they showed off knee breeches and yellow stockings. Other Bluecoat schools were opened in different parts of England but the original, which moved to spacious grounds in Sussex at the start of last century, is alone in maintaining Tudor dress. For the Edinburgh foundation envisaged in the goldsmith's will it was laid down that scholars were to be clothed in 'sad russett cloathe doublettis, breikis and stockingsis or hose and gowns of the same colour, with black hattis and stringis.' Here 'sad' is merely a Scots word meaning firm but – by way of contrast – it may be presumed that High School boys of a later Georgian age were glad to sport jackets and waistcoats of blue, green and scarlet.

19. *Heriot's Hospital boy.*

The public liked to see the Heriot's boys in uniform as they marched to Greyfriars Kirk on Sundays, although concern was expressed about the appearance of shoes ruined from kicking balls indoors and out. Eventually it became possible to supply two suits per annum, and of better cloth, instead of the three suits over two years provided at the start. When regulations came to be laid down for John Watson's Hospital, metal buttons were obtained from a Sheffield firm on the same terms as those afforded to Heriot's. An illustrated collection of Edinburgh characters shows a Heriot's boy generously supplied with jacket and waistcoat buttons. The russet colour of these upper garments (trousers grey, shoes black) is a paler version of the maroon now associated with George Watson's College – the French *marron* for chestnut making the link. Hospital boys of Heriot's and Watson's wore broad-topped woollen caps with shiny peaks. Watson's leavers were photographed individually – indoors and bare-headed – to register the fact that they were by this time regularly passing the University's entrance exams. But the 'livery' had become (in Les Howie's words) 'a mark of shameful charity and the crushing of individuality'.

Robert Gibson who entered George Watson's Hospital in 1864 recorded the start of the process: 'After the bath we discarded our own clothes and donned the George Watson's livery, viz. flannel undershirt and drawers, woollen socks, white shirt with unstarched collar, black and white woollen tie, long grey tweed pants with coat and vest to match, dark, almost black peaked cap, and good strong leather boots. On each article your number was stamped. The clothing contractors brought the goods in bulk, and each boy picked out a size suitable for him. Any little alteration was done by the tailors, who came on Saturdays to mend or alter: but we were all expected to sew our own buttons on, while the servants darned our socks when necessary.' Gibson, who kept photographs of hospital boys senior to himself, became an emblem of the new George Watson's College in a double-breasted suit, wing collar and bowler hat. This became the preferred headgear of the Classical VI.

20. *Watson's College boy.*

When the hospital boys who benefited from the charity of George Watson moved into the Merchant Maiden premises in 1871, there to lose all prominence among eight hundred new fee-payers, there was a natural prejudice against uniform: 'We wore long stockings with tight garters above the knee, and our short breeks were puckered with another elastic round the knee. Some fellows appeared in Norfolk suits complete with belts, and a cap to match… A Glengarry or Balmoral hat was also much used.' In general boys went to school in clothing and head gear of the parents' choice, but never more so than in the case of former hospitals.

The Edinburgh Academy demanded nothing by way of uniform for pupils when it opened in 1824, nor did that alter during most of the century. However an illuminating exchange took place some forty years on when a parent persisted in sending his son to school wearing a pork-pie hat. Rector 'Goudie' Hodson's brother had personally shot the sons of a Delhi Mogul during the Indian Mutiny, and the schoolmaster was not one for backing down in face of rebellion. A letter went out to the father: 'He is the only boy in the School who has not at once attended to my speaking to him about wearing a Cap of some sort which has been the *custom* of the Academy from the first, even if not a "rule".' The matter was taken up with the Rev. Dr Hodson's Directors and the Rector defended his position: 'I found in the Rules (or Customs) of the Academy ten years ago that all boys should wear Caps at School, the kind being left to themselves. This I have from time to time enforced and in several cases recently.' But Hodson was considered to be at fault for the tone of his letter and for punishing the boy. The incident helped to prolong the period of no uniforms, the Directors having made it clear that 'there is no rule and no imperative custom in the Academy as to the dress of the boys.'

However in England the rising prestige and popularity of public schools led to the spread of dress codes: Mill Hill began the process and by 1880 most others had adopted some form of uniform, although Oundle went no further than straw hats in summer. By the turn of the century, as Jonathon Gathorne-Hardy has observed, Charterhouse was using clothes to denote hierarchy: 'A new boy had no distinctions and no privileges. The second term you were allowed a knitted tie instead of a plain one. Second year, coloured socks. Third year, turned-down collars, coloured handkerchiefs, a coat with long lapels, etc. Fourth year – still more distinctions… But the blood's dress was unique and peculiar: light grey flannel trousers, butterfly collars, coats slit up the back, and the privilege of walking arm-in-arm.' The 'bloods' at the top of public school hierarchy were members of the first football and cricket teams. These variations might be interpreted as an escape from uniform by stages rather than an imposition of it, but at any rate photographic evidence shows fully ten distinguishing articles or variations of dress among a typical English public school group of the time.

In those Edinburgh institutions which had largely English teaching staffs (three boarding-schools and the Academy) there was a tendency to adopt similar customs, but also considerable range of response. A key figure influencing schoolwear in Scotland was Hely Hutchinson Almond who left Merchiston in 1862 to begin forty years in charge of Loretto. Almond was an imaginative thinker concerning all matters educational who placed great value on health. A bronze statue created in modern times shows a boy in open-necked shirt, one sleeve rolled up and the other trailing in casual Lorettonian fashion. Its other notable feature is the fact that the boy wears short trousers – to be discussed. But as Frank Stewart has made clear, this innovating head was at the forefront of what soon became shared assumptions about *esprit de corps*:

21. *Almond and others on Sunday.*

'When Almond came he immediately decided that a uniform would be good for morale and would encourage a feeling of belonging to a community. He had little difficulty in choosing what it should be, for he always liked bright colours and strong contrasts ... and selected scarlet and white. At the start, every-day dress consisted of a Glengarry, a white flannel shirt, tweed knickerbockers with red or red-and-white striped stockings, a waistcoat and a red jacket. But this did not satisfy him for long. The waistcoat and the Glengarry were soon to go, the first on the grounds that it restricted chest expansion, the second for the simpler reason that it was always being mislaid or exchanged, so it was easier to do without it. A protest was raised by some anxious parents who feared that their sons might suffer from chills but, as usual, Almond had his reasoned answer ready. He pointed out that the Bluecoat schoolboys at Christ's Hospital never wore any hat and took no harm.' The School Song testifies to the success of Almond's morale-building through 'free and jolly dress':

> The Old Red Coat is a glorious sight,
>> Then a song to the praise of the Scarlet and White.
> Far better than brown, or magenta or blue,
>> To the Red of Loretto we'll always be true.

Chorus
To the Old Red Coat, and the open throat,
    And the School where we can wear it;
And we always shall bless the free and jolly dress,
    And be glad that we still can sha-are it.

Though it's out at the elbows and spotted with ink,
    And faded away to a delicate pink,
Yet we cannot give up such a charming old rag,
    And we stick to it still like some battle-worn flag.

Blue blazers for summer came early to Merchiston along with shorts of the same colour, but in 1896 the area's second boarding school diverged from Loretto by introducing a school cap – 'with crest, the previous cap having been plain blue without any mark to differentiate it from the other blue school caps then to be seen in Edinburgh.' This must refer to private schools since closed. Heriot's boys had yet to acquire the distinctive striped cap in

22. *Homer's Head.*

two shades of blue. At the Academy Rector Mackenzie was keen to introduce official school head-dress, but it did not become the cap of blue with a laurel wreath badge until six years after the Merchiston crest was added. Silver braid round the peak and lower rim of the Academy cap came later. Mackenzie's original required item was a Glengarry decorated with Homer's head. Even when the second was devised pupils were left free to wear one or the other. There was also the third option of a straw boater in summer with a ribbon in the blue and white of the school's sporting colours.

The tight-fitting caps with peaks which became almost universal among pupils of Edinburgh boys' schools had originated with the cricketers of England, being pulled down over the eyes. For cricket they were generally white to match the flannels. High School boys competed on the games field in bright combinations of blue and orange, then scarlet and blue, until black and white was adopted with all due solemnity from the 'colours' of the city. A black cap with the intertwined monogram RHS followed. To begin with Daniel Stewart's boys wore blue and red striped scarves – comforting items hardly mentioned elsewhere, although Fettes boys later sported long ones for athletic awards. But at Queensferry Road 'in 1895 the cap became black with a version of the Stewart arms embroidered in front, and the colours changed to red, black and yellow.' A Romanian visitor was 'very happy to see my country's colours at the necks of little Scotch boys.'

Much later Miroslav Sasek, Czech illustrator-compiler of the delightful *This Is Edinburgh* (recently reissued) wrote: 'Edinburgh is by no means dark. It has many bright streets, mews and school uniforms.' The chapter title 'Caps, Blazers and Shorts' is confirmed by a group of boys in Melville College red. The Princes Street of Sasek's post-war era provided a late afternoon pageant of day school pupils, from the maroon blazers and headgear of George Watson's boys and girls (and Gillespie's girls) through the mainly black of Stewart's and the High School to different shades of blue provided by Heriot's, the Academy, John Watson's and Queen Street, otherwise Mary Erskine's Merchant Maidens. But only the Cranley girls' striped blue, red and green blazers rivalled the brightness of Melville scarlet. Returning to the start of the century, at the other Merchant Company boys' school (after Stewart's) the new headgear for schoolboys became so popular that guests at a Watsonian Dinner of the Edwardian era were asked to imagine that 'when the proverbial Scotsman does get to the North Pole, he will find the ubiquitous *maroon* cap on the top of it!' An indication of how the French-derived word was pronounced by Scots appears in a blazer advertisement: 'In the correct shade of Marone Flannel with School Badge…'

'Brown and magenta' in the Loretto song made reference to the striped jerseys worn by Fettes rugby players as rivals on the field. When it was proposed, ten years after the 1870 opening of Fettes College, that yellow and blue colours should be adopted instead of those which were already 'time-honoured', the response was once again in verse:

> Let them be a bit dearer, and fade if they will;
>   The original colours have charms for us still,
> And in spite of the schemes of the cunning inventor,
>   Let's stick to our Brown and our faded Magenta.

Ten years further down the line a second attempt was made to alter colours which were inclined to fade despite costing more. It was defeated by the increasing army of past and present Fettesians, 'and the only result of the discussion was that the arrangement of the colours in the School

23. *Tassels and top hats.*

caps was slightly altered.' Fettes pupils evacuated to the Lake District because of diphtheria were photographed wearing peaked caps except for a couple with boaters. Colours awarded to members of early Rugby Football teams at first took the form of tasselled skull-caps without peaks. A drawing of an early pupil's study shows one of them.

It also displays a top hat. As with Etonians, Fettes boys were required to wear these whenever they went into town. That happened most regularly on Sundays for Presbyterian or Episcopalian service – either St Stephen's in Stockbridge or Holy Trinity beside the Dean Bridge. Tail-coats (or Eton jackets for younger boys) were part of the 'up-town' outfit: 'Morning coat and striped trousers were put on, the garments having been collected, smelling of moth balls, from matron's room the night before.' Umbrellas safeguarded the shine. A well known photograph shows cheeky London urchins being ignored with lordly disdain by Etonians in top hats. The custom persisted for seventy years at Edinburgh's closest approach to Eton: 'We were, in fact, dour, patriotic and proud. Even the "lum" hat was, to our minds, a distinction, though an incongruous one. The ridicule poured upon it by the inhabitants of Stockbridge and by our neighbours at the Academy, who regarded it as presumptuous and unnatural, stimulated rather than damped us.'

There is evidence from photography as well as art work. At the end of the school's first year a photo of Fettes masters and pupils shows only the former in uniform dress – that of black gown and mortarboard. But the same J. W. Parsons who drew his study in 1878 recorded the vertically-striped blazer already in use, cricket spectators wearing it in the shade of an old beech tree. Horizontal stripes had been adopted as early as season 1873–74 for the football XX (as it was then – to be followed by the XVs of subsequent seasons). That transition was accompanied by a move from trousers into knickerbockers, equally white despite the frequent muddiness of the sport. These were still in use at Sports Day 1893, but by the following year white shorts below the knee are to be seen on capped and blazered spectators. A gymnasium photograph at the turn of the century shows that white shorts and dark stockings were mandatory.

There are also memories in *A Hundred Years of Fettes*. Away from the sports field and the greater freedom of summer, Fettes pupils dressed like gentlemen – it was customary to refer to even the youngest boys as 'men'. From an 1887 leaver we learn that 'for school wear, dark suits only were permitted with black ties. On the breaking-up days the "bloods" used to appear in the most dazzling light checks of sponge bag pattern and ties of every hue.' Rank brought its privileges: 'Unless you were a thoroughly established "dook" of a particular class you might not wear a bow tie or carry a walking-stick to church, or "up-town".' Dooks occupied a place below prefects. Athletic prowess could be acknowledged as early as the fourth form stage which was the focus of many school stories: 'I remember getting a Third XI Cap, and it was the most marvellous event... I was listening for omens (I had taken some wickets against Loretto Third), and as I walked down the gangway furtively scrubbing up my right hand on my Sunday bags, I could almost hear my heart drowning the organ voluntary. Then came the long descent, as it seemed, from Chapel door with one's eyes fixed somewhere on the Sixth Form Library, and finally, everything was merged in the magic words from the Olympian height of H. S. H. Wallace, "Congrats on your Third."'

That memory came from one who survived the trenches. War, which enhanced the significance of uniform, also led to a softening of its school requirements: 'Shortage of starch made clean hard collars a luxury, and the wearing of a soft collar a patriotic duty... War-time restrictions were not relaxed for some time; the chimes were restarted, the College clock painted, the green lining to the windows removed, the Sports held once more, the soft collar supplanted by the stiff collar – all symbols of peace.' Collars, stiff as upper lips, mattered at Fettes, and studs were fastened early

24. *Mortar-boards for masters.*

in the day: 'At 7 a.m. exactly the houseman battered on cubicle walls and thrust open dormitory doors. Then followed a rush for the obligatory cold shower and the struggle into the uniform of tweed suit, flannel shirt, stiff collar and black tie. The suits worn by most people came from a well known firm of Edinburgh outfitters. "Functional" is, I think, the appropriate adjective. They came in two shades of closely woven herring-bone tweed, blue-black and slate grey, of quite remarkable toughness. Ink stains and streaks of dirt blended imperceptibly with the pattern. The collars were rounded at the front and of a type then worn only by our grandparents. Collars with points were the privilege of prefects except in College, if I remember correctly, where a square cut collar was allowed.'

Maroon jackets were already being purchased for George Watson's boys in the Edwardian era, on the evidence of an article about advertising in *The Watsonian*: 'Is it a blazer for your boy of six, madam? You shall have the best for as many shillings. His older brother of seventeen, madam? That comes a little dearer, madam, seven shillings and sixpence to be quite candid, ma'am.' At the Academy it was decided in 1911 that 'the ordinary "blazer" of the School should be an all-blue blazer of Academy blue, with the School crest, and the blue-and-white blazer at present in general use throughout the school should be confined to the first three XVs and the first three XIs.' Parents were informed that 'the School colours may be obtained at various outfitters in Edinburgh. Care should be taken that they conform to the standard pattern and material, as supplied by Messrs Gulland & Kennedy, 35A George Street.' At a later stage an Academy Clothing Shop took over the stock, undercutting commercial outfitters despite protests from the Scottish Drapers' Federation.

Department stores like Jenner's, as well as dedicated outlets like Aitken & Niven at the West End, played a part in advancing uniformity according to each school's regulations. In 1927 the Watson's blazer, which until then had white piping in some Edinburgh shops, became standard and compulsory for summer term as far as the second top class: 'Several new summer fashions have come into being – as, for instance, the wearing of blue shorts and cricket shirts and the pernicious habit of turning up the collar of one's blazer.' Eleven years later Headmaster George Robertson's dress 'recommendations' to parents included the command that it 'must be worn.'

Between the wars blazers became regulation wear at most Edinburgh fee-paying schools, in marked distinction to those attended by the majority of children where uniforms were unknown. The Royal High's new badge featuring the heraldic three-turreted castle of Edinburgh was used first on caps and then blazers, but neither was compulsory by 1930: 'When the decade began, we were still allowed to wear lounge suits, plus fours, kilts or riding breeches instead of School uniform.' Merchiston's move to Colinton in the following year coincided with major sartorial change: 'Even the boys looked new and strange clad in the winter in blazer and shorts, clothing only seen in summer before.' Merchiston prefects alone were granted the privilege of wearing long grey flannels.

Edinburgh Institution pupils became brightly associated with scarlet about the same time as the name was altered to Melville College. Daniel Stewart's caps with red, black and yellow stripes designed by the Vice-Convener were issued free to all boys in 1924: 'With the cap went a black blazer with embroidered badge and red and yellow piping.' It became compulsory by the same Merchant Company order which was passed on to Watson's parents. When Scotland's international rugby ground was moved from Inverleith to Murrayfield, schoolboy tickets were restricted to boys wearing caps or sporting school badges. Half a century after Daniel

Stewart's boys took possession of their caps in three colours, the merged Stewart's and Melville Colleges agreed on a black blazer with minimal red piping. Later a scarlet blazer was introduced to recognize sporting and other distinction by senior pupils. At sixth year level Stew-

25. *Stewart's caps in the playground.*

art's Melville is now merged with Mary Erskine, so that gifted girls are equally liable to finish their schooldays in red blazers.

'The Old Red Coat' came to represent Loretto School although no badge was ever added. Short trousers were firmly associated with it, which probably gives Loretto something to answer for as the custom of wearing blazer and shorts (and uniform stockings) spread to other schools in Edinburgh. Loretto historian Frank Stewart: 'Cricket trousers were long and white but shirts were not necessarily white. Those of Loretto were of red and white stripes, the stripes being vertical. The Edinburgh Academy had similar shirts with blue and white stripes… Some care had to be taken over dress at the Interscholastic Games because they were held in Edinburgh, where there was a strong prejudice against any sense of "indecency". It was made a rule that competitors must be completely covered from neck to toes and elbows. The custom for Lorettonians was that those competing wore knickerbockers of grey flannel and above them a jersey of scarlet and white stripes. Then, in 1872, a daring boy from the Royal High School appeared in shorts and no socks. He ran in the open quarter-mile race and won it. There was some talk of an appeal against him for wearing an illegal costume…'

Lorettonians rode their bicycles all over the Lothians, and summer terms produced a spectacle in the 'red jacket, red stockings and white shorts in which all boys would cycle up to a School cricket match at Fettes, Merchiston, the Academy or Watson's.' They also wore straw 'bashers' for shade. Surprisingly perhaps, Almond was not personally responsible for the shorts: 'What he did introduce was knickerbockers for football, strapped below the knees. Nor was there any song and dance about them when they did arrive. All that happened, it seems, is that one day some football players cut off the bottom straps of their knickerbockers. Photographs of the XV as late as 1900 show the "shorts", or "cuts" as they were called, well below the knee and as far down as the top of the stocking. Even in the 1930s boys often wore shorts which covered their knees. Since then shorts have got shorter and boys, apparently, have got longer…' The Merchant Company diktat of 1938 made it clear that 'shorts, of a colour as laid down, must be worn by all boys up to 16, boys above that age to be at liberty to wear long trousers of grey flannel.' But next year Watson's went further: 'Robertson's last piece of absurd Anglicisation was to force all into shorts, including S6. This foolishness, unfortunately, lasted until the late 1940s.' A Watson's prefect photo shows the rulers of the school in navy blue shorts and

maroon stockings. Senior pupils of other schools (Merchiston a case in point) waited a further quarter century for their equivalent liberation, at which stage uniform stockings for daily wear ceased to exist beyond the primary school level. Many years before this, boys

26. *Watson's in shorts.*

at 'ordinary' schools had graduated to long trousers before entering their teens.

The title *Ties That Bind* (apart from being popular with romantic novelists) is mainly intended as a reference to the old school tie, and the tradition of networking by professional and business men in adult life. The basis of whatever that may still amount to is established during schooldays, but the ties which were worn after the demise of the hospitals were not of uniform design. The earliest George Watson's College class photo of 1874 exhibits a range of neckwear on senior pupils, but within a decade or two of entering the new era small maroon and white bow ties began to appear under stiff collars.

Despite the emphasis on 'rational clothing' at Loretto, Sundays were different: 'Almond hated lugubriousness, so light coloured trousers, the lighter the better, if not exactly enforced were strongly encouraged… Ties were slate or lavender while certain school distinctions gave the right to wear a red and white one.' Later the distinction for dressed-up Lorettonians was between grey ties and 'red-and-whites'. Among those who wore the latter (along with athletes and exam-passers) were prefects, 'permitted to wear long grey flannel trousers after games and to smoke a pipe at weekends.' The latter custom was introduced by Almond, in all other respects a fresh-air fiend.

Ties invariably had horizontal stripes at first, presumably because they could be knitted that way. A photograph of ten Serbian boys attending George Heriot's School during the Great War shows all of them in that style with Eton collars. These venerable items appear incongruous above the newly adopted short trousers. The combination of jacket, waistcoat and shorts (knickerbockers going out of fashion) was advertised as the Lothian Tweed Henley Suit 'for those notoriously hard on Clothes. Fitting Boys 7 to 13 years. 15/6 all sizes.' A group visit by the Serbian youngsters to the department store Patrick Thomson's, courtesy of the Heriot Trust, may be imagined. In contrast a contemporary photograph of the Royal High School First Form shows three kinds of black-and-white striped tie: horizontal, and diagonal in opposite directions. High School boys came from homes all over the city and their parents shopped accordingly. The photo appears to illustrate a period of transition for school outfitters, although it was a prolonged one on the evidence of 'mixed' tie-wearing by Junior Watson's boys in the Thirties.

"REYNARD"
JUVENILE CLOTHING

THE "REYNARD" SERVICE
in the Meeting of Boyhood's
Needs is Thorough——Sincere
—— and does not overlook
one Single Point, making
for Comfort for the Boy——
Quality in Appearance and
Wear of the Clothes
And Value, which is
decidedly the Best in
Boys' Wear.

THE LOTHIAN TWEED
HENLEY SUIT

(as sketch)

Recommended for those
notoriously hard on Clothes.
Fitting Boys 7 to 13 years,
15/6 all sizes

27. *Best in Boys' Wear.*

Ties were one of the first items of uniform to be made compulsory at boys' schools, along with caps. Soft collars came to predominate, but no slack was allowed on how they should be worn: tightly knotted at the neck. No lack of respect was implied – rather the reverse – when a Melville College rugby captain used the red and black item to hold up his shorts. The influence of one scarlet-blazered school on another was felt around the time of the Edinburgh Institution's centenary, when Norman Barber arrived from Loretto to take over as Headmaster. Although the blazer's colour was established already, white shorts and open-necked shirts now accompanied it in summer. Other day schools followed.

Ties continued to be worn when other items of uniform were hard to obtain in wartime, and also during the period of austerity which followed the Second World War. Once clothes rationing ended there was a lengthening of the uniform list. Among the optional items – but which, if worn, had to conform to school regulations – were V-necked jerseys which allowed ties to be seen. Towards the end of the Fifties there was a new development in boys' school wear when prefect ties began to be awarded, usually plain in the dominant school colour with a version of the school badge. By this time the wearing of caps had ceased to be compulsory above the junior level at several boys' schools, reflecting a change in adult fashion. Office workers rejected the advertiser's 'If you want to get ahead get a hat', and peaked cloth bonnets were also given up at all social levels. But rugby caps, tasselled and velvet, were still awarded to schoolboys for wearing to Murrayfield – and away matches by coach. There were plainer untasselled versions for every day.

The Royal High was one of the first schools to allow secondary pupils to go bare-headed, but the 1964 magazine *Schola Regia* shows eleven Olympians (captioned 'School Celebrities') under the Greek colonnade. Most have prefect ties and lapel badges; several dated athletic 'colours' can be seen on badge pockets. Early in the previous decade Stewart's had pulled back from 'letters and dates, like long-service medals or the festal dress of an American confraternity', substituting a simple badge with XV or XI below it. Letters and dates were taken up by all but one of the blazer-wearing day schools (the Academy) but the High School hero who captained both Rugby XV and Cricket XI represented the trend at its peak with both sides of his blazer embroidered. Seated at an angle which makes dress distinction impossible to detect is the beardless Robin Cook. Later to tender his resignation to Prime Minister Blair as Leader of the House of Commons over the Iraq war, Cook was then President of the Literary and Debating Society.

28. *High School celebrities.*

Tony Blair offers a link with Fettes College. Seven years younger than Robin Cook, he never met him in inter-school debate but is said to have regularly talked his way out of encounters with authority. This was a time of teenage rebellion and the future politician was identified (perhaps only in hindsight) with Mick Jagger. The Beatles had launched a fashion for longer hair, and the wearing of caps by schoolboys was one of its casualties. When Blair arrived at Fettes Ian McIntosh was Headmaster, after a brief period in charge of George Watson's. Robert Philp describes his time at Fettes, which ended in the same year as Blair's, in a chapter headed 'Keeping the Lid On'. McIntosh sought to maintain respect for authority while young Blair was among those who questioned it. Faced with a rule that hair should be cut four times a term, he made four appointments in the first week. However on one occasion McIntosh encountered Blair, A. C. L. near the school barber's shop: 'He took him straight in and stood there, unrelenting as the cherished mop was trimmed.'

Not even 'the Eton of Scotland' was immune from changes in society. An Old Fettesian observed of the post-war period: 'Increasingly as home life becomes more liberal for many boys, the pressures on boarding school life grow, and during this period those in authority were endeavouring to allow more freedom.' Due to clothing shortages uniform at Fettes had given way to tweed jackets during the war, and regulation dress returned in the form of something resembling an army tunic, but grey. Some thought it looked well with the kilt which a few pupils wore. Others disagreed: 'Post-war Fettesians were clothed in a costume which would have debased the morale of a convict... From the chrysalis of Top Hat and Tails erupted a prodigy called a "lumber-jacket" in a preference, which seemed perversely inappropriate, to tweed jacket or blazer in everyday dress. Blazers were of course worn to games; but chocolate and magenta stripes, being in short supply, were the prerogative of Bigside.' Brown blazers (with bee badge for industry) came in after the war, with the 'sports' jacket a permitted alternative: 'Although teenage fashions and dress had not reached the peak of the 1960s there was undeniably a growing self-consciousness in this direction.'

1968 was the year when Lindsay Anderson's film *If....* portrayed an old-fashioned school where the pupils turned automatic weapons on their teachers. At Fettes there was a simmering resentment in the air, and Ian

McIntosh gathered his new prefects to discuss the situation. Previously the twelve seniors who helped to run the school had been addressed by pupils as Sir. Now the prefects themselves were inclined to voice objections – to compulsory rugby, restricted leave out, and to 'piddling' dress rules about al-

29. *McIntosh and his Fettes prefects.*

ways having the middle jacket button fastened. That rule was dropped, and prefects were no longer required to check boys with hands in pockets. Senior boys apart, housemasters were the key agents of greater flexibility: Headmaster McIntosh (to borrow from another area of management) never 'lost the dressing-room'. Fettes had a happy Common Room and support from an excellent staff, many of whom went on to headships at major public schools. At the centenary celebrations just before his retirement, which helped to generate positive morale, even the critics of McIntosh's authoritarian style were ready to praise him.

The question of authority is taken further in the following chapter. Here it is enough to follow resistance to uniform as it was manifested in other schools, and one in particular. R. B. 'Rab' Bruce Lockhart (an Edinburgh Academical) was Headmaster of Loretto during the Sixties and early Seventies. He put a stop to the wearing of tartan shirts but recognised the need for change. Making its appearance at Loretto through the Officers Training Corps, the kilt had been adopted as formal wear for Sunday chapel. Black jacket and silver buttons now gave way to hairy jackets as used for walking out, saving parents £40. The kilt was also required travelling dress at the beginning and end of term, but with English pupils in mind Bruce Lockhart relented, allowing a dark grey suit to be worn. Soon this was permitted to Sixth Formers going into Edinburgh or elsewhere. Nobody had objected to the Old Red Coat or Almond's 'open throat', but there was another issue to be resolved:

'For many years boys had refused to be seen outside Musselburgh in shorts, or had at least protested strongly if forced to wear them. There was

30. *Loretto – last into longs.*

less opposition to wearing them within the school grounds, but even this began to provoke fierce argument. It was an emotive subject. Those in favour of shorts claimed that they were a practical and healthy garment, and they earnestly believed that shorts had become such a hallmark of Loretto that if they were abolished some O.L. parents might immediately cancel their sons' entry to the School. Those against could see no reason for retaining them. Other boarding schools had recently given them up – Merchiston, Sedbergh and Gordonstoun – and long trousers were being worn at an increasing number of prep schools. There was evidence that some small boys were persuading their parents *not* to send them to Loretto and the indignity of reverting to shorts.' The decision was made in September 1974: 'The formal school dress, for such events as School Plays and Concerts, and for Chapel in warm weather, will no longer be red and white, but red and grey, the grey being long and dark.'

The wearing of caps was still compulsory at Melville College in the latter part of the Sixties, the school becoming more traditional by the year. Compulsory cadet corps, after all other local schools had abandoned it, was another aspect linked to uniform which helped to gain admission to the Headmasters' Conference. The Royal High School was still laying emphasis on correct dress after it ceased to be a boys' school and moved to leafy Barnton. The challenge was all the stronger since parallel rules had to be laid down for girls, but 'Any question on the matter of dress should be submitted to the Rector whose decision is final.' Co-education's most obvious effect on school uniform in general is that kilts (and mini-kilts) have become the preserve of girls. The question of uniform is still a live one in schools of all descriptions and many state schools see value in it. The received wisdom is that a shared dress code can still play its part in developing school spirit – or ethos.

Chapter 4

Authority and Ethos

'Headmistresses presiding majestically over assemblies belong to a world of school songs and prize-giving ceremonies. School mottos also played their symbolic part, and badges were designed with care. School rules provide a rough guide to the intangible heart of the matter. There were sanctions against breaking them, but never the corporal punishment which was such a feature of boys' schools – nor were girls spared the strap in normal co-educational schools throughout Scotland. Only in fee-paying girls' schools did ethos come first. Elsewhere the heading would have to be "Authority and Ethos".' The extract from *Crème de la Crème*'s 'Ethos and Authority' chapter explains the heading for this one. Attention has just been paid to a time when authority was questioned over the wearing of uniform in one of Edinburgh's stricter boys' schools, but Fettes came late on the scene. The High School provides a better starting-point.

Down the years from 1595 pupils of 'The Tounis Scule' were regularly reminded of the incident when a leading Councillor was killed by one of their forerunners. It occurred during a traditional 'barring-out', when boys refused a week's holiday arrived early to barricade the school against all-comers. Modern sit-ins are tame by comparison. Scholars brought food to withstand siege and weapons to deny entry. Scions of turbulent noble families took the lead, and it was the Earl of Caithness's grandson who responded to a battering ram by shooting Bailie MacMoran in the head. King James intervened, and the murderous pupil was dealt with by a genteel, temporary exile. Lest folk memory failed to keep the deed in mind, one of the twenty-two school rules read out at the start of each session at Regent Road was that 'No gunpowder, fireworks or firearms of any description are to be brought within the grounds...'

'Barring-out' was replaced by 'bickering' or street fights with nearby college students and also the boys of Heriot's Hospital. Bickers involving Heriot's boys were endemic in the days before rugby offered an alternative to breaking the windows of George Watson's Hospital. From the viewpoint of those across the road, 'Heriot's always had behavioural problems among its inmates… Theft, violence, bullying and desertions on a vast scale plagued the Hospital.' Heriot's modern chronicler confirms this. A form of bullying saw new boys introduced by seniors of the house into the 'Garring Law' by which they were sworn to secrecy about acts against adult authority – a sort of malign prefect system. Accustomed to running affairs in this way, those who moved on from school formed themselves into a 'Decorating Club' – ostensibly to decorate the Founder's statue for June Day but also giving freedom to invade the premises and harass staff. Floggings, expulsions and suppression of wholesale mutiny by the Town Guard all featured by way of response.

Other boys were also controlled with difficulty. At the High School each master was a law unto himself in matters of discipline, since he kept the same class for four years before handing it over to the Rector. Henry Cockburn, nicknamed 'Cocky' and destined to become a Law Lord, was particularly unlucky with Alexander Christison: 'Out of the whole four years of my attendance there were probably not ten days in which I was not flogged, at least once.' There were also harsh masters after the move to Calton Hill. Hardened by a previous spell at Heriot's, Samuel Lindsay was notorious for his use of Scotland's divided leather belt: 'Mr Lindsay had, in particular, a fine playful way of waking up the class when its attention was languid by going between the forms and making the tawse come down with a raking sweep on the legs of the boys.' On the other hand Dr James Boyd sometimes went a month without taking the 'adjutant' from his desk. More than one High School rector tried to ease discipline. Ending the school day at three o'clock made it possible to substitute detention, with 'tasks to be performed'. And monitors from among the abler pupils were given responsibility for helping to teach the rest, with beneficial effects on the master's temper.

The Edinburgh Academy founders agreed with Cockburn's condemnation of physical punishment for failures in school work. The Directors laid down that it 'should be reserved as much as possible for extreme cases, or for serious moral offences.' However Academy teachers in most of the decades to come wielded the tawse for 'palmies', so it may be presumed that the injunction was meant for caning on the body. This remained a Rector's privilege. D'Arcy Wentworth Thompson, a nineteenth-century

Academy teacher who expressed his progressive ideas in *Day-dreams of a Schoolmaster*, recalled the reproach in his wife's eyes on seeing the tawse he took to work. He rarely struck a child in class, but regarded it as 'almost innocuous' compared with the cane- and birch-flogging that went on in English schools: 'We have gone a great way already in Scotland in the way of civilised teaching, in forbearing to use an instrument of acute pain and an instrument of indecent brutality.'

Teachers used the strap in all the Edinburgh boys' schools, but the Academy went further when a prefect system was introduced in the form of 'Ephors', a term borrowed from ancient Sparta. There was initial reluctance to allow them to administer corporal punishment, rejected as an English innovation. Rector R. J. Mackenzie was persuasive on a wide range of issues but on this occasion they refused to go along with him. His successor 'Reggie' Carter was more successful, however, persuading them in 1903 that the change should be introduced on condition that the Rector's approval was always obtained and due procedure followed.

Arnold Kemp was one of the many who suffered, on one occasion for being seen out of school without the compulsory cap on. The other offence was refusing to run round Fettes when the ground was too hard for rugby. The ephors, assembled in the room which was theirs by right, behaved like the judges that some of them were destined to become before punishment was administered. Kemp recalled the charge of the chosen ephor from across the room, clacken in hand, while he was bent over with his head under the table. The evident pleasure of the punisher was to affect the future journalist's attitude to authoritarian personalities.

In the experience of Magnus Magnusson, himself an ephor before Kemp's time, up to six blows might be imposed – the punishment being a collective one in which left-handed ephors were valued for variety of stroke. There was much discussion of the practice in the post-war period at the Academy, public opinion beginning to turn against corporal punishment, while ephors argued that their authority would be undermined without it. By the end of the Sixties it had been quietly dropped, bringing to an end the practice of 'Ephors' beatings' which Magnusson himself seems to have regarded as barbaric

Other senior day school pupils were allowed to punish junior ones physically – at the High School (with a slipper) and also at Melville College. There untidy desks, and running on the mid-morning Walk (round the block) were the commonest offences in a system where 'crosses' were accumulated:

> Here come the Prefects snooping around,
> With their canes and their crosses, they're sure to be found.
> Be wary! Be wise!
> The snoopers have eyes.

Melville punishment was not so carefully regulated as at the Academy, but prefects (also introduced from Loretto by a new head, as in the case of Mackenzie) were less likely to use the cane than a gym shoe. Blows were administered on the backside by one prefect in the presence of others when the warning of a final cross in the Prefects' Book was ignored.

In the early days of Merchiston's expansion under John Rogerson there were no prefects, 'the only boy with any authority being the Captain of the School who was elected to his post by those members of the previous year's football team who had returned.' Following the end of

31. *Melville prefects, capped and caning.*

blue shorts at Merchiston (the rulers of the school hitherto being distinct in grey flannels) it became difficult to identify a prefect – although they were allowed to wear tweed jackets along with shirts and pullovers of non-uniform colour. Looking back from the 1970s Merchiston's chronicler recorded a sea change: 'The School Captain and his team of Prefects remain the most important influence in maintaining standards of behaviour but in some ways to do so has become more difficult… Though bearing on their shoulders just as much responsibility over the day-to-day running of the School, their disciplinary powers have been curtailed with the ending of corporal punishment even by the School Captain.'

Outside the classroom (where teachers are in charge) punishment tends to be about breaking school rules. The High School's list for solemn reading out included several on avoiding damage to 'the splendid building provided by the munificence of the City.' As timetables became more complicated, movement on stairs and corridors had to be controlled: 'Stewart's College in 1882 was a small school, badly equipped and ill-disciplined. When classes changed from room to room there was scrumming and confusion almost inconceivable. Few of the old staff had any real control even in the classroom… [The Rector] called together the senior boys and asked them if they liked the existing state of things. They assured him they did not, and he enlisted their sympathy and support. With their support and help, and some necessary changes in the staff, discipline was restored and maintained.' Sometimes, as at Merchiston in Victorian times, boys were asked to recall how they behaved at home: 'No loud talking is permitted during meals. The same quiet and gentlemanly demeanour must be observed that characterises the family parties in a well-ordered private household.'

Although Fettes arrived late on the Edinburgh scene, its first Headmaster Alexander Potts was steeped in public school traditions and keen to apply them in a new setting. He came north from Rugby, where Thomas Arnold's ideal of 'godliness and good manners' still prevailed. Fagging, whereby junior boys carried out domestic chores for seniors, was important within an ethos which was rapidly established. One of the accounts from *A Hundred Years of Fettes* sums up the fags-to-Sixth-Form progress: 'The pride of increasing seniority, as the years went by, made the return to School after the holidays an exciting and delightful moment.' Potts valued sport for creating a school spirit which was truly spiritual. Arnoldian in outlook, he told the guests at an Edinburgh dinner party: 'I should like my boys and all boys, and all men, to be ever mindful, in the hottest scrimmage and in the most exciting period of the game, that they are not only football players but Christians and gentlemen.' Although personally devout, Potts raised eyebrows by insisting that no school chaplain should be appointed. According to him every master and prefect had a religious role, not least housemasters and house prefects.

The House system was one in which boarders of all ages lived in groups of about fifty during their time at school. Fettes boys joined the rest of the school for classes, chapel and – a Potts innovation – eating in a central dining hall. Neither of the other Edinburgh boarding schools had anything like this. Merchiston's six-storey castle and nearby dwelling-houses lent themselves to a division by age which was continued at Colinton. Almond opted for a Room system at Loretto, with boys put in charge of bedrooms of varying size. Pupils merely slept in boarding-houses which lacked recreation and study areas, and they could be shifted from one house to another at the start of a term. Housemasters with little to do by way of a pastoral role had less opportunity for promotion to headships of public schools. When Loretto became too large for the Head to know every boy, as in Almond's day, Bruce Lockhart readily persuaded his governors to introduce four all-age houses with sixty boys in each.

It is worth staying with Loretto for Almond's radical views on ethos. Frank Stewart again: 'From the very start he was determined to break down the great barrier between masters and boys… At night he would come round the bedrooms between bed-bell and lights out and sit chatting to the boys on their beds. In the earlier years he would often rag with them, taking part in a pillow fight, or struggling to free himself from the clutches of half a dozen boys… From the very start Almond took a strong line against fagging, on the grounds that it was bad psychologically, both for the fag and for his master… Similarly, bullying of any sort has always been severely stamped on.'

This is reminiscent of another well known head, A. S. Neill. After three-quarters of a century his Summerhill in Suffolk still bears the child-centred accolade of being a 'free school' run, to a considerable extent, by pupils. Attendance at class is voluntary and there has never been corporal punishment. Its relaxed atmosphere was based on a rejection of authoritarian Scottish education, Neill's father having been a Forfar dominie who used the tawse on a regular basis. Within his Spartan regime Almond had no qualms about physical punishment by masters and senior pupils, threatening to haunt Loretto if deadening 'lines' replaced it, but in all other ways he deserves to be seen as a progressive educator:

'There was developed a highly organised system of government of boys by boys which has been carried further at Loretto, probably, than at any other school before or since. Prefects, house-prefects, heads of bedrooms and heads of formrooms comprised four sets of authorities who had their several duties to discharge… A promising boy could be appointed head of a small bedroom at a young age and gradually progress up the ladder to become head of a large room in another, house prefect, and then prefect in a third… Of no little importance, too, were the heads of forms. Not only were they responsible for order and discipline within the formrooms

32. Almond's Head of School.

during lessons if the master happened to be called away, but there being no studies at Loretto, a good deal of free time had to be spent in formrooms and at such periods the heads of forms were in charge. Progress up the school was mainly according to age, so some of these heads of forms were very small boys indeed. It happened therefore that at any one time there could be as many as twenty-five boys out of a hundred or so with some position of authority…'

'Nippers' or junior school boys could aspire to a first step on the ladder of self-government. It rose very high, with Loretto's Head of School given more authority than head boys elsewhere: 'Until the creation of the office of Viceregent he was a more important person than any master. The Headmaster consulted him on everything to do with the School… On one occasion when Almond was away and the Viceregent took ill, the School was left in the Head of School's charge for a fortnight, during which time everything proceeded with the utmost regularity.' Although there were so many of them, Arnold's attitude to the selection of those in authority was also radical. In contrast to other schools, powerful athletes would be passed over as readily as able scholars in the absence of 'qualities which make a boy respected and influential among his fellows.'

Houses as introduced into the boys' day schools of Edinburgh may be regarded as an act of homage to the boarding-school system. The Academy was the first to make it when four Divisions 'for games and other purposes' were created in 1905. Three were named after leading men associated with the school while the fourth, for boarders, was called Houses. Two of these buildings, each accommodating twenty-eight boys, had been built beside the school's New Field north of Inverleith Park so that boys from afar no longer had to live in the homes of masters. Two other boarding-houses followed. The inclusion of a residential element heightened the sense of competition: boarders had more time and opportunity for practising together.

Heriot's and Watson's both created four houses in 1908. The Watson's House Championship expanded after the move to more spacious conditions at Colinton Road and took in seven sports, plus cadets and 'scholarship'. The High School set up four Nations – Angles, Britons, Picts and Scots – for which there was an element of 'mental' achievement from the start. Stewart's followed on with three houses, and in course of time had a record eight named after Scottish firths.

33. *GWC house badge.*

A former Tay housemaster provided an extended humorous account of the start to each day in the all-age House Room: 'It is often held to be one of the great spiritual rewards of Housemastering, the matutinal confrontation with those rows of scrubbed and shining faces, haloed by unruly spikes of hair recalcitrant even under the ministrations of brush and brilliantine, and to hear the ringing youthful tones of the dawn chorus – "Good morning Mr Housemaster, Sir" – shouted in high good spirits and unison. Why this is often held to be so I don't know, for it is neither spiritually rewarding nor true.'

After the Stewart's-Melville merger, co-educational links were made with the Mary Erskine School. These led to complications – readily overcome – during outdoor education at Carbisdale Youth Hostel, 'where the entire programme operates on a House basis, and although each House at Carbisdale combines with half a Clan from MES (where they have four Clans as distinct from our eight Houses) it seems as if the House spirit not only prevails but communicates itself to the girls.' The Institution never developed houses due to numbers being so small, although a recovery to about 150 secondary pupils was made by the time it became Melville College. In general the pupils of preparatory or junior departments, such as all day schools added at various times, were not admitted to house membership. Large numbers lay behind the trend as well as concern for *esprit de corps* through inter-house competition. When Heriot's and Watson's divided into four, their rolls were in the region of 1,300 – about half the pupils being of senior school age in each case.

As shown at the start, in *Crème de la Crème* the ethos of girls' schools – more important than rules or sanctions – was discussed largely in terms of symbols and impressive occasions. On the evidence of memories and histories, these were less significant for boys: no doubt the greater emphasis on authority, plus the compulsory sports and cadets still to be considered, go some way to explain it. Certainly there is nothing in the records equivalent to senior St George's girls 'waiting breathless to hear the decision' on their school motto and 'immediate recognition that Chaucer's description of his knight was the inevitably right one'. Perhaps the contrast also stems from the greater age of the boys' schools, mottos and the badges associated with them having come down from a distant past.

The High School's *Musis respublica floret* ('The State flourishes by the Muses' – or education) was carved in a stone dated 1578 and taken from building to building like a totem. George Heriot's arms are surmounted by *Impendo* and supported by the translation 'I Distribute Chearfullie'; likewise those of George Watson whose *Ex corde caritas* expresses the founder's charity from the heart. The Edinburgh Institution which became Melville College demonstrated that its modern approach implied no disrespect for Latin with *Doctrina vim promovet insitam* ('Learning promotes inner strength') around the head of Minerva, Goddess of Wisdom. None of this survived the merger with Daniel Stewart's College, whose founder's arms serve the joint institution along with the Stewart's motto 'Never Unprepared'. During the

34. *From building to building.*

middle years of last century John Watson's School celebrated the achievement of senior secondary status and a roll which peaked at 346 by adopting the motto *Stabimus*, 'We shall stand'. It proved to be ironic when the school closed.

The Academy's Directors had Greek letters engraved early beneath the pediment of the building for a motto which meant 'Education is the mother of both Wisdom and Virtue'. It has been used in association with Homer's head on the 'Accie' (or old boy) blazer but never on the school one. Fettes, with admirable brevity, combined the image of a busy bee with *Industria*, while Loretto's *Spartam nactus es: hanc exorna* ('You have obtained Sparta: adorn it') is linked with a wreath of Scottish thistles and St Andrew's cross. 'Ready, Ay Ready' (so spelled) was adopted by Merchiston when the Napier arms were matriculated

35. *Industria.*

as a crest for the First Eleven blazer. That took place in 1883 marking the first fifty years. By then 'the school had developed certain ways of doing things, hallowed by time so that they were already accepted as traditions.' (A 'touching hands' ceremony after evening prayers, for example, recalled the school's second headmaster John Gibson who shook every boy's hand then took to his bed and died.) The words of the motto featured in a hearty chorus:

> Ready, aye ready, this shall be our song!
>   Ready to be gentle, ready to be strong,
> Ready to uphold the right and redress the wrong;
>   Merchiston for ever, hip, hip, hip, hurrah!

As with Loretto's 'The Old Red Coat', the verses (first sung at the Golden Jubilee) mainly emphasised sporting achievement.

School songs can be difficult to maintain over long periods of time, as noted by Dr John Thompson in his account of Daniel Stewart's College: 'To the three houses – Belford, Dean and Ravelston – of 1910, Drumsheugh was added in 1927 and the words of the chorus had to be altered. The cheers which ended it have happily been forgotten… [The song] has survived in suspended animation, to be revived once or twice a year.' The Merchiston one with its 'hip, hip, hip, hurrah!', though fully expected to be 'mellowed by age and become the perfect school song,' was replaced by a better one in due course. A new custom then began whereby the Captain of School sang the first verse at the Prizegiving.

The commemoration of George Heriot's birthday on June Day was associated from early Hospital days with fine singing in Greyfriars Kirk. More than a school affair, this annual social occasion drew a great crowd and the need for a special anthem was felt: 'By the 1790s they were being composed annually and an Old Herioters' Anthem Club grew up. Two anthems were used; one was written especially for the celebrations, although it was sometimes repeated and sometimes adapted, while the other anthem was standard.' The boys of George Watson's Hospital also attended the church service, as they did on Sundays, and in the 1840s objections were raised by governors on their behalf. A compromise was suggested whereby the whole congregation would join in the anthem, as at normal Sabbath worship. The Heriot governors refused to budge. After a 6–4 vote at their own governors' meeting, Watson's boys were required to continue singing along with their old rivals. The contentious words have not come down to us.

Around the turn of the century the old boys of new George Watson's College were stimulated into action by a letter to *The Watsonian*: 'Why should a School which occupies such a position as ours in the realms of education not have a school song?' A series of efforts were submitted and printed, until the editors were able to produce a four-page song sheet which they anticipated would grow to book length. Watsonian Day (a January affair) would benefit, they believed, from the new musical element 'in the programmes of the many gatherings on that night.' Wider still and wider was the imperial mood of the time, with jobs for Edinburgh boys everywhere. A common theme of the versifiers was of Watsonians 'far in the jungle, far on the snow' gathering to remember their schooldays. Out of all this creative effort there emerged a School Song to the tune of 'Hail to the Chief' as used to greet American presidents:

36. *Maroon Supplement.*

> Hail to the Old School that claims our allegiance!
> Gladly we yield it, whole-hearted and strong,
> Here we acclaim her with loyal devotion,
> 'Queen of the Meadows' and theme of our song.
>
> *Chorus* – Watson's the name we sing,
> Long let the echoes ring,
> Dear to her sons are her praise and her fame,
> 'Neath home or alien skies,
> Loud shall the chorus rise,
> 'Watson's for ever' again and again.

Just as *Gaudeamus igitur* has resonated with university students, so Latin works well for schools with classical traditions. Rector James Marshall wrote the words for *Scholae Regiae Edinensis Carmen* while he was actively broadening the High School curriculum and introducing modern subjects. The School Song was launched by a Royal High choir formed for the purpose in 1895. The music had been composed by Alexander Campbell Mackenzie, who was knighted that year in recognition of his high place among the musicians of Europe: Liszt, Gounod and Dvořák were among his regular correspondents. By then Mackenzie was operating between London and Florence, but during a sixteen-year return to his native city he had (among nobler works) given piano lessons in Edinburgh Ladies' College, Queen Street, for up to six hours a day teaching eight pupils simultaneously on eight instruments.

A year later the Academy Rector provided music for *Floreat Academia* to words by a master who taught History. The multi-talented 'Bob' Mackenzie was a fine singer; but in the judgement of Magnus Magnusson (who numbered the Balfour Music Prize among his many school achievements) the range of notes was too demanding for the average Academy boy. *Floreas Fettesia* reached its peak when one verse (only) was sung by a breathless Fettes party on the summit of Mont Blanc. More enjoyable but no less ritual was the Founder's Day 'Vive-La' (by no means unique to Fettes) in which the year's events were sung to awful rhymes by the Head of School. It began in June 1871:

> We're starting a song which we hope will be annual
> *Vive la compagnie!*
> About Midsummer-day, when the hot sun doth tan you all…

It is unlikely that songs in Latin or English (or French choruses) retain their full power to stir the emotions of generations which follow on, but the final rendering may leave an impression for all that. High School historian William Ross provides a context:

'There is one School ceremony that is unique in character. No one who was present at the Dedication of the Memorial Porch will ever forget that supreme moment when, as the last note of Reveille died away, the Memorial Door was opened wide and a flood of sunshine poured into the Hall. Was it then that the idea was born? Year by year, at the close of Prize Day, the senior boys say farewell to the Rector and pass through that Memorial Door into the world outside… It is the crown of a school career, the perfect symbol of that unity of past and present which is our glorious heritage.' A lone piper later replaced the bugler. Drama of that kind, for boys in the audience as well as those who exit the stage, is a fine expression of ethos. Many adult lives are mundane by comparison.

The external appearance of school buildings has already been celebrated here, but interior spaces like the Heriot's quadrangle and the assembly halls and chapels of several schools probably had more effect on those who spent long years inside. And daily familiarity makes its effect as well as the grand occasion. The High School Hall was so evocative that the Memorial Door (along with memorial windows and boards with names from the past) was reinstated in a modern setting when the school moved to Barnton. The oval seating-plan at Regent Road no doubt influenced those who campaigned for the High School building to be used for a Scottish Parliament. The Edinburgh Academy Hall is also oval. Reminiscent of a Greek amphitheatre, it was modelled (by way of St Cecilia's Hall in the Cowgate) on the opera house at Parma. An elliptical cupola sets it off, admitting ample daylight without over-heating the area below. Having looked up to one Greek motto outdoors, assembled Academy pupils are faced with another exhortation in the language. The transliterated *aien aristeuein* above the organ means 'Always strive to excel.'

Elsewhere boys assembled for morning-prayers and announcements in less exalted surroundings. At Loretto it was the dining-hall after breakfast had been cleared away, at Melville the gymnasium. Fettes used the Chapel

37. *The High School Hall.*

as an alternative to outdoor assemblies in front of the school. It could accommodate the whole community even when rising numbers required the addition of a cramped gallery accessible by ladder. Loretto's equivalent

for Sunday services was to become strikingly decorated with carved wooden panels by Sir Robert Lorimer, paid for by grieving parents after the Great War. Merchiston's Memorial Hall at Colinton served for worship twice on Sundays, with visits to churches at Holy Corner ceasing after the move to Colinton.

It may fairly be said that boarding schools exhibited a stronger Christ-

38. *Fettes at worship.*

ian commitment than day schools. This was particularly so at Fettes, as expressed by the message which Alexander Potts dictated for the Head of School to read out: 'I wish as a dying man to record that mercy and loving-kindness have followed me all the days of my life; that firm faith in God is the sole stay in mortal life; that all other ideas but Christ are illusory; and that duty is the one and sole thing worth living for.' Almond set the tone of muscular Christianity at Loretto. Although anything but 'preachy', his talks to the boys (carefully prepared and well received) were published afterwards in books like *Sermons of a Lay Head-Master*.

The idea of a lay headmaster was something of a novelty at the time, most English heads taking Holy Orders at Oxford or Cambridge. Some moved on from schools to ecclesiastical livings including bishoprics. The Rev. Dr John Hannah was more than happy to accept the headship of Episcopalian Glenalmond (at a lower salary) after seven successful years in charge of the Academy. Magnus Magnusson described the religious culture of the Academy as Presbyterian but hardly Calvinist, even in evangelical times. Dr Hannah, by contrast, was an Anglican clergyman. Never narrow-minded, he went no further than replace the class prayers of masters at the start of the school day with a more imposing assembly.

Parents of Melville pupils were later told in the school prospectus that religion was not taught, 'as merely another subject', because it was better caught at assembly. Hymns were never sung, however, and wall-bars made it difficult to generate an atmosphere of prayer. At George Watson's the reading of Scripture passages by prefects may have heightened levels of devotion.

With such a remarkable setting, it has never been difficult for Heriot's to create a sense of occasion. The Tercentennial June Day of 1923 extended beyond the school premises with a procession to St Giles' Cathedral. Worship was all the more deeply felt thanks to a ceremony, earlier in the year, dedicating the Heriot War Memorial Pillar. Other schools paid their own forms of respect to the glorious dead, but Founder's Day was always special. It is curious, by contrast, to read in the summarised 'landmarks' of George Watson's College that the first Founder's Day celebrations were not held until 1947. Perhaps the War Memorial taken to Colinton Road and the annual ceremony associated with it put George Watson in the shade. Either way, whether in sadness for lost lives or commemoration of a benefactor, ceremonial offers something to remember.

A chapter in *Crème de la Crème* was given over to the idea that girls' school stories influenced the way pupils felt – ethos absorbed from literature – and no doubt Edinburgh schoolboys enjoyed reading about Billy Bunter when boys' school stories were at their peak. That peak came earlier for boys. A fine overview of the genre appeared in *The Lighter Side of School Life* by Ian Hay which was published in 1914. The author John Hay Beith, himself a Fettesian, had completed six years as a master. His comparison of old and new school stories ends: 'There is another marked characteristic of modern school fiction – its intense topicality. The slang, the allusions, the incidents – they are all *dernier cri*. But the more up-to-date a thing may be, whether it be a popular catch-phrase or a whole book, the more ephemeral is its existence… Books, speeches and jokes – very few of these breathe the spirit not only of the moment but of all time. When they do, we call them Classics. *Tom Brown* is a Classic, and probably *Stalky* too. They are built of material which is imperishable, because it is quarried from the bed-rock of human nature, which never varies, though architectural fashions come and go.'

This judgement would have been approved by Selkirk-born *litterateur* Andrew Lang, who recalled his Academy schooldays: 'I remember saying, in an essay, that *Tom Brown* was the best book extant – after the *Odyssey.*' But even ephemeral stories affect the way school life is regarded and experienced. Those which appeared in weeklies like the *Magnet* and *Chums* were especially liable to rejoice in schoolboy mischief and the breaking of rules. The 'ragging' of teachers was regularly depicted in a way which inevitably affected school ethos. Perhaps that should be 'culture', or even counter-culture. In his gallery of form masters Ian Hay provided a caricature German, 'a survival of the days when it was *de rigueur* to have the French language taught by a foreigner of some kind. Not necessarily by a Frenchman … but at least by someone who could only speak broken English.' At Fettes the young Beith, J. H. had been taught by 'Froggy' Goldschmidt, whose methods of control included throwing the books of careless boys out of the window. A weaker 'Johnny foreigner' target – Beith's teaching contemporary – was provided by the Czech art master whose classes regularly descended into pandemonium.

Something should perhaps be said about 'unnatural practices' as an aspect of boarding-school life, although Robert Philp is the only chronicler of Edinburgh boys' schools to do so. These were genuinely rare at Fettes due to the late start as a reformed boarding school under the Christian banner of Thomas Arnold. Ian Harvey, a Fettesian who resigned from the Macmillan government after being caught with a Coldstream Guardsman in St James's Park, claimed that 'homosexual practice was almost non-existent, compared with what one has heard of other schools.' Bullying was another dark area. Half a century later Philp noted that the end of fagging and other aspects of hierarchy led to a 'decline in bullying and homosexuality'.

In day schools and boarding institutions alike, however, the older boys of Edinburgh schools embraced a Rabelaisian culture which thoroughly degraded the female sex through 'rugby songs'. These echoed in communal baths where mud was washed away and filth proclaimed. 'Mademoiselle from Armentières' suggests male bonding in wartime as a source. Shared summer cadet camp with other schools of the same type certainly widened the repertoire in a way that 'ordinary' schoolboys never knew. Schoolgirls were among the innocent objects, unaware of 'We are the Queen Street girls' as a local example. And all this out of the mouths of spotty adolescents, whose acquaintance with girls was so slight as to require cousins and friends' sisters as partners for the school dance.

39. *Jinglin' Geordie.*

40. *Heriot's Hospital, main door.*

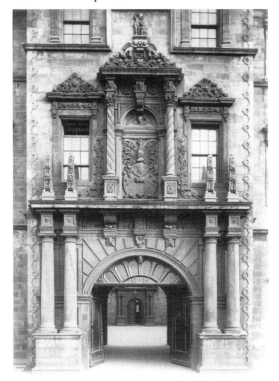

41. *George Watson, Hospital founder.*

42. *A new prospectus, 1870.*

GEORGE WATSON'S COLLEGE-SCHOOLS
FOR BOYS.

43. *High School Yards.*

44. *The Edinburgh Institution.*

45. *Alexander William Potts of Fettes.*

46. *Glencorse House, Fettes.*

47. *Thomas Harvey of Merchiston and the Academy.*

48. *John Rogerson of Merchiston.*

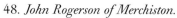

49. *Watson's at Archibald Place.*

50. *Back gate, Heriot's to Greyfriars.*

51. *Heriot's Free School, Cowgate Port.*

52. *Academy pavilion at Raeburn Place.*

53. Stewart's pavilion at Inverleith.

54. Day boys beginning at Stewart's.

Chapter 5

Schoolboys at Work

In these days when there is so little Latin taught (and hardly any Greek) it is quite difficult to imagine what 'classical' schools were like. They began in medieval times when Latin was the shared language of European scholars. For Edinburgh there are records of courses of study from the sixteenth century onwards showing books by Roman authors which High School boys – and later their counterparts in private schools – studied at different stages. Grammar and syntax, the necessary 'rudiments' of literary studies, were traditionally learned by rote. Physical punishment often accompanied this, and historian William Ross widened the context of a twelve-hour High School day: 'This is as barbarous as anything that the Industrial Revolution produced. It is little wonder that the same inhuman method of flogging the tired horse was employed in both cases.'

But the largely Edinburgh-based Scottish Enlightenment owed a good deal to classical education. After years of what D'Arcy Thomson condemned as 'gerund-grinding', all came to fruition in the Rector's class. This can be demonstrated through the career of one Rector, Alexander Adam, who spent a remarkable forty-four years with the High School's top classes until his death in 1809. Walter Scott had been one of Adam's pupils: 'It was the fashion to remain two years in his class. I had by this time mastered, in some degree, the difficulties of the language and began to be sensible of its beauties, nor shall I forget the swelling of my little pride when the Rector pronounced that, though many of my school-fellows understood the Latin better, Gualterus Scott was behind few in following and enjoying the author's meaning. Thus encouraged, I distinguished myself by some attempts at poetical versions from Horace and Virgil… It was from this respectable man that I first learned the value of the knowledge that I had hitherto considered only as a burdensome task.'

An alternative chapter title might be 'Teachers at Work'. No one worked to greater effect than Alexander Adam, who pioneered a new approach by encouraging his pupils to understand as well as memorise. A row over textbooks illustrates the difference. Thomas Ruddiman's *Rudiments of the*

Latin Tongue (every page in perfect Latin) went into many editions during the eighteenth century and became the standard grammar throughout Britain. Ruddiman himself, who combined the roles of printer, scholar and keeper of the Advocates' Library in Edinburgh, joined with High School masters in literary debate at the heart of the Enlightenment. When an alternative text became available they were loyal to him, refusing to make use of Adam's *Principles of Latin and English Grammar*: the Rector's book sought to lead pupils into the subject through their own language. Adam also fell out with the University Senate for

55. Alexander Adam, High School Rector.

introducing Greek to his classes (a professor claiming monopoly rights) and with the Town Council for his radical political views. After fourteen disputed years the alternative grammar was finally allowed to be used throughout the High School.

Grammar was by no means the whole story, which was principally one of presenting the high culture of the ancient world. Benjamin Mackay, who later taught at Regent Road, described Adam's method: 'The class appeared very numerous (120 boys) and in the finest order. The Doctor was calling up pupils from all parts of it, taking sometimes the head, sometimes the foot of the forms… The boys construed and answered with extraordinary readiness and precision, illustrating every allusion to Roman or Grecian history, antiquities, geography, mythology, etc. Nothing was omitted necessary to bring out the author's meaning and impress it upon the class. This exhibition gave me a valuable lesson, and made an indelible impression on my mind.' Adam's 'explanatory' or 'intellectual' system was taken up by John Wood, who brought education to the urban poor of Edinburgh, and Wood's Sessional School in Market Street became the model for teacher training in Scotland. Adam was seized at the last by an apoplectic fit in the classroom. He died soon afterwards saying, 'But it grows dark, boys – you may go; we must put off the rest till tomorrow.'

It is worth going back half a century to encounter the same Alexander Adam, not yet out of his teens, being appointed head – or first – master of

George Watson's Hospital. Boys were men in these days, and Adam had already been placed in temporary charge of a parish school in his native Moray. However it must be acknowledged that there was a house governor senior to him at Lauriston Place who was responsible for running the Hospital. Adam moved on after three years to pursue the classical studies at Edinburgh University which brought him to High School Yards. Latin was also the staple diet of Watson's boys although most had no intention of continuing with it. More to the point were the skills of writing, arithmetic and book-keeping which had formed the basis of the founder's prosperity.

Heriot's hospitallers were exposed to much the same curriculum which widened in time to include French and science. Entry standards were raised, with boys requiring a clergyman's certificate to show they were instructed in the principles of religion and had attended English classes. Most left at the age of fourteen in order to learn different skills through apprenticeship. In 1839 the American Alexander Bache of Philadelphia devoted a section of his report on European schools to George Heriot's Hospital. His highest praise was for religious education (excluded from the American common school) and he also approved of Heriot's drawing instruction based on the Prussian system. Bache's main criticism was that pupils and teachers spent too long in the classroom. The Rev. Dr William Steven, who in the year of Bache's visit was named as the

56. *George Heriot in stone.*

Hospital's first Head-Master with authority over others, agreed with him that 109 boys studying Latin out of 180 was too many. Steven laid greater store by reading and writing in English, and on the practical mechanics which had recently become available for senior boys.

In the following decade Horace Mann of Massachusetts provided a memorable description of what appears to have been the High School: 'The room, unlike the schools of the common people, was large. Seventy or eighty boys sat on deskless, backless benches arranged on three sides.' It may well be supposed that Benjamin Mackay was carrying on the Adam style: 'To an unaccustomed spectator on entering one of these rooms, all seems uproar, turbulence and the contention of angry voices – the teacher traversing the space before his class in a state of high excitement, the pupils springing from their seats, darting to the middle of the floor, and sometimes, with extended arms, forming a circle round him two, three or four deep – every finger quivering with the intensity of their emotions… I have seen a school kept for two hours in succession in this state of intense mental activity.' Elsewhere Mann wrote: 'The most active and lively schools I have ever seen in the United States must be regarded almost as dormitories, if compared with the fervid life of the Scotch schools.' But also, having observed the boxing of ears: 'Could the Scotch teacher add something more of gentleness to his prodigious energy and vivacity … he would be a model teacher for the world.'

By now the Edinburgh Academy was well established as a classical school for the New Town. It was intended from the first to resemble the High School with masters keeping the same pupils for four years before handing them over to the Rector, but the fifteen founding Directors also had improvements in mind. A preparatory 'Geits' class was added at the start (the word a Scots one for child) and it was possible to spend two years in the Rector's senior division. A key concern was to make the school more classical, with Greek taught earlier and to a higher standard so as to match the best schools in England. Nine-year-olds were introduced to the idea of Greece through the Athenians and Spartans described (in Latin) by Cornelius Nepos. Their literary studies culminated with Xenophon's *Anabasis* under the Rector. In his class Virgil, Horace and Livy represented the peak of Academy Latin which had begun with pupils passing from Ruddiman to Adam's *Latin Grammar*. By modern standards classes were large at fifty-plus, but smaller than those of the High School: monitors were never used at the Academy.

The Academy Directors were astonished at the welcome accorded to their school. More than five hundred boys enrolled in the first session, although numbers settled at a more manageable 360 by the 1840s. Despite the school's classical emphasis several modern subjects were on offer: French, astronomy and Natural Philosophy (or physics), along with geography, writing and arithmetic. These subjects, mostly optional, were put in the hands of full-time teachers to provide a level of staffing beyond that of English public schools. This is partly what earned the Edinburgh Academy of Victorian times the name of being the best school in Scotland. An additional Writing master was employed to ensure that no more than thirty-five pupils were required to share an adult's attention. The teacher of English (along with history) attempted to fulfil Walter Scott's dream of having boys compare ancient and modern civilizations in an imaginative way, but the subject remained a minor one. When times were hard in years to come – as when the roll fell to 211 in face of Merchant Company competition – the English master's work was returned to the Classics teachers.

A particular responsibility of the one member of staff required to have 'a pure English accent' was to improve pupils' speech through Elocution lessons – the old Scots language having begun a process of social decline. Scotticisms had been ridiculed for half a century, with help advertised to correct them in adults. The Academy existed partly to improve prospects for careers based in England and throughout the British Empire. Cockburn lamented the change, although he was renowned for his prose style in the increasingly fashionable language: 'English has made no encroachment on me; yet, though I speak more Scotch than English throughout the day, and read Burns aloud, and recommend him, I can do no more than get my own children to pick up a queer word of him here and there.' Not all the masters had pure English accents. James Gloag, who came from Gretna by way of a teaching post at Heriot's, had no time for social pretension: 'You think because your faither's a duke you can mak' a moke of me!' But his subject was mathematics, where speech mattered less. And thanks to Gloag's forty years there, the school produced an unlooked for quota of mathematicians and scientists including James Clerk Maxwell.

The amount of time spent with Latin rather than English in their schools was one reason why educated Scotsmen were sometimes ill at ease in London. Embarrassment was even felt about the way they pronounced the Latin tongue. The founding Academy Directors laid down that it should be taught 'according to the accustomed mode of pronouncing that language in Scotland,' which was also the way of continental Europe. However boys at the top of the school were also to be made familiar, 'as far as is practicable, with the English mode of pronunciation.' This Eton standard rhymed *qui* with 'why', and was associated with the start of received pronunciation in English. The Rev. Dr John Williams who became the Academy's first Rector (a Welsh

57. Classical languages at the Academy.

clergyman of the Anglican communion) was strongly in favour, so the compromise of using two styles at different stages did not last. Hard Scots sounds gave way to softer English ones. 'Cocky' again: 'There are Scotch schools (the Edinburgh Academy, for example) from which Scotch is almost entirely banished, even in the pronunciation of Latin and Greek.' Much later a general agreement among the world's classical scholars (accepted at Oxford and Cambridge) came down in favour of the system given up by the Academy.

However the languages were pronounced, George Harris (the school's resident historian today) believes that Latin and Greek provided little more than 'a necessary badge of gentility' for many pupils. He cites John Hay Macdonald who rose to the top of the legal profession – and Edinburgh society – after studying under Rector Williams: 'Smart, clever and more studious boys formed a set by themselves, and a long string further down constituted what the huntsman would call a "rubbishing tail"… There is a cruelty in the force feeding of young boys on literature that is sweet to the palate of the Oxford graduate who is set to teach, and who loses his temper over their blunders.' The *Day-Dreams* of D'Arcy Thompson rejected the methods of his colleagues: 'Having a keen sympathy with boyhood, I succeeded more and more… But the more I gave satisfaction to myself, the less I gave satisfaction to the majority of my so-called patrons: the guardians of my young

58. *RLS.*

pupils.' Some were removed 'without a word of explanation', to the concern of those responsible for the school. However the Rector's 1857 report made it clear that Thomson's Fourth Class – which was about to become his – had grown, 'contrary to all precedent'. One sickly youth who benefited from Tamson's Class was Robert Louis Stevenson.

Most of the pupils who were removed from the Academy did not go in search of more rigorous Latin grammar. In 1832 Robert Cunningham resigned as the head master at Watson's Hospital in order to set up a private school on lines of his own devising. As the Edinburgh Institution it was to

59. *Robert Cunningham.*

become a formidable third force in the New Town: 'The Institution is intended for those Young Gentlemen destined to employments for the successful prosecution of which a critical knowledge of Greek and Latin is not indispensably requisite... The branches proposed to be taught are:— Languages, including English Literature and Composition – History – Geography, with the Elements of Astronomy – Mathematics, Theoretical and Practical – the Elements of Natural Philosophy and Chemistry – and Drawing. The age of the pupil at entry is supposed to be from twelve to fifteen... The time necessarily devoted to the minutiae of the learned languages in the classical schools leaves comparatively little time for other studies. The private classes for Modern Languages, Mathematics, Drawing, etc., are scattered over the town, unconnected with each other and consequently without any unity of system.' No more than two hours a day of Latin and one of Greek were on offer at the new Institution, amounting to far less than the time devoted to these subjects in the classical schools. Gallingly for Academy and High School masters, the standards of attainment at the Institution turned out on inspection to be very similar.

Natural Philosophy (or physics) was delivered to a number of schools by outside lecturers, but the touring American Alexander Bache pointed to a particular area of contrast with the Academy: 'The courses of science are raised into a high comparative importance in the Institution... That of Chemistry is one of the most useful and interesting exercises of the student. The professor assembles a class from the Institution in his laboratory, places them at tables with the materials for experiment before them, orders different experiments by the several groups into which the class is divided, receives their explanations of the operations in the hearing, and inspects the results of each within the view of the whole class.' Lab work of this kind was far ahead of the times, but there were costs. Thirty years into the experiment a jar of nitric acid was dropped by the science teacher, and the janitor who helped with the spillage died after breathing in fumes. Near the end of the century the Institution's headmaster Robert Ferguson (who had studied under Bunsen at Heidelberg) lost a leg as the result of a laboratory explosion.

Practical science apart, what made the Institution challenging to other schools was the open curriculum at No. 8 Queen Street. A six-year course was on offer but a majority of the pupils only spent two sessions there in order to complete their schooling. These older boys (or their parents) were free to choose from what was on offer. Having everything under one roof was a definite improvement on going to this or that master's 'classes'. Rule 6 at the Institution made it clear that 'Pupils who join classes in the course of the day are required to come punctually at the hour; and if they have to remain outside for a short time until the door is opened, they are forbidden to ring the bell, make a noise, or in any other way give annoyance.' The Institution masters judged the level appropriate to each pupil, so that it was acceptable for a boy to be in the fifth class for English and the third for mathematics. Academy boys were assigned by age (though it became controversial) with automatic promotion at the start of each session.

During the 1870s the Edinburgh Institution became one of the largest schools in the city. Since the high numbers were based to a great extent on the short-term attendance of older boys its influence became widespread – through former pupil rugby as well as among members of the business community. But ironically it was competition from the Merchant Company day schools which brought this golden age of commerce to an end. Dr Ferguson was in no doubt that the new system did 'much more to cheapen the highest secondary education to those who need no cheapening than to render it accessible to people in humble life… £10 a year for a girl, and £6 for a boy, are sums that cannot be paid by working people.' The loss was felt in Edinburgh teaching circles. As one High School master put it to a 'Stution old boy at the turn of the century, 'The Institution has had a lean time for some years, but during the period you were a pupil it was, I should think, the best school in Edinburgh, and I have no hesitation in saying that it was possibly the best school in Scotland. What a splendid staff of masters it had!'

Alexander Graham Bell of telephone fame would have been happier at Queen Street instead of Regent Road: 'I took a very low rank in my classes. The subjects in which I really excelled, such as music, botany and natural history, formed no part of the main school curriculum. For Latin and Greek I felt no taste.' Mid-century High School head teachers followed the example of Rector Leonhard Schmitz (from the educationally-progressive Rhineland) by adding new subjects in an attempt to hold the interest and attendance of senior pupils.

Old prejudices were strong, however. Rector James Donaldson had to oppose the idea that 'nearly all the clever boys took the classical side, and the idle or stupid took the modern.' He was in charge when the High School came under the Edinburgh School Board after the 1872 Education Act. New regulations ended the dominant position of classical masters whose income had been largely based on the fees of their pupils, since government inspections now affected all High School teachers equally. In due course pupils found themselves taking the same broad range of subjects (still a feature of Scottish education) until the final year when specialisation was allowed. Under James Marshall, who retired in 1909 as the longest-serving Rector since Adam, the modern side finally achieved parity with the classical. Greek now came under threat, partly because it was no longer a requirement for admission to Edinburgh University.

Unusually for the 1830s (we return there for the boarding schools) Merchiston's first headmaster was a mathematician and scientist. Son of a practical Fife ship owner, Charles Chalmers studied these subjects at St Andrews University like his older brother Thomas. (This Dr Chalmers it was who led ministers and congregations out of the Established Kirk into the Free Church of Scotland.) The younger man, regarded as a 'brilliant and original thinker', stumbled into school teaching by taking in boarders and coaching them while he was pursuing his own studies. With Merchiston Castle leased as a school from the Napier family, unusual importance was accorded to maths and science. Chalmers took boys out weekly on botanical excursions and they also made visits to local factories. Under his successors 'the study of Chemistry and Natural History continued as before' – this although Thomas Harvey, who came from a teaching post at the Academy and returned there as Rector, was a classics man. A 'Chemistry House' was established – for safety's sake in the garden – during the time of John Rogerson, Merchiston's inspirational head for thirty-five years. Rogerson arrived as an assistant master at the same time as Hely Hutchinson Almond, whose even longer headship of Loretto began in 1862.

Almond's ideas on education were at first regarded as peculiar. As his successor (and brother-in-law) H. B. 'Tim' Tristram put it, 'For ten years he was laughed at, for ten years he was watched, and for twenty years he was imitated.' Almond regarded examinations which tested a syllabus as the enemy of free thought and enquiry. For him the five great objects – in descending order – were character, physique, intelligence, manners and information. He had no strong preferences as to which subjects provided the 'information' and was persuaded by Tristram (as Viceregent) to follow a gifted maths teacher called Marzials in the direction of science. As a boy Tristram had left Loretto for Winchester in order to study the ancient languages more effectively. He came north again for the wider experience of education in East Lothian. Tristram was Lorettonian enough to gain renown for his drop-kicking off either foot, and for tackling which won him the nickname of 'Octopus' at Oxford. He won five England caps at full-back before returning as a Loretto master. An old pupil was full of praise:

'How can one bring back to view that magnificent figure; the massive shoulders and hips, the beautifully formed thighs and legs, the straight piercing look? ... He was a great schoolmaster, and a sensitive scholar. In addition to his sound knowledge of the Classics he was widely and deeply read in English literature, and his culture was a decided asset to the School at a time when, if truth be told, the *litt: hum:* were not eagerly pursued by the many. He took the Fifth and was a really good teacher who saw to it that boys in his Form worked, and that while those who had the ability to go further were given the grounding necessary to their progress, others of lesser scholastic power were taught to use their brains and develop their capacities for reasoning and deduction. He had an amazing memory, and could quote whole books of the Odyssey by heart... The pages of the Greek grammar we used were etched on his brain, so that he could refer us off-hand to "Page 23, third line in the fourth paragraph".'

60. *The Chemical Lab, Loretto.*

Sad to report, this Greek god wore himself out early. He resigned after five years of supervising a large building programme while bringing Loretto through a post-Almond transition. The sciences became a full option against Latin and Greek, and numbers reached equality in the top classes of the school. Under 'Sconnie' Smith more laboratories were provided after the Great War, although elementary 'bottle and squirt' science was postponed until the fifth form because the Head believed it was useless to teach the subject until boys had reached a fair standard in maths and English. At sixth form level they kept on these subjects along with electricity, mechanics, chemistry and heat. As a final comment on Almond's schoolboys at work, however, Frank Stewart observed that in the Thirties 'any Loretto boy who was seen studying outside normal working periods was looked upon with suspicion, and even with pity, by his classmates most of whom genuinely believed that all spare time should be devoted to physical exercise.'

Fettes would have become a very different school if another leading candidate had been appointed to the first headship. Frederick Farr, author of *Eric, or Little by Little*, was an enthusiast for school science. Instead the post went to Alexander Potts who agreed with Thomas Arnold that science was liable to divert pupils from 'more important matters'. Potts hesitated about including modern languages at all: 'Classics reigned supreme, with maths and languages very much a side-show. Science was notably absent… Being a strong academic, Potts aimed from the start to drive the School towards the highest goals of scholarship. The Classics were to dominate the curriculum for the first 75 years of the School's life. The excellence of the teaching and the impact of Fettes scholarship at Oxford and Cambridge were the mainspring of the School's astonishing early success.' It continued under Potts' successor William Augustus Heard, who dismissed those who opted for other subjects as 'barbarians'. He was no doubt the origin of Ian Hay's fictional head who 'lamented at a masters' meeting the impossibility of procuring a science master who was a gentleman.'

As the school roll reached three figures and continued to rise, Potts reluctantly created a modern side while shuddering at the very idea of 'bifurcation'. One pupil was nevertheless apt for science. After reading about the invention of the telephone Allan Swinton set up the first connection in Scotland between two of the Fettes houses but was required to send the machinery home lest this absorbing interest might interfere with his Latin verse composition. After school Swinton went on to produce the first X-ray photographs, and as early as 1908 had developed 'an all-electronic concept for the realisation of television, having every claim to be regarded as the father of modern, electronic television, as against Baird's short-lived mechanical system.' His former teachers would have attributed this to the mind-training benefits of a classical education.

At Fettes the 'Mods' were despised for having opted for an easy life in preference to the challenging demands of the Upper Fifth Classical, and they lacked all standing in the community: at its most senior level they were not allowed to sit at the Sixth Form Table. It was only when Donald Crichton-Miller became headmaster after the Second World War that things finally changed – and in very evident fashion. As a Fettes pupil Crichton-Miller had won an Exhibition in history to Pembroke College, Cambridge. By the time he returned to a position of authority the old verities had been shaken. Without ceremony 'the classical Sixth was ejected from its time-honoured home in the "Upper" where the horseshoe desk was carved with the initials of generations, and dispatched (significantly) to the Museum, where, as *The Fettesian* noted, it was watched over no longer by Juno and Apollo but by a bearded goat and a stuffed python. It was to end up later in a converted changing-room beside the west lavatories.' *Sic transit gloria mundi.*

Daniel Stewart's Hospital arrived late on the Edinburgh scene and then, well placed to the west of the West End, Daniel Stewart's Institution flourished on low fees rising to £2 a quarter. An initial roll of three hundred trebled in twenty years, although this scarcely matched the staggering 1,600-plus boys at George Watson's College. The Company's original intention had been to make Stewart's intermediate between the James Gillespie's Schools (elementary – boys' and girls') and Watson's which charged two guineas a quarter at the top of the school. However in 1888, as part of a new endowment scheme authorised by Parliament, Stewart's was granted parity with Watson's. A stream of clever bursars arrived from poor homes by way of Gillespie's, most proving themselves well suited to the purposes of an academic institution.

School historian John Thompson gave evidence of high standards at Stewart's by citing the texts used in English, Latin, Greek and mathematics ('Few Scottish schools of the time did more') as well as in the distinctions won by former pupils – a Lord Lyon King of Arms was amongst them. Examination results provided a yardstick after the introduction of the Scotch Education Department's Leaving Certificate. Dr Thompson took pride in Stewart's successes at the Honours level (above Higher) but went on to cast doubt on the whole process: 'No figures are used more frequently; no figures are more deceptive. A table of passes would not show that [at the start] in 1889 many candidates came from primary schools, children of eleven or twelve, and that in some subjects, at least, the standards must have been very low… Nor do the figures distinguish between teacher and crammer. Our own figures show too plainly that one of the dullest and least competent teachers we ever had was quite the most successful in getting boys through the examination.'

Government was now encouraging and controlling schools through syllabuses, grants and regulations. The technical and commercial education of German schools was much better in states newly united under Prussian leadership. In imitation of this British boys with less scholarly pretensions were now pressed into book-keeping, short-hand and typing. Stewart's ran a Commercial 'side' for teenage pupils in the top two classes. Technical workshops provided a longer-lasting alternative to academic subjects but the school, like many another, did best by its brightest pupils. When C. H. (later Dr) Milne arrived as head-master in 1911 from Arbroath High School he found that progress among the majority of pupils was slower at Stewart's than what he had been used to in the state sector. His strong

61. *Dr Milne of Daniel Stewart's College.*

leadership over several decades restored the school to 'its old position'.

Charles Thomson was successively head of three state schools before becoming President of the Educational Institute of Scotland. His *Scottish School Humour* provides a counter-point to *The Lighter Side of School Life*. (It is perhaps worth adding here that another humorist who emerged from Fettes was W. C. Sellar with *1066 and All That*.) As a young man Thomson took up a post at George Watson's College teaching English, Latin and German at the end of the Victorian era. His description was not funny: 'The School was a strange mixture of excellence and inefficiency. An upper stratum of pupils did splendid work and maintained a first-rate reputation for their school at the University, but there were under-strata of comparatively neglected pupils who would have faired better in almost any Board School in Scotland… The maintenance of good order was exceptionally difficult, as the boys had learned the power of the "team spirit" in practising every sort of trickery… One session at Watson's sufficed me.'

It was Classical studies, for the most part, which distinguished the work of Edinburgh boys' schools from the rest. That hegemony did not come under challenge until the start of the twentieth century, and even then the change to a wider curriculum was less than wholly modern. A High School FP looking back on the inter-war period could have been speaking for boys' schools generally: 'We received an old-style liberal education, with a few concessions to the growing importance and respectability of science. It suited me very well… Backward-looking or forward looking, classical or non-classical, we enjoyed ourselves.' Exams had not yet achieved the status of being all-important: the 'group' Leaving Certificate (all or nothing) was generally passed in fifth year by those deemed capable of higher education. There was no sixth form in day schools apart from the Academy.

Boarding schools were different. Boys were virtually guaranteed a place at an Oxbridge college on passing the School Certificate (or 'Matric') at fifteen or sixteen. The Higher School Certificate was a sixth form option alongside sport. In 1932 there were thirty-two Lorettonians at Cambridge, mostly there on the basis of college entry requirements and interviews concerned with 'character'. There was no sense of strain at Loretto until after the second war, when Headmaster Mackintosh's 'first objective was to make the boys work harder… Examination for School Certificate must be taken as early as possible so that more time could be spent on preparation for the Higher Certificate. Science must be given a greater emphasis in the curriculum, since the many boys wishing to enter medical, science and agricultural faculties and colleges must be prepared for standards of entry which would become more and more exigent.'

Secondary Education for All was introduced by government at much the same time as the National Health Service, so that a similar range of subjects was offered in schools of both private and local authority sectors. Throughout the Fifties and Sixties, however, the post-war 'bulge' in birth rate provided fee-paying schools with a ready market. Competition was with senior secondary schools, entry to which depended on passing a 'Qualifying' test in primary seven. For children of average ability, chances of doing so were reduced by the large size of classes in neighbourhood schools. Passing an ill-defined test at age five for a fee-paying institution eased the tension, and it became common for day school boys (and girls) to spend up to fourteen years identified by the same badge and tie.

In schools of all kinds new subjects were added to the curriculum. If only to offset the idea of a straightforward confrontation between the classics and science there, a word is due on Fettes: 'I remember boys taking Economics (the timetable alternatives being Geography, German, Greek or Art) and a select band of Russophiles were taken to O Level standard by a retired army man who had picked up the language while serving against the Bolsheviks at Archangel. Music tuition cost extra but was encouraged. Latin was still compulsory, but so were English, maths, French and science under various options. There was a workshop with lathes where boys could learn to turn wood and metal. We had a number of lively characters on the staff. One had a stable of Icelandic ponies in the Pentlands. Another constructed a bizarre apparatus in one of those "temporary" wartime sheds using lights and mirrors to be able to see on a panel at the "desk" what his maths pupils were writing. It never quite worked.'

Nowadays journalists unravel exam results from SED information on each local education authority and – separately – for independent schools in Scotland. Edinburgh figures tend to show the Royal High maintaining its academic traditions near the head of some twenty comprehensive schools. Two other secondary schools with rolls of over a thousand, Boroughmuir and Gillespie's, are at much the same level with more than forty per cent of pupils passing three Highers in fifth year. At Heriot's, Stewart's Melville and Watson's the proportion achieving this basic qualification for further (but not higher) education is generally twice that.

Most pupils now stay on for a sixth year. At the Edinburgh Academy the brightest are not troubled with Highers in fifth year, and the boarding schools are even more fully committed to Advanced Level GCSE. Here comparison becomes difficult because day schools prepare their pupils for Advanced Higher while Fettes, Loretto and Merchiston focus on A Levels. On 27 August 2005, however, the Scottish Council for Independent Schools provided *The Scotsman* with good evidence that 'the discrepancy between the state and private sectors remains as high as ever.' This was demonstrated at the 'top-grade' level of A passes at Higher and Advanced Higher, and explained by a pupil:teacher ratio of 8.5 to 1. Others would say that many of the best pupils are 'creamed off' into independent schools.

There is more to education than exams, of course, but boys' schools responded to demand before there was anything in the nature of league

62. *Sir Roger Young and Watson's prefects.*

tables. In the case of one, the response began before 1958 when Roger Young entered his long reign at Watson's. A Westminster and Oxford man, he set out to alter the reputation of Edinburgh's largest fee-paying school as a crammer or 'sausage machine'. Young's campaign for real education was unwelcome: 'He would be taking on some very entrenched conservative attitudes right across the board from parents, teachers and, indeed, pupils.' Most changes were accepted in time, however, to create a healthier learning community at Colinton Road.

One innovation was abandoned, although Sir Roger (as he became) deserves credit for an imaginative '6-Day Cycle' which offered relief from the timetabling limits of a normal day school week. Though rather different in intention, this recalls Dr William Dewar as Young's opposite number at Heriot's. Dewar objected to the loss of one afternoon period three times a week so that sports-minded staff could take classes at the Goldenacre playing-field. As a compromise each class in the senior school was released one afternoon a week for games, with the school day lengthened by one period on Mondays. That did not long survive either, but it serves as a link with sporting chapters to come.

Chapter 6

Rugby the Defining Sport

The first rugby football match between Scotland and England took place in 1871 at Raeburn Place, Edinburgh Academy's playing-field near the school. Several years before that an inter-school game was played on the same pitch below the spectators' Mound. It took place on 11 December 1858 between teams of twenty boys representing the Academy and Merchiston Castle. A hundred and fifty years later a closely fought contest reaffirmed the event's significance as 'the oldest regular fixture in world rugby', according to sports journalist Allan Massie. A prior match was played between Merchiston and the High School on 13 February – but where? The Town Council had not yet granted use of the Holyrood field to the High School so it must have been on ground near the Napier tower-house. A wall on one side and a paling fence on the other were all that Merchiston boys knew of 'side touch', which became a point of dispute at Raeburn Place.

According to the High School's latest chronicler John Murray, 'Evidence exists to show that some form of the handling game had been played by the High School boys from as early as 1810.' This is surely a claim too far, from a time before William Webb Ellis at Rugby School. The Edinburgh lads would have been engaged in an older game equivalent to Kirkwall's Uppies and Doonies heaving back and forth in the street. Struggling while upright made it feasible to play on hard gravel, as in the pre-rugby 'muddles' of the Academy Yards in front of the school. What makes the Raeburn Place encounter interesting is the full *Merchiston Chronicle* report which followed. It shows that 'the Rugby rules', as written down by boys of that school for their spacious green, had just reached Scotland:

'Last year there was no order in the game whatever; it was each for himself, each kicking recklessly straight ahead, very little running with the ball, and "off-side" scarcely heard of. Now it is far different; each one has a place assigned to him for which he is most suited, whether goal-keeper, muddler, dodger, or as a member of that useful body the light-brigade.' The charging pack is here linked with Tennyson's recent poem. 'Last year we were disappointed in playing the Academy; but now, to our great delight, it

63. *Merchiston XX on home ground.*

was fixed as the first match of the season.' More than one prior match is implied. 'Comparisons are odious, yet we could not help observing that the Academy goals were a good deal easier to kick over than ours, being both lower and broader.'

There was no turn round for a shot at the easier goal posts, nor any idea of a half-time break – though play stopped often. An Old Fettesian described the 1870s when 'umpires and referees were unknown, and the two Captains argued out all disputes; a dispute sometimes lasted for fifteen or twenty minutes, so that a plausible tongue and an obstinate mind were valuable qualities for a Captain to possess.' The Raeburn Place match went on for two and a half hours, with spectators wet and cold. Tries counted for nothing unless a goal was achieved by the ball being kicked over the bar between posts which might rise as little as a foot above it. The whole affair was reminiscent of a school playground dispute, although knee-grazing gravel was exchanged for grass. The Merchistonian chronicler praised toe-stamping in mauls by 'the sturdy Campbell', along with the spotlessly-trousered McFie who kicked the ball an unlikely '80 or 100 yards' out of defence. Unfamiliarity with rules was the main theme of this 'Foot-Ball Match' report:

'All of a sudden Lyall made a rush, and to our great astonishment runs into "touch" right behind our goal. Here an expostulation was made on the plea that the rules prohibited running into "touch", but, finding that it only related to side touch, we were obliged to yield and allow the "try at goal". Fortunately for us the wet had so completely saturated the cover of the ball and made it so slippery that, when kicked, instead of going between the goal-posts, it flew out to the side... A little after one the game was all at the Academy's goal; and here we thought *we* had a goal, for the great MacFie kicked the ball easily over; but it stood for nothing as it was handed to him "off his side"… A few minutes after time, 2 p.m., was called, and the match was over without a goal being scored by either side.'

This unpromising version of football became rooted in Edinburgh through the enthusiasm of three headmasters – Rogerson, Harvey and Almond – who met as teachers in the tower-house before taking charge of Merchiston, the Academy and Loretto. Hely Hutchinson Almond only had about forty boys to call on at the start, fewer than half in their teens, and the first match against Merchiston was lost by three goals and five tries to 'a goal kicked by Mr Almond by a very good kick'. It was common for masters to take part in the early days of the game, leading by example. Almond was an umpire at the first Scotland-England match at Raeburn Place and wrote about it: 'I do not know to this day whether my decision which gave Scotland the try from which the winning goal was kicked was correct… When an umpire is in doubt I think he is justified in deciding against the side which makes the most noise. They are probably in the wrong.' A painting of a later Scotland-England match on the same ground shows a bowler-hatted umpire holding up his flag in recognition of yet another appeal.

When Fettes College opened its gates in 1870 the football enthusiasm of Headmaster Potts at once found expression in a game involving fifty-

64. *Flagging up a foul.*

two pupils (all those enrolled except one delicate boy) and three masters. Adults apart, the average age was barely twelve. Soon afterwards a twenty-a-side game took place, probably against the Academy which a young diarist described as (Walter?) 'Scott's School'. According to him 'It was a dirty game. We won, but they said we didn't, so we came away.' A team mate dropped a goal but the other side said it was punted without hitting the ground, and two watching Fettes masters flung down their coats to join in 'a very sanguinary encounter'. Two years later a team consisting mainly of fourteen-year-old Fettesians held its own with Merchiston, Loretto, the High School and Craigmount, although the Academy proved too strong for them. The last Fettes XX which took the field in 1873–4 (recorded in the first team photograph) still had a youthful look, but by the following season it was fifteen young men who faced the camera. Opposing XVs became standard. Numbers in Fettes College passing two hundred, additional accommodation was called into being and in 1879 a match to decide 'cock' house was captured in water colours for posterity.

The Academy was not the only New Town school which played. When George Watson's College opened its doors to day pupils, boys transferring from Circus Place School brought the game with them and also a rugby-playing teacher. Canonmills House Academy played rugby, and the Edinburgh Collegiate School in Charlotte Square had a field out at Ravelston. Collegiate were strong enough to take on the Academy, Merchiston and Fettes first teams, although it was Loretto's second string which received them at Musselburgh. At that time wearers of the Old Red Coat were particularly strong and there were seven Old Lorettonians in the Oxford XV. In a later Varsity match both captains came from Almond's school in Scotland.

In the last season before whole teams of former pupils went off to the Kaiser's war, a Collegiate man looked back on Scots school rugby for a *Boy's Own* compilation. Having emphasised the prior role of the Academy and

THE TRIUMPH OF LORETTO.
Scene: *Queen's Club, December 12th, 1900.*

THE OXFORD CAPTAIN: "Mr Greenlees, I believe?"
THE CAMBRIDGE CAPTAIN: "Mr Swanston, I presume?"
BOTH (together): "I think we've met before!"

65. *Varsity match.*

the boarding-schools and singled out George Watson's, he provided an overview of other schools: 'We played the Edinburgh Institution which in those days was renowned for the exploits of its FP's. Also we played the Royal High School which has turned out even more internationals than the Institution. And, as it was at the High School and the Institution and us and the defunct Craigmount and Blair Lodge, there were "football-daft laddies" (as the Scots phrase runs) at Heriot's and Stewart's College. We held our heads high above these last-named because we could claim at least one international player.'

The interest of the last sentence lies in the late development of Heriot's and Stewart's rugby, for there were to be many Scotland caps in years to come. H. H. Johnstone was a Collegian capped for Scotland, and a Loretto man also started his rugby there. This was at a time when the Institution still flourished through lively forward play. Blair Lodge Academy, set in thirty acres at Polmont near Falkirk, was Robert Cunningham's second foundation after the Institution. Along with Glenalmond in Perthshire, Blair Lodge played city schools on a regular basis. Craigmount School in Dick Place was a boarding institution catering for boys who studied Oriental languages for the Indian Civil Service. After becoming 'defunct', Craigmount reopened as a girls' school.

George Watson's College grew to rugby greatness in time, but the early days were difficult. Thanks to the enthusiasm of some boys on the Classical side, a team was quickly raised to play against a club called 4th Merchiston. Influenced by the Castle school, that district already favoured the new game. Jackets were used for goals in the Meadows for want of better playing conditions, but the result of this pleasingly casual encounter has not come down to us. Drop-kick practice in the play-ground had been driven out with threats and insults by Commercial pupils who preferred the other kind of football. When Rector George Ogilvie was persuaded to ask the Merchant Company for a field, its primary purpose was cricket. Summer seemed to him the natural time for sport.

An unsatisfactory ground was leased at Bainfield north of Myreside. A tree encroach-ed on the football pitch and the changing hut was dismantled by local youths for a bonfire.

66. *All for Watson's.*

Players entered from the canal path by 'louping the dyke.' On 2 November 1872 the first recorded match took place there between Watson's and a combined team from Warriston. A narrow victory was achieved by a goal to nil, as also in a contest with Collegiate. Other proprietorial schools refused to play Watson's, however, the owners' property having lost value to what local snobbery dubbed (for its low fees) a 'middle class charity school'. Games against nearby Glengyle and Carlton took place, and at least one trip was made to Portobello where there was a long walk between the railway station and Lady Napier's Park.

No difficulty was encountered over Daniel Stewart's as the other Merchant Company boys' school, first and second teams of twenty playing each other until numbers were curtailed: 'A list of fixtures was drawn up and the Stewart's Fifteen had an undefeated first season, playing with a team of a full back, three half backs, two quarter backs and nine forwards.' The original Stewart's pitch was clinker-covered on sloping ground in front of the school, although it had goal posts of the approved width and height: 'On the north side this rugby pitch was bounded by a thorn hedge. The touchline ran within a foot or so of this hedge and gave scope for gamesmanship; opposing wing halves came to dread the tackle into touch. Not that many opponents visited us. Heriot's were brave enough to face it, but the Academy boys who called us "cads" and fought with us along the Water of Leith declined.' At Fettes College sloping ground was seen as evidence of inferiority: 'Beyond Stockbridge in those days there were but few houses, and one passed practically into the open country, with fields on the right, including the Academy playing-grounds, and on the left a green expanse stretching right up the hill to Buckingham Terrace, called by us with singular lack of proper democratic delicacy, "the Cads' Park".'

Social class came early to Edinburgh rugby, but from one perspective the game actually helped to heal divisions. The man who brought it to George Watson's certainly thought so: 'I am convinced that the introduction of Rugby Football did more for the elevation of the School than appeared then upon the surface. It brought it into line with other schools and was the means of overcoming prejudices which were actual and deep-seated. In its subsequent development it instilled an esprit-de-corps which must have worked for good. In its later stages, it brought together the "Commercial" and "Classical" sides of the school on common ground where antagonisms could be sunk and in time forgotten.' By then George Watson's College was competing in 'the Public Schools Championship Competition'.

The rules of rugby football changed through time and with them the tactics. Fettes captain Gerald Campbell described early days on the College's Bigfield: 'The game consisted of interminable tight scrimmages, varied by equally prolonged mauls in goal. These gladiatorial wrestling matches, which have long since been disallowed by the rules of the game, were certainly not football but none the less extraordnarily thrilling, both for those who took part and for the spectators. The way of them was this: If a player carrying the ball crossed the goal-line and was then collared by one or more of the opposite side, he fought his hardest to touch the ball down and to secure a try, while his collarer or collarers did their level best to take it from him and touch down themselves. The only rule was that once the attacker or defender failed to keep at least one hand on the ball he was out of the fray.'

One such maul had a heroic Fettesian finally scoring after seventeen minutes, despite the close attention of four opponents: another rule pre-vented team mates from joining in after the ball was over the line. Scrimmages required heads down for shoving and searching: 'Without any elaborate 3-2-3 arrangement of the forwards, you plunged into the scrum where you could, but somehow or other stalwarts like Jenny Henderson … always managed to be up first and then, if they could not get hold of the ball, solemnly proceeded to kneel on it regardless of the vicious hacks of the opposing forwards. When the ball did get out of the scrimmage you dribbled or sometimes, if you could, picked it up and then if you were collared hung on to it like grim death till you were tired of being scragged and were forced to call "down", when another tight scrimmage was formed.'

The game was mainly about forwards going forward, although Fettes began a new trend by 'hoicking' (or hooking) the ball back. Middle-aged men 'frowned on the practice.' The ball was still round when teams of twenty gave way to fifteen: group photos show that change taking place in Scottish schools some time before it became official in 1877. It was several seasons before the referee had a whistle, since play only stopped when one side appealed. Until new laws began to have their effect, 'hacking' or tripping an opponent (with or without the ball) was allowed. 'Fisting' a ball thrown in for a line out from touch was banned in Scotland while still legal in England. This led to a fiercely disputed English try and a prolonged cessation of matches between the two nations.

For a while it was a rule that the ball had to be kicked over the line before being touched down, emphasising the importance of the charging light brigade of forwards: 'Feet Scotland, feet!' encouraged dribbling for years to come. It was Almond of Loretto who pioneered the passing game. Those designated to stay clear of the heaving pack sometimes wore caps and kept their heads up. The start of passing was accompanied by the cry 'Chuck when you're collared' – in the Archibald Place playground Watson's boys regularly played this as a game at intervals. Almond went further: 'If only they would pass constantly and systematically to each other they would baffle any side unaccustomed to such tactics, but they refused to try it for many years to come because it would look like funking.' Blair Lodge impressed with a line of backs taking the ball at speed, but it was Fettes boys (on the basis of pre-match planning in the Common Room) who countered a formidable Academy half-back by withdrawing a man from the pack. He became 'an extra half or three-quarter' in the system of eight forwards and seven backs which became general.

The Academy soon struggled against boarding-schools whose Oxbridge connections encouraged pupils to stay on till nineteen or even twenty, but for a while the day school was stronger. On one occasion Fettes conceded seven tries without reply but none of them was converted into a goal: 'It was rather a weird game… They scored their last try at the College end of the field just on the stroke of time, when it was almost too dark to see the goal,

67. Kicking practice at Loretto.

and some wag relieved the tension by shouting out in a broad Edinburgh accent, as the ball was being placed for the final attempt to lower our colours, "Why don't you light the gas?" The try however, like the six before it, failed and strictly speaking we, or rather the Academy placekickers, had drawn the match.' Scoring by points was later introduced into Scotland, being settled at 5 for a placed goal (or converted try), 4 for a dropped goal and 3 for a try. Penalty goals came in later, giving schoolboys further incentive to practise their kicking.

Boots were basic. Before the game emerged from the Academy Yards 'the most cruel "hacking" with iron-toed and iron-heeled boots was allowed.'

Tackety boots came in when it became important to get a grip on soft ground, and team photographs show these polished for the occasion. It was some time after knickerbockers were cut to shorts that school teams wore uniform stockings. Leather cross-grips

68. *Getting a grip.*

for forward traction were used in the first XV put out by the Edinburgh Institution. If a pair of Glasgow High School groups may be used in evidence, it appears that in season 1904–5 boots were still equipped with cross-grips. Five years later studs are on view in token of back play liable to include the jinking side step.

With spacious pitches available to the leading schools, progress into rugby by others came to depend on decent grass. The name 'Puddocky' suggests wet conditions suitable for frogs, and Warriston did indeed leave much to be desired. One touch-line ran parallel to Eildon Street, off Inverleith Row, at a level ten feet below grass verges on each side of a tight pitch. Changing took place in a tent. The Edinburgh Institution played there until the generosity of a parent obtained Coltbridge, opposite Murrayfield Polo Club which is now the international ground: 'In the days of Institution success their field was looked upon as the best in Scotland, but unfortunately the railway cast envious eyes on it and in 1891 the Institution had to look out for fresh quarters.' At that point, according to Melville headmaster Roy Young, it was the most successful day school in Edinburgh apart from the Academy. Losing Coltbridge contributed to the decline in 'Stution rugby along with a falling pupil roll.

Bainfield was abandoned after six seasons when Watson's took over part of a farm at Myreside. The farmer tendered cheaply to prepare the ground for sport and the result was summed up as 'Quag-Myreside'. Boys took the lead in raising money for a pavilion – fire-proof in brick – and the second fifteens of several schools deigned to change there: 'It was not until 1879 that they met the mighty Royal High 1st XV which was the signal that they had at last "arrived" in Edinburgh rugby circles.' The result, disputed for lack of a referee, was close enough to establish the High School fixture. By now the team which had been dubbed 'Invincible Ragamuffins' was smartly turned out in maroon and white stripes, some members to the extent of striped stockings. The Athletic Club run by Watsonians (former pupils who also used Old Myreside) soon passed the thousand mark, of whom six hundred members were pupils. When the move to New Myreside took place in 1897 there were sixteen rugby teams, twelve of them for schoolboys.

By then the Daniel Stewart's fixture had become a 2nd XV one for Watson's. Stewart's took over Honeyman's field at 'windy Ravelston with its hills and dales', behind the houses of what became Queensferry Terrace. In 1895 the members of a successful 'Scholars' Stewart's FP team persuaded the governors to acquire Inverleith. The Scottish Football Union was soon to enter into twenty-six years of hosting international matches on the neighbouring pitch, which was bought by the Merchant Company after the move to Murrayfield. To celebrate an upgrade which eventually produced Stewart's international players, the school's rugby team adopted red, black and gold jerseys: 'With the new jerseys came the new ground at Inverleith, level ground, where the grass was cut and wily lads could no longer tie together the tops of tussocks to make snares for their opponents.' Five years later Watson's were persuaded to send their 1st XV to a pitch as good as any at Myreside, when the Stewart's roll of 573 (having fallen) stood at a third of their opponents'. The home club's defeat was narrow, and Rector Milne regaled the gallant losers with a high tea, but the fixture between these two Merchant Company boys' schools did not become established until the Twenties. By then there were six senior fifteens at Stewart's and six junior ones.

Stewart's rugby has been strengthened in modern times by the merger with Melville College, and Ferryfield across the road from Inverleith provided the precursor Edinburgh Institution with a solution to its ground problems. The High School was one of eight founder members of the Scottish Rugby Union but changing facilities were primitive: 'What special sins have members of The Royal High School Present Pupils' Football Club committed that, when they have the misfortune to attend a football practice, they must dress not only in Stygian filth but also in Stygian darkness? Would it ruin the Club to have a lamp, or some other illumining agent, introduced into that abode of darkness, the dressing room at Holyrood?' After many years of ground-sharing the High School found a satisfactory solution at Jock's Lodge. As for Stygian filth, Fettes prefects were the only players who had hot water after games during the school's first heroic period. Conditions were warmer for Watson's boys at Myreside, but a bath nine feet by seven had to suffice for eighty at a session.

Of all the school playing-fields on the north side of Edinburgh, none is greater than Goldenacre. Despite this name in the singular the grounds of George Heriot's School extend to many acres. Rugby was slow to develop at Heriot's with the transfer from hospital to day school coming so late. When the first day boys were accepted a triangular piece of ground was obtained near the gate of Warriston Cemetery: 'Logie Green or Warriston was a miserable field. There was a sort of horsebox of a pavilion – one part for the visiting team and one for us... The only facility for washing was a tap at the end of the field. You can imagine what it was like after a game on a muddy ground in the depth of winter.' As with Puddocky the ground was soft and much work was needed to provide pitches for two kinds of football. Soccer enjoyed greater popularity, but the coarse language of visiting supporters came to the ears of school authorities. When the Scottish Football Association declared their version of the game professional Heriot governors dropped it for 'turning a good game into a trade'. When Goldenacre was purchased, weeks before the end of the century, three rugby pitches were laid out. There was no place for football.

While playing-fields spread, pioneers kept ahead of the game. Loretto played on ground taken from Pinkie Farm until Newfield was acquired on the left bank of the Esk – this when Oxbridge undergraduates only had to appear in Loretto red jerseys to be given a trial. Further acres to the Forth were added for a Memorial Field. Merchiston's last pitches in town suffered the fate of having George Watson's College built on top of them, but there was to be ampler scope for rugby at Colinton. Fettes used its lower playing area for less gifted players who made unrefereed 'House Belows' a watchword for ferocity. After buying additional land beyond the Jordan Burn, Fettes was more than amply supplied, and a field was set aside for members of the Fettesian-Lorettonian Boys' Club whose homes were in closes off the Canongate. Finally on fields, Raeburn Place proving inadequate for a school of almost five hundred boys to share with the Accies (or former pupils) the Academy purchased New Field from the Fettes Trust – by means of a loan from the Heriot Trust.

As the Heriot's example demonstrates, not playing the round-ball soccer game became a defining characteristic of fee-paying boys' schools. But there were exceptions. Roger Young played for a Watson's Staff XI against pupils, and the man he followed as Rector, Ian McIntosh, was a Cambridge soccer Blue: after his move to Fettes McIntosh was spotted by pupils (skipping their touch-line duties in support of the 1st XV) at Easter Road, the Hibernian FC ground. Previously an Old Fettesian had written to the school magazine: 'Our famous rugby Blues would be shocked to see some of our senior rugby men playing soccer on a summer's evening.' He was referred to the first issue of *The Fettesian* in which the captain of the Fifteen reported: 'In addition to our rugby matches we also played two under Association rules… It greatly improves dribbling.' Four Blues came from that team. In the following season Fettes played a home game against Heart of Midlothian and lost 8–2. At the Academy soccer became established as the official game of choice at Prep School level, allegedly because a nursemaid pulled the family's schoolboy to safety from a scrum.

The hero among Magnus Magnusson's Academy rectors is undoubtedly R. J. ('Bob') Mackenzie who turned round a failing school during the last decade of Victoria's reign.

69. *R. J. Mackenzie – compulsory games.*

Coming from a teaching post at Loretto he was a thorough 'Almondist', and wrote a biography of the man who brought sport to Scottish education. Mackenzie's first Report to the Directors made his position clear: 'Vigorous exercise of some kind is, I think, a necessity for boys, and it would be difficult to find more wholesome and recreative forms of it than the School games afford. They develop physique, endurance, presence of mind, qualities of the highest value in practical life... If I were asked what was the most dangerous occupation for a boy's hours of leisure, I should at once name loafing.'

Compulsory games were thus introduced for the first time into an Edinburgh day school. For three afternoons a week Academy boys played rugby in winter and cricket in summer unless they exercised the right (as very few did) to undertake a course of drill under the sergeant instructor. Senior practices were conducted by the ephors. At the end of session 1893–4 the Rector praised a XV which 'for the first time in nearly twenty years raised the football of the School to a level of that of Boarding Schools.' Victory over Fettes finally made up for the seven-try 'draw'. A year later Mackenzie went further: 'Any reference to published lists of successes won by examination shows that in this sphere the Day Schools more than hold their own with the Boarding Schools. In all forms of manly exercises, however, it is commonly admitted that they are inferior. The tradition of the Academy has been different, and the successes which our boys have won in the field are, I think, worthy matter for congratulation.'

Mention has been made of the impact made on the Varsity match by Almond's young men. At international level, the compilers of a 1954 centenary booklet on Raeburn Place showed that forty-six Academicals had played for Scotland and three for England in the first half century to 1904. During that period the Institution had eleven capped players (one playing for both Scotland and England) and the High School seventeen. Watson's began to produce Scotland caps in 1884, when the Institution stopped, and eleven Watsonians had won them by the Accies' chosen end-date. As for the boarding schools, thirty-one Merchistonians, twenty-one Lorettonians and nineteen Fettesians played for Scotland during this early period and two each for England. So closely was international rugby football tied in with these few centres of education that several caps were won by schoolboys. An Academy forward known as 'Hippo' Reid was chosen to play for Scotland in 1881. At the same time one of the school's quarters Frank Wright, 'a Manchester boy', was drafted into the English team at the last moment to take the place of a player who had missed the "night mail"… On the following morning (the game was played on a Tuesday) the Rector was forced to abandon Prayers, so prolonged was the cheering for the two boys when they entered with their class.'

That morning readers of *The Scotsman* had been told that young Wright 'saved England repeatedly' – the result was a draw. Full press coverage was soon being extended to school matches. Robert Philp has drawn attention to the stoking up of public excitement over 'the school rugby Championship. It was fought out by the six public schools of Scotland, each playing each other twice. On Fridays the *Evening News* or the *Evening Dispatch* used to survey the prospects for the next day's games, with reports on them in Saturday's late editions and on Mondays. They went in for headlines like "Schoolboys Astounding".' Magazines for schoolboys made all this a matter of more than local interest: '"The immense force of rivalry," according to a 1911 article by George Wade in the *Boy's Own Paper* ("The Greatest Football Schools") "has gone far towards making Fettes what she is today in football"…

'He puts down Fettes' pre-eminence to (1) excellence in pitches, practice arrangements and coaching (by old boys as well as others), (2) the enthusiasm and encouragement that makes every boy want to do well and get into the 1st XV if he can, and (3) tremendous local opposition.' House prefects chose hymns like 'Fight the good fight' before the Merchiston match; afterwards, if Fettes won, it was 'For all the saints who from their labours rest'. The national team benefited. Two years after the Accie 1904 cut-off point seven Old Fettesians were selected for Scotland. There were three OFs at Murrayfield against Wales in 1930 when one of them, Herbert Waddell, gained a first Grand Slam for Scotland with a drop goal five minutes from time.

By then rugby had become established in all the boys' schools, and fixture lists grew longer as motor coaches took teams out of Edinburgh. As the years passed, results were analysed in terms of opponents and periods of time: Watson's offered a double comparison: before and after 1927 as well as Archibald Place and Colinton Road – where ready access to pitches became a feature. The 'Golden Age of School Rugby' was identified as the early Twenties, however, one Watson's season marred only by a draw with Loretto. Meanwhile Heriot's Former Pupils won the Unofficial Championship in an unbeaten season and a member of the team,

Charlie Broadwood, joined the school staff as an English teacher. Over the decades which followed he produced six unbeaten rugby XVs, and during a seven-year period no school won a game against Heriot's at Goldenacre. Merchiston has always been a strong rugby school with unbeaten seasons in three centuries. The High School had good teams each side of the move to the suburbs, and in 1963–4 the 1st XV won all twenty-three matches scoring ninety-nine tries.

70. *Charlie Broadwood of Heriot's.*

The Watson's XV immediately after the Second World War was said to have 'broken all records', the achievement measured by nine boys playing in the inter-city match with Glasgow. Fettes soon entered an even more golden age, however, by being unbeaten in Scotland for nearly six years until 20 October 1956 – when 'the captain of Merchiston drop-kicked a late penalty from the touch-line which bounced on the bar and crept over...' During Ian McIntosh's final year of maintaining standards which included compulsory rugby, he braved a backlash by widening the fixture list to the point where it was no longer possible for Fettes to meet their three traditional rivals twice in a season. A curious fact associated with the post-war period is that during McIntosh's five years as Watson's Rector Fettes were never beaten, but the boys in maroon and white then proceeded to win every Fettes match during his first five years there.

Another remarkable story concerns Dr Dewar and the Goldenacre rebellion. William McLachlan Dewar was an exception to the rule that only Herioters could be appointed as Heriot's headmasters, and one of his first acts was to enrage a close-knit community by interfering with their rugby. At the urging of Charlie Broadwood the practice had begun (in session 1947–8) of releasing classes early for training three times a week. Dewar persuaded the governors that the timetable could not stand the loss of three periods. Broadwood submitted a letter on behalf of fifteen teachers stating their intention to resign from voluntary supervision and instruction at Goldenacre. A compromise was reached (winning staff back to referee games before darkness fell, which was part of the argument) by lengthening the school day on Mondays. Although Dewar was concerned about academic work, he also introduced compulsory games and with them the first full-time games master in Scotland. Tense times followed over a period of years but Heriot's rugby survived Broadwood's withdrawal from involvement at Goldenacre. By the time Dr Dewar reached retirement age no fewer than thirty teams – boys of all ages – were playing there.

A particularly attractive aspect of Heriot's rugby is the number of attacking full-backs who have played for Scotland, and none more so than Andy Irvine. His home was in the outer suburb of Liberton: 'I felt odd at first, putting on a uniform and going away to school when all the boys I knew went to local schools. The first thing I did when I got home every day was to strip off my school uniform and go out and play football... I played my first game of rugby when I was thirteen and went to George Heriot's School. I had only watched one game of rugby before that. I was taken to Murrayfield, but was so small that all I could see were the heads of the crowd and occasionally the ball sailing up into the sky. At Heriot's we were given a choice of rugby or cross-country. I opted to run the shorter distances, and found myself in the trial for the first-year fifth and sixth teams. After ten minutes, during which I scored quite a few tries, I was promoted...'

Changes have come upon Edinburgh schools' rugby since then. At the Former Pupil level most clubs are 'open', offering membership without too much concern for the old school tie. Boroughmuir is often the city's most successful club despite never having been a boys' school or charging fees. Girl rugby is more than a beer bar fantasy, but the main effect of co-education has been to lower standards at schools with half the number of boys to choose from. By concentrating on what boys' schools have always done, Merchiston achieved great success under future Scotland coach Frank Hadden: during one four-year period 54 victories were achieved from 58 matches. Early in the twenty-first century, however, the premise behind this chapter's title was yielded up when the rugby schools (including Merchiston) began competing in a Scottish Independent Schools' Football Association Cup. Fourteen of them participate, with Heriot's predominant. Watson's have even ventured into league competition against state schools: end of an era indeed.

Chapter 7

Cricket and other Games

Rugby football has been given priority for its autumn to spring importance in creating the sporting ethos of Edinburgh boys' schools, but cricket came first. In a sense it came from England, where inter-school matches had been on the increase since Eton and Harrow began to meet on a regular basis in the Regency period. In another sense it emerged out of longer days and warmer weather – a feature of the outdoor summer term. Bat and ball came together naturally without assistance from adults. Although cricket, like rugby, also became a compulsory school-approved activity in time, boys needed no encouragement to play 'other games'. Elsewhere girls performed stately movements while singing or amused themselves with ropes for skipping and balls for bouncing, or raided classroom chalk to play hopscotch. *The Singing Street* by James Ritchie, an Edinburgh science teacher, evokes all that.

Boys' games by contrast – in a way which no longer divides the sexes to such an extent – were distinctly masculine. They took place in the streets, where High School and Hospital boys 'bickered' aggressively or disturbed the citizens with 'Hare and hounds' through the Grassmarket. The Meadows were near at hand for other wide-ranging games, but school 'yards' offered a daily arena. Teachers did not supervise play in Scotland, but rules read out to High School boys at the start of session below the Calton Hill reminded pupils that 'All climbing on any part of the building, all playing against it with marbles, balls or anything else, is, on that ground forbidden. You are, also, cautioned against carrying on any of your amusements so near to the building, as to expose you to the hazard of breaking any of the windows.'

Ball games apart, schoolboys' playground activities were strenuous and breathless by turns. 'Cuddy-hunkers' had one side jumping on top of the other as it scrummed against a wall, while 'Goosie' or Prisoner's Base was a vigorous game of interception. When it came to morning interval there was no time for counting-out rhymes to decide on the first chaser: 'Last up's het at cockie-rosie' signalled the arrival of spring at Stewart's – the Scots language proving apt for rough and tumble outside the classroom.

The single combat of 'Hoppy-bowfie' (one-legged shoulder-charging) alternated with paired contests, one boy carrying another in what the South Side called 'Tilting' or 'Tournaments'. The commoner name of 'Coalie-bag fights' suggested a link with the smoke-encrusted buildings of Auld Reekie. A breather could be requested in any game by holding up a thumb and calling out 'Barleys'. This parley or truce went back to the days of real tournaments, and to public friction in the reign of James I:

> Thocht he was wicht, he was not wyss,
>   With sic Jangleurs to jummill;
> For frae his Thoume they dang a Sklyss,
>   Quhile he cry'd Barlafummil.'

Club and ball came together in Loretto shinty as ash sticks were wielded among golfers on the links, golf itself being a more spontaneous activity in those days. Loretto boys also played a summer game akin to cricket: '"Puddex", often shortened into "Dex", was a much more popular sport. It was generally played in the Orchard. Basically it is single wicket cricket but was played with a hard tennis ball and a porringer [porridge spirtle but larger]. A degenerate age has introduced modifications and has robbed the bowling of much of its skill by rejecting anything short of a full-pitch and, to prevent scores being too great, the laws insist that a batsman must retire on making twenty-five. But in its old style it was a fascinating game. Enthusiasts were even known to leave their beds at six o'clock of a fine June morning and make the Orchard ring to their shouts of "Pyjamas versus Nightshirts". For those who were not so wakeful the half-hour after prayers in the long twilight of Scottish summer evenings was the golden time for "Dex".' The Quidditch of Hogwarts Academy is just an imaginative step away.

Puddex also flourished at the Edinburgh Academy, but the game which became most fully associated with that school's Yards was 'Hailes' in which boys used a 'clacken' – eighteen inches long with a spoon-like head for lifting the ball. These were sold by the janitor's wife along with biscuits and milk. Academy boys carried them to school and back for security against the Stockbridge cads of Stinky Lane. Originating in the old Scots Hand-and-hail-ba', this was a form of shinty in which the ball could be carried on

71. *Clacken and ball.*

the clacken. Finding that the game had died out among senior pupils – while deteriorating at the hands of juniors – Rector Mackenzie revived it by introducing an annual Silver Clacken competition. Clackens were also used in a form of 'Fives balls' against the school walls and even classroom walls. Robert Louis Stevenson made them into a symbol of lost schooldays:

> The roll-book is closed in the room,
> The clacken is gone with the slate…

Tip-and-run was another Academy playground game which came close to the major sport, and cricket itself was adapted to hard surfaces as recalled by a Lord Justice Clerk: 'When summer came round, cricket was played with balls covered with thick, coarse leather to withstand the stones. As a substitute for stumps we chalked the size of a proper wicket upon the wall, and the chalk acted as umpire. The batsman was out when there was chalk on the ball.' An early drawing shows a boy in front of the portico with cricket bat, not clacken.

72. *An early Academy batsman.*

Eight years after their school was opened Academy boys played two proper cricket matches against the High School and the Scottish Naval and Military Academy, and in the following decade High School teams were challenged regularly on Bruntsfield Links beyond the Meadows. Arrangements were left to the players, as recalled by an old Academical army man: 'The Elevens doffed their jackets, laid them in a heap, and the game went on. There were no flannels, fielding jackets, cricketing caps, pretty ties, nor newspaper paragraphs in those remote ages. Pads were rarely used, and hardly necessary seeing that the bowler's hand was strictly kept down by law.' Newspaper paragraphs followed, as the fashionable new game brought out 'a splendid display of private carriages'. The Grange Cricket Club (largely consisting of former Academy pupils) helped by bringing an All-England team to their Grove Street field near Fountainbridge. On another occasion W. G. Grace played in a United South of England XI against eighteen Gentlemen of Scotland.

Recognising that the carriages were those of potential Academy parents, the Directors made the momentous decision to lease Raeburn Place. The ground was much larger than required at the time, and scarcely more than half of its ten acres were levelled and re-sown for cricket. Turf for the square was brought from Fisherrow at Musselburgh. Outside the fenced sports area the ground was sublet for pasturing sheep and cattle – so close to the country was Edinburgh's New Town in these days. Fourteen years later the Argyll Commission on Burgh and Middle-Class Schools in Scotland made an appeal for better recreational facilities: 'With the single exception of Irvine Academy, which has three acres in extent, there are not to the best of our recollection two acres of grass set aside for the use of any of the schools, except the Cricket Field of the Edinburgh Academy.' After giving up Grove Street, the Grange Club played on the Fettes estate. Then the projected building of a school there brought about a move to the East Haugh beside the Academy ground. Fettes College inherited pitch, pavilion and scorers' box.

The Royal High School benefited from having Edward Prince of Wales as a pupil for three summer months in 1859 by being given the use of land in front of Holyrood Palace. A Former Pupils' Cricket Club was promptly formed, its first three members allegedly meeting in a sentry box which was also to serve as a changing-room: 'One could hardly imagine a more fortunate choice of ground, if only it had been an acre or two larger. The turf is old, the view of Salisbury Crags and Arthur's Seat is magnificent, and by reason of its central position and open surroundings the School's Park attracts more cricket lovers than any other ground in Edinburgh.' This had not been achieved without difficulty: 'The southern portion of Holyrood Park, near the Crags, was very uneven, and at considerable labour and cost this was levelled.' In the Thirties of the following century the Rector was able to report seventy-five per cent of High School boys taking part in cricket 'fixtures' – mostly between Nations of the house system.

The agricultural origins of Loretto's ground were evident from the nature of the pitch which became notorious among the cricketers of one rival school in particular: 'Fettes batsmen – not for the first time, or the last – found themselves all abroad on the slow ground at Pinkie after their own hard and fast wickets.' Merchiston laid out their first cricket square in a field to the north of the school. When it was sold for housing, stumps were removed to the future George Watson's College site, and a better ground was eventually created at Colinton: 'After the levelling process boys were brought out from the old school several afternoons a week to clear the biggest stones before grass could be put down. It is estimated that by 1927 over 200 tons of stones had been lifted by hand.'

Nearly two hundred Academy pupils paid the field subscription in the summer term of 1854 – six shillings for seniors, four for juniors. Early games were mostly in-school affairs, but the High School match was trans-ferred from Bruntsfield Links to Raeburn Place. At first only home games were played for want of proper playing-fields elsewhere. In particular the idea of boys heading off to play Trinity College at Glenalmond was rejected, a Director arguing that 'such matches are calculated to bring Schoolboys too much forward, and to give them higher ideas of their own competence than is good for them.' Nine 'external' matches were played in 1857 – the first year with a true fixture list – all but one of them at Rae-burn Place. Merchiston was met home and away that summer and for many years to come. A train journey to Glenalmond was also allowed, after reconsideration, to complete a second double-header for the calendar. Games were of two innings each, scores tending to be low: 'Few sides who have made thirty runs need begin their task in the field with despair.'

Glenalmond's team included one of the College's teaching clergymen. Other schools had their professional coach take part along with a master or two, and in Loretto's case the Head: 'Every year up to 1880 the first named player and captain was H. H. Almond… To Almond cricket was fun, and he made it fun for others. His own merriment and energy made certain of that. Perhaps, as in so many things he did which he thought worth while, he carried his enthusiasm to excess, for in summer Loretto was all cricket, and nothing but cricket; it was sides twice a week and matches most Saturdays, with nets on the other days. With little talent at his disposal, at least in the early years, he concentrated on proficiency in fielding… He spent much time making the boys learn by practical experience what was a possible run and what was not… It was not until 1875 that the game against Fettes became a two-day fixture.'

With a good pitch nurtured by the Grange members, Fettes were able to take up serious cricket in the school's first summer. Because of small numbers and the age of pupils the first inter-school match was against the

Academy's youngest senior class known as the Geits. Fettes achieved a comprehensive victory. Two more wins were achieved that term against the same 'Gites' (as the Fettes chronicler had it) and one against the Academy's Moderns. The majority Classicists stood apart. Finally, 'with the aid of masters and professional, we beat the Academy 2nd XI by 62 runs.' The young Fettes College's strength was reduced when their professional coach (whose brother toured Australia with W. G. Grace) was dismissed after returning drunk from Glasgow. His sober replacement could neither bat nor bowl, however, and as a result the Academy Seconds won the return match. In Fettes' third season 1st XI fixtures were granted by Loretto and the High School: 'The Academy and Merchiston, however, stipulated that we should first beat their 2nd XIs… In the returns with their 1st XIs the Academy were beaten by 60 runs and Merchiston by 86. The High School were defeated by 24 runs, and these results firmly established our position on an equality with the other schools.' Five years later the Fettes team had nine players who achieved batting averages of 13 or above, boosted to a considerable extent by scoring 370 against Craigmount.

In the last quarter of the nineteenth century Edinburgh's boarding schools became locked into a series of testing matches each summer along with Glenalmond, Blair Lodge and the Academy. There was a family feeling about the rivalry. The shared Merchiston origins of Almond, Harvey and Rogerson have been noted in relation to rugby football. As for cricket, it was Dr John Hannah (as Rector) who approached the Academical Club about 'a field for the use of the Pupils for Cricket'. Having left to become Warden at Glenalmond, Hannah must have taken satisfaction when a team of that college's best cricketers (out of sixty-eight boys and several clergymen) won their first match at Raeburn Place. A Loretto master, J. Cooke-Gray, played in the school's early elevens along with Almond and his pupils before going on to become headmaster of Blair Lodge outside Falkirk. The roll there topped three hundred before Cooke-Gray died at the start of the following century, bringing its time to an end. Blair Lodge outgrew Loretto, in other words, but the balance of results in winter and summer sports always remained with the Musselburgh school.

Craigmount disappeared from fixture lists some time before it became defunct. Apart from the Academy, other day schools featured occasionally in what was otherwise a closed shop. Edinburgh Collegiate played once against

Fettes, their Former Pupils twice. The Royal High School contrived a single victory against Fettes through the bowling of their professional, but the fixture was dropped after a series of heavy defeats for the day boys. The Edinburgh Institution scarcely features, although its former pupils were to achieve consecutive seasons undefeated. Daniel Stewart's boys found themselves playing an extended game at Inverleith: 'In these days the only cricket boundaries were the walls and fences and the cinders in front of the pavilion so that batsmen and fielders had much more running than now. There was one occasion at least when the batsmen ran five for a leg hit to the pavilion which if it had travelled two feet more on to the cinders would have qualified as a four.' Heriot's had a professional and groundsman before the move to Goldenacre, and his work was pursued more effectively there, but inter-school matches were slow to follow.

Watson's also took some time to develop the summer game. Pupils at Archibald Place came from homes all over Edinburgh, and many found that the long walk to school and back was exercise enough. Masters with large classes to contend with took little interest in cricket, and playing conditions at Bainfield left much to be desired. When Old Myreside was made ready for use out of plough-fields, however, its pavilion with dressing rooms was regarded as the Cricket House. The first professional to be taken on was a veteran who could only bowl underhand. (A Merchiston captain of the early days 'bowled slow, well-pitched underhand balls, which were apt to twist and caused much trouble to the other side.') His successor was much better, and interest gradually grew among pupils and Watsonians. By the time the College entered into possession of New Myreside there were eleven schoolboy cricket teams.

Encouraged by the *Wisden Cricketers' Almanack* there developed an English tradition of fine writing on the sport, and Edinburgh schools embraced it. The Fettes 1875 season produced two catches to inspire the scribe. One concerned the Lorettonian R. J. Mackenzie who later brought compulsory games to the Academy. As a schoolboy his spin-bowling (or 'lobs') was deadly and J. F. Carruthers did well to score 49 before being 'caught and bowled by Mackenzie from a tremendously hard return which rendered the catcher insensible though he held the ball.' However Fettes gained 'a glorious victory amid scenes of wild enthusiasm... All the Schools were decisively defeated, and we were "cock" school for the first time.'

73. *In the shade of a Fettes beech tree.*

(Club matches against such as Brunswick, Grange, Edinburgh University and Lasswade also featured.) The other dismissal, from earlier in the Fettes season, was so dramatic as to enter the opposing side's records as well: 'In the match with the Academy at Raeburn Place Carruthers made his immortal catch. Ninian Finlay, a tremendous hitter, made one of his biggest and loftiest smites and Carruthers, fielding in the country, ran a long way at full speed and caught the ball with his left hand close to the hedge near the entrance.' The batsmen were crossing for a third run when Finlay was given out.

Loretto's two-day matches with Merchiston were generally hard fought and the Loretto-Fettes match near the end of term often decided the championship. *Wisden* also encouraged record-keeping: results, as well as batting and bowling averages. Between 1880, when Almond ceased to lend increasingly dubious support on the field of play, and his death in 1903 Loretto played 133 matches, of which eighty-three were won and only thirty lost. Given the Scottish climate, the low number of draws gave testimony to the sporting spirit (on all hands) of going for a result. As Loretto's

74. *Almond retired unhurt.*

latest historian Frank Stewart noted, these figures represented not only a clear advantage over other Scottish schools but also parity with Rossall on the Lancashire coast, 'one of the top cricketing schools in England'. Sedbergh near Kendal has also provided a benchmark for Scotland's schoolboy cricketers over the years.

Despite the glories of Raeburn Place, and then the acquisition of New Field under Rector Mackenzie, the Academy found it difficult to keep up. In 1884 Loretto scored 407 leaving the Academy an hour in which to make 21 for 4 wickets – this in the days when it was against the rules to declare an innings closed, and the scorer of the first Loretto century against Fettes sat down on the pitch in order to be run out. Andrew Lang (who admired *Tom Brown's Schooldays* next to the *Odyssey*, and whose subsequent writing covered cricket among much else) opened a new library at Henderson Row in the first summer term of the new century. He sat down to an ovation after offering 'to give cricket bats to the boys who were most successful in batting and bowling against Merchiston the following day'. Mackenzie persuaded the Directors to employ a second professional, and 'his cup of happiness overflowed when he was able to announce, in his last Report in 1901, that the Academy XI under G. L. D. ("Gibbie") Hole, had won the "Schools Championship"'.

By this time Watson's had widened the basis of competition, and two years later were hailed by the press as Day School Champions. Members of the team wore white blazers (all five buttons fastened) with maroon piping and collar turned up, along with white peaked caps. In 1906 the College's cricketers shared the more prestigious Public Schools' Championship due to victories over Merchiston and Loretto, and in the following 'halcyon' year they won it outright. However as *The Watsonian* editor Hector Waugh put it, 'While we have more than held our own with the day schools of Edinburgh and Glasgow, we have suffered many more defeats than we have gained victories against the Academy, Merchiston, Loretto, Glenalmond and Fettes. There have been seasons when Watson's have been easily superior to their day school rivals, winning by eight or nine wickets, dismissing teams for 20 runs or less; and yet they have, in those seasons, been unable to extend their public school rivals at all.'

From that journal of record comes a humorous item of the Thirties: 'I am a perfervid and aggressive Watsonian, always insisting loudly – and I don't care who hears me – that George Watson's College, of all the schools I have attended, is easily the finest… But I must admit here with sadness that nowadays when I see a team, wearing white trousers which reach from the waist to the middle of a white boot, playing against my old School, my sympathies turn the wrong way and I find myself distressfully supporting the enemy.' The sartorial aesthete went on to abhor his old

75. *Under the stand at Myreside.*

school's 'truncated trousers, and these boots in all their nakedness, and those fat maroon Rugby-legs in between.' By the time an indoor wicket was added to the Myreside pavilion in mid-century senior knees were decently covered. Cost must have been a consideration, with no other use (as with tennis shorts) for white flannel trousers. The High School 1st XI still wore shorts at the time of the move to Barnton, as did Melville and Stewart's – although members of the top team adopted long flannels at the start of the combined school.

George Heriot's School cricketers followed the same fashion at about the same time. The pitch and outfield at Goldenacre have long been recognised as among the best in the country, and there were 'glory years' in the post-war period. During seven seasons from 1953 Heriot's lost only six matches, playing up to nineteen fixtures in the short summer term, and from these school teams there emerged several long-term Scottish international cricketers. As with rugby, Heriot's were late arrivals on the Edinburgh cricket scene and the only 'public' school to play them was Merchiston in the Seventies. This was at the point where co-education reduced the number of boys available so that results were less than glorious.

Even Fettes, who generally disdained day school fixtures apart from those with their neighbouring rivals, experienced lean years: 'Presumably Scotland is by nature unsuited to the game, as is the climate of Edinburgh in particular.' Despite being even more fully exposed to the Firth of Forth, however, Almond's heirs continued to flourish. Between 1959 and 1968 Loretto lost only once each to other boarding schools and the Academy. Merchiston were the main rivals, providing stiff opposition in a series of draws – now mercifully reduced to one-day matches: 'It is natural to ask whether the School's post-war success at cricket was due to the main-tenance of a high standard at Loretto or to a lowering of standards among her competitors.' Reassuring wins were gained against Sedbergh, but even English schools were losing enthusiasm for the game. Loretto paused to consider. As Headmaster Bruce Lockhart put it, when reducing compulsion to one term of trial with bat and ball, there was little to be said for boys without aptitude 'spending their afternoon chewing grass waiting outside the boundary for their own side's innings to end, or chewing grass inside the boundary waiting for their opponents to get – or be umpired – out.' But the playing of compulsory cricket was coming to an end. In recent

76. *Merchiston at the crease.*

years no Scottish school has been able to live with Merchiston's continuing level of dedication to the sport.

At an earlier time, when sport meant a more positive liberation from the compulsory classroom, there were other games beside rugby and cricket. Closest to these as a team game was hockey, which took firmer shape at Fettes when regulations arrived from England. Ian Hay (Beith, J. H.) recalled his involvement: 'Enthusiasm reigned, and a challenge was sent to Loretto for a match under the new Association rules… On Monday before the match five Loretto boys went to Fettes to take part in a practice, and, no doubt, spy out the land. They found, according to the contemporary *Lorettonian*, "that with a heavy ball our short shintie sticks were no match for their long heavy ones, and that if we were to make a match of it we should have to change both our shinties and our style of play." By brilliant staff work the revolution was accomplished. New sticks were got out in time for a try-out beforehand, and on the Saturday the shinty-trained boys won the first hockey match in Scotland by nine goals to five.' Even so, five years passed before the less dignified 'shinty' ceased to be used at Loretto and 'hails' were reclassified as goals.

Another ball game to become popular was Rugby fives – named after the school, and distinct from versions originating with Winchester and Eton.

Overtaken by squash in modern times, the game relied on the construction of suitable courts. Once Almond became persuaded that sufficient fresh air was available from the back of the playing area Loretto took up fives in earnest. Merchiston's results were discouraging over many years until two new courts were presented to the school: 'During the years 1952–62 we lost only one school match, and our first pair's performances in the Public Schools Rugby Fives Championship has been unique in the history of Scottish schools and even enviable by English schools of double our numbers, bringing the coveted Mappin Cup over the Border.' Tennis courts also became available, but the racquet game never enjoyed the same cachet in boys' schools where it was said that 'you did no one good but yourself.'

The Royal High's basketball team won the championship when Tony Blair turned out for Fettes in the name of new – North American – sport; there is no reason to suppose that the day school's Robin Cook (older, smaller) ever bounced a ball on court. Some activities were more sport than game, or else hard to classify. At the Academy, where Magnusson's repeated observations on the lack of a swimming pool have been ignored, there was inter-division competition at Drumsheugh Baths. Cycling, recently raised to Olympian glory by Watsonian Chris Hoy, began with the penny-farthing. There was a handicap two-mile race on these ungainly vehicles while Stewart's were at Ravelston, and the back marker who overtook all opponents to win by fifty yards was still an Inverleith regular in his nineties. Some contests such as boxing and fencing took place in the gym. Winter sports like sledging, skating and curling relied on cold weather: among Royal High FP record-holders (lists having been compiled for pupils past and present) there is a playful entry concerning the winner of a snowshoe race at Winnipeg.

Before coming to athletics and the sports days which exhibited their events from mid-nineteenth century, a parallel indoor occasion deserves to be noted: 'At this time also began the function known as the Annual Assault, a gathering at which the High School, Loretto, the Edinburgh Academy, Dreghorn College, the Institution, Canonmills House, Blair Lodge and Merchiston met in inter-school competitions in fencing, singlestick and gym. Right from the start it must have been a popular entertainment for parents and others, as it needed the Music Rooms in George Street to house both the large number of visitors and the military band which was always brought in for the occasion.' Singlestick was widespread enough to become an Olympic event before giving way to sabre and épée. Merchiston boys were to achieve notable fencing success about the same time as their fives triumphs. Both were regarded as minor sports 'in that they are practised at odd times during the school day.'

Athletics emerged out of the simple activity of running: Watson's boys, for example, instituted a March Hare round the outside of the long buildings at Colinton Road. School authorities sometimes made road-running an alternative when the ground was too hard for team games, as with Academy boys being sent on 'dreary runs' to Davidson's Mains and back

77. *Watson's March Hare.*

or (less demanding) round the Fettes railings. Inside the Fettes grounds a gruelling race took place in spring (before the days of Health and Safety) 'around the Below Fields area over various walls, fences and through or over vast water "jumps", fifteen feet in width and five to six foot deep. Competitors had to be either swimmers or long-jumpers – preferably both.' This Steeplechase varied for different age groups, and the pond was made shallow enough to run through. The Paperchase was another Fettes run, with Hares scattering the 'scent' over a marathon which sometimes encompassed the Pentland Hills. At one High School assembly, just before the Leaving Certificate took control of Scotland's day schools, 'the Rector complimented the boys on their run, and remarked that they would have a different kind of paper-chase all the week. He hoped everyone would show as good form in the examinations as they did on Saturday.' Loretto boys took things more seriously than others with a daily run on the Links before breakfast, regardless of weather, as well as longer trails round Three Hills and Fa' Side.

Almond gave deep thought to the question of athletics. He was delighted when the Academy made Raeburn Place available in the spring of 1866 for Interscholastic Games – distinct from the school's own games which were by then in their eighth year. Both of the classical day schools took part along with Merchiston, Glenalmond and Loretto. Almond appreciated the fact that there were competitions for all sizes of boy at a time when most Lorettonians were too young to succeed in open events. His considered view was that boys should take exercise for the sake of fitness, and to achieve defined 'standards' in running, jumping and the rest. As with exam passing, he was not interested in individual winners – although their performance was valued for contributing to success in inter-school competition.

Great was Almond's disappointment when the Raeburn Place meetings stopped after six years. This was due to the Academy Rector, his former colleague Thomas Harvey – and 'the very man who at Merchiston had imbued in him the importance of games in education.' Harvey felt that undue credit was being given to schoolboy 'gladiators', and he was also wary of the betting and drunkenness which pervaded other meetings. Almond revived the Interscholastic Games at Pinkie, close to the Race Course, and then at Corstorphine where the University (partly at his urging) had acquired a playing field. In the absence of support from other schools, and an outright ban on Fettes boys taking part, Almond fell back on team games. In the words of Frank Stewart (who welcomed the revival of athletics during his own time at Loretto), 'the third sport on Almond's list, after football and cricket, was athletics, but it was a poor third.'

That view was held quite generally among those who encouraged the games cult in schools. Classical men who might have been expected to admire the Greek ideals of Olympus opted instead for contests more akin to Roman circuses. At sports days which followed in the wake of the Academy Games, drop-kicking and place-kicking competitions were prominent. For years Fettes sports day had a 'XV Race' for the rugby elite. Later, when the summer term came to be preferred, throwing the cricket ball paid a separate homage. But athletic records were kept and published along with rugby and cricket ones. At Fettes the sixteen-pound hammer was eventually exchanged (on the advice of a visiting athletic club) for one of twelve pounds, and the height of hurdles came down by stages to three feet. These changes helped school times and distances to be broken, but old cricket-ball records (up to 118 yards at Merchiston) remained so curiously unbeaten at most schools as to raise a question about the missile then in use.

The Interscholastic Games failed partly because Musselburgh and Corstorphine were too far away for supporters. These gathered readily enough at more convenient spots. The High School sports at Holyrood were popular, and Warriston drew many to the Institution Games: 'These banks provided natural grand-stands, and their green surroundings made an admirable frame for the picture supplied by the contests in running and jumping that took place in the centre. The sports were widely attended by friends of the school and by strangers to it... When Warriston was abandoned and Ferryfield became the Institution field the popularity of the sports, which had been showing a decline, still further suffered. The ground lacked the homely comfort of Warriston...'

Watson's went there in May 1876, 'starting at 1 p.m. on the school field of the Edinburgh Institution... Thousands turned up and the event soon became "an occasion" as the girls made it into a fashion parade. Indeed, each year Watson's Ladies College provided some of the prizes with echoes of a romantic medieval tournament. Spectators stood around the ropes, picnicked on the grassy slopes or packed the soft drinks Refreshment Tent in readiness for the 100 yards, the great mile race, throwing the cricket ball, high leap, long leap and 60 yards sack race. There were also Consolation Races for the losers and a Band Race... Music was provided by the "Castle band of the moment, the Queen's Own Highlanders." ... One winner wrote: "Nor do I forget how proudly I held my cup as, seated on top of an old-fashioned horse tramcar, I returned home with my equally proud parents."'

Trophies like the silver Burma Cup, presented by Academical sons of Empire and supported by three elephants on an ebony stand, lent prestige to prize-giving ceremonies. Memorial ones were added, as for a Watsonian who died at Gallipoli: 'John Ranken was a great runner, gaining Scottish athletic international honours for four years. He was killed while leading a bombing raid on a Turkish trench.' Athletic 'standards' as a basis for sports day awards were transferred from New Field to Ferryfield by Norman Barber as incoming Institution head. A spirit of seriousness also reached Inverleith on the other side of the road: 'A laudable innovation is

78. *Running and jumping.*

the presentation to boys over fourteen of medals, in place of the cake-stands, jelly-spoons, egg-cups and such like domestic utensils which we used to take home… The medals are of bronze and bear on one side a replica of the Stewart's arms.'

The appointment of gym teachers, though described as games masters, helped to advance the cause of non-team sports. Inter-school matches began to be held on an annual basis, starting with Merchiston versus the Academy in 1922. Loretto, now imbued with 'an entirely new attitude to athletics', challenged Watson's and the Royal High. Coaching raised standards, and running spikes replaced gym shoes. Times, distances and heights became more precise – and eventually metric. At some cost in boypower – six personal hours per term in support of a bulldozer – Fettes created a flat cinder track out of sloping ground. Long and narrow with tight bends, it served for forty years until (in what some regard as a desecration) the land was sold for a housing development called Fettes Village.

Other playing fields or parts of them have gone the same way, but the old boys' schools of Edinburgh still have tracks and pitches second to none. Goldenacre lives up to its name a hundred years on with excellent facilities for rugby, cricket, athletics and hockey. To mark the ground's centenary the Governors endorsed a 'Goldenacre 2000' initiative which provided a K. J. F. Scotland Hockey Pavilion and an artificial hockey and football pitch. There has also been realignment and drainage of the cricket square to improve playing conditions for both cricket and hockey, girls' sport no less important than that of boys. As elsewhere, an old ground tended with care has been brought up to date. Wider access to playing-fields, it may be observed, provides one of the strongest arguments for retaining the charitable status of independent schools.

Chapter 8

Schoolboys in Khaki

Throwing the cricket ball as a sports day event seemed to offer a curious chapter link, with the Mills bomb or hand grenade supplied to British troops on the Western Front owing something to the cricket fields of Eton. It seemed obvious that German stick grenades (which British soldiers were still calling potato mashers in the second great conflict of last century) would be more efficient because of technical know-how and the leverage effect. The Hun could hardly be expected to know about glorious returns to the top of the stumps but he took war seriously. Unfortunately for the theory it appears that the Mills bomb could be thrown further, even by Scotsmen unfamiliar with infield and outfield.

A truly significant link between this chapter and the last, however, lies in the fact that the establishment of cadet corps in boys' schools was hindered by the belief that games provided the best training for battle. Eton formed a Volunteer Corps early under the appropriately named Dr Warre; Wellington took half its pupils from army backgrounds so naturally had officer cadets. But these two were exceptions. Westminster's headmaster explained to a commission of enquiry that the school corps was 'necessarily officered in the main by boys who are not very good at games, and consequently not much respected.' As for games, the unsporting Hun was to become a theme of letters sent to headmasters. According to a Lorettonian who transferred from infantry to RFC, above the trenches of the Western Front, 'The German Flying Corps is the only part of that degraded nation's military machine which plays the game.'

Scotland's first school cadet corps was established at Glenalmond in 1875. The man behind military training was William Edward Frost, Master of the Junior School who went on to found Ardvreck – still flourishing as a preparatory school outside Crieff. Frost held a lieutenant's commission in the local militia, acting as CO with the support of sergeant instructors from regular units. Glenalmond was soon competing at Bisley: the Ashburton Shield still challenges school shooting eights. Despite the chapter's title, Glenalmond's change to khaki lay far in the future. For its first fifty years the

Perthshire school's uniform featured kilts of Murray tartan, white spats and grey doublets.

A second kilted unit was established at Merchiston in 1884, although it took a while before uniforms and rifles were available for all three companies. The first inspection was of a joint Corps with George Watson's and it followed the retiral of the day school's first head. Dr Ogilvie had accepted a rifle club with reluctance, and when school teams won prizes for swimming and shooting he commented: 'This is for saving life, that for destroying it.' Under his successor, however, Watson's volunteers were soon drilling in style: 'The Cadets were not then subdued to the habiliments of the monotonous khaki which clothes the army of today. It was a Highland array – jackets of rifle green, kilts and hose of Stuart tartan, sporrans, flashes, spats, belts and badges, on top the Glengarry; pipers with flowing plaids and blackcock feathers.'

Although Glenalmond began the military project, Edinburgh Town Council had earlier supplied its High School with a hundred constabulary carbines (plus bayonets and scabbards – Heriot's also got them) for boys to 'learn the Manual and Platoon Exercises and Bayonet and Position Drill'. No permanent corps resulted, although a teacher of fortification was recruited. When the Edinburgh and Midlothian Rifle Association started a competition for schools, the oldest of them regularly triumphed over teams from the Academy, Collegiate, Craigmount, the Institution, Loretto and Merchiston – this before Fettes and the former hospital schools came fully on the scene.

Academy Rector Hodson had campaigned for a cadet corps after his brother's heroics in the Indian Mutiny. Military drill, linked to fencing and gymnastics, was introduced but boys could not easily be persuaded to give up their rugby and cricket. During the opening years of the twentieth century the Academical Club urged consultation with Merchiston to set up a cadet corps on similar lines – answer to queries, £280 a year and £3 each for uniforms. Members provided a miniature rifle range, and in October 1908 an Officers' Training Corps was started with the enthusiastic approval of Reginald Carter as Rector. A mathematics teacher was the first officer in charge.

The War Office's OTC scheme was introduced at the same time as the Territorial Army, and the Edinburgh Academy had a particular reason to join because an Accie was Britain's Secretary of State for War. Once uniforms had been acquired Richard Haldane returned to his old school. He congratulated the contingent on its Seaforth Mackenzie kilts and newly learned drill movements, and his speech about looking to 'the young brains of the nation' for a reserve of officers drew loud bursts of applause. Haldane went on to invite the boys 'to take a serious view of the duty that might some day be incumbent on them, to fight and if necessary die for the Empire.' Fettes entered the scheme at the same time under the command of another maths teacher. Lieutenant Jock Beith 'shared with him some of the toil and anguish of converting a mildly-amused and thoroughly self-conscious herd of Rugby football players into a smart and keen little military machine.' As Ian Hay, Beith was to describe life as a volunteer member of Kitchener's Army in *The First Hundred Thousand*. The War Office provided a start-up grant and £1 for every efficient cadet on parade at annual inspection. Public schools now found it necessary to provide an OTC in order to attract those parents with army careers in mind for their sons – and the deteriorating international situation offered the prospect of good ones. Watson's and Heriot's also joined the scheme.

Loretto hung back. In Victorian times Almond had been angered by army regulations which insisted on high-necked tunics buttoned to the top, especially when men died from heat exhaustion at Aldershot. Headmaster Allan Smith wrote to the War Office in 1910 offering to start a Corps under modified dress regulations. These were never formally sanctioned but in the following year a Loretto OTC company paraded along with 15,000 cadets in Windsor Great Park. King George V, recently crowned, inspected the ranks of those who would soon be fighting for him and country. The Loretto boys were unique in their open-necked khaki tunics. Also in the spirit of Almond's 'rational dress' (with a nod to Baden-Powell) the uniform was topped off by a slouch hat as worn by Lovat Scouts in South Africa. Fettesians fainted in the sun while Lorettonians stood firm. Officers from the neighbourhood school – Eton – wondered about War Office approval and asked to borrow a hat. Loretto also ignored the injunction to wear spats with the kilt, which was of Hunting Stewart

79. *Loretto on the march.*

tartan because of a link with the Royal Scots. Instead the 'free and easy' uniform was completed by stockings and brogues, not boots. Khaki spats were accepted in time, however, and the slouch hat was exchanged for a Balmoral – as happened with the Lovat Scouts.

The Edinburgh Institution's Cadet Company came next, and members of it promptly went to Canada as part of a Scottish shooting team. Although not part of the OTC scheme (senior numbers too small) some members of the contingent were recognised as 'cadet-officers' while still at school. There is no record of masters being involved, an old 'Stution boy merely recalling that the 'first two colonels were delightful men.' The Institution Corps was affiliated to the 9th Battalion Royal Scots, then acting as Guard of Honour at Holyrood, and 'their smart appearance attracted much attention.' Daniel Stewart's College wore the same uniform: 'At a meeting in March 1913 Colonel Mackenzie, the CO of the Royal Scots Cadet Battalion, spoke to the boys about the Cadet force. Volunteers came forward and on 11th March 1913 Stewart's cadets were embodied as C Coy of the 1st (Highland) Cadet Battalion, the Royal Scots Regiment. They carried the carbine in place of the rifle and wore a uniform that 1914 was to drive out of the army – well-fitting scarlet doublets, hunting Stewart kilts, white belts and spats, red and white hose tops and a serviceable leather sporran.'

Between dress-parades and training sessions, the Corps took root in Edinburgh schools. Fettes raised a company whose four sections were based on houses, with prefects featuring as cadet-officers and NCOs. MacLeod kilts honoured a cadet-officer's family. Loretto did drill movements without weapons and unrealistic 'skirmishing practice' on the neighbouring estate. When rifles arrived things became serious, and Fa' Side Castle was defended against a notional enemy landing at North Berwick. A band of seven pipers and six drummers was assembled without difficulty, and buglers practised battlefield signals while actual signallers exchanged messages in the Orchard. Soon after returning from the Windsor event Loretto met up with other OTC contingents at the Army's Barry training camp near Carnoustie. Bell tents gave shelter after close-order drill, route marches and tactical exercises. The senior Lorettonian present later recalled that 'Hadge Almond, who was on furlough from Rhodesia, came as a sergeant.' This was Henry Tristram Arnold, the

CADET **NOTES**

80. Field day firing blanks.

Doctor's middle son and a colonial officer. Like both his brothers, he was soon to be killed in action.

Senior boarding-school boys, for whom Corps was compulsory, worked for the Army's Certificate 'A' which provided a short cut to a lieutenant's commission. Academy day boys all failed at the first attempt but nineteen passed on the eve of war. For a hundred and twenty Watson's volunteers, field days felt like an escape from the classroom: 'As the Corps marched away on a bright summer morning, I fear there were envious thoughts rising in the breasts of those left to fulfil the scholastic time-table. Dreghorn, Campend, Swanston, Dalmahoy and the remoter fields of Dumyat and Sheriffmuir were the scenes of memorable, if indecisive, warfare. Umpires were generally charitable and evasive as to the results obtained but we returned well satisfied with our own performance, very hungry and thirsty, and convinced that we had won the laurels of the day.' As many as 1,200 cadets could be involved on these occasions, during which there was increasing talk of war. Then the Fettes contingent arrived at 1914 summer camp to find their officers away being mobilised for it.

As a fighting soldier Lieutenant Beith continued to produce remarkably cheerful books while winning a Military Cross and moving up the ranks, with an Edinburgh Academical as junior officer until a sniper shot him at Ypres. Beith's account of the war dead commemorated in Edinburgh Castle was to be sombre by contrast. As an Old Fettesian, master and OTC officer, his view of the transition from school to service carries authority: 'The Great War was largely a war of Second Lieutenants… There are sixteen platoons to a battalion, and most of those platoons were officered, fathered, and inspired by boys barely out of their 'teens. Some day, when we have outlived our present attitude of mild apology for having participated in the war at all, we shall realise and recognise what we owe to the Officers' Training Corps. When the storm burst in 1914 – when everybody was willing to do something but no one was quite ready to do anything – that Corps provided hundreds of young officers both ready and willing to undertake the training of our new, leaderless armies. They did not know much, but they knew enough to lick a platoon into shape, and subsequently to lead it to wherever duty called.'

The first volunteer subalterns – the most junior commissioned officers – came mainly from boarding-schools. Senior pupils were closer to eighteen and a half (as laid down by Army regulations) than boys who sat Highers, and even without Cert. A it was possible to 'wangle' a commission: many fathers of boarders were career soldiers, often in the Indian Army. Apart from licking platoons into shape, second lieutenants were expected to lead them into battle. Soon that meant going over the top from front line trenches to face barbed wire and machine guns. On 1 July 1916, the first day of the battle of the Somme, 20,000 British soldiers were killed. Many of them were young officers. Over the battle as a whole, which dragged on into autumn without any sort of break-through – progress measured in yards – the life expectancy of a second lieutenant was two weeks.

The first Edinburgh schools old boy to fall in the Great War was a Lorettonian at Mons, a few days after he arrived in Flanders with the British Expeditionary Force. Nine former wearers of 'the old red coat' followed him to the grave by the end of the year, all but two of them career officers. Schools made careful records of those who served and casualties were announced at assembly. The missing and wounded hindered calculation at the time, but the names of the Glorious Dead eventually appeared on war memorials. *The Watsonian* for December 1914 published the first of several tableaux by the school's art master with five names on it – in Les Howie's words 'a design for a war which would be over by Christmas'. As late as July 1915

81. *Over by Christmas.*

only forty-three Watsonians had been reported dead out of a final awesome total of 605. Regiments of Kitchener's New Army were then going ashore at Gallipoli, otherwise the Dardanelles. There was grimmer reaping to come.

The regular army's 'Old Contemptibles' saved the Allied cause at Mons by disciplined musketry. They were almost wiped out for it, but in the following spring public school volunteers were far from downhearted. Jock Beith again: 'In August 1915, when troops were being concentrated in the La Bassée area for the battle of Loos, the 9th and the 15th Divisions found themselves side by side. The *place* of the little town of Bethune, where we forgathered in our moments of leisure, might have been Princes Street on the morning of an International. Those were probably the happiest days of the war for most of us. We were all volunteers, we were all optimists, and we were all embarked upon the adventure of our lives. So far, few of our friends had "gone west". So far there had been no great military disappointments.'

The capture of this mining village was achieved at terrible cost to the largest Scots battle assembly of all time. Eleven Watsonians died in one day, including the school's first head boy who had also captained the XV. This was Sandy Morrison, who pressed for OTC status and was given the rare schoolboy rank of cadet-lieutenant. Gallipoli was even worse, but the same blithe spirit pervaded letters home. A High School FP reported himself 'very pleased to see in a dispatch that the School beat Watson's at rugby. I got hold of it in the trenches and went up with great glee to show it to a Watsonian who was in the dug-out next door.' Two brothers from the rival school were killed within yards of each other in Gully Ravine on 28 June. Among the 204 Royal Scots who lost their lives that day were six 'Stution men. To this record of wartime carnage may be added seven members of the last pre-war Academy cricket XI. The other four were wounded.

Parents mourned sons, as did the headmaster of Heriot's his own. The loss of teachers had a wider effect on pupils, however, as Brian Lockhart shows for Jinglin' Geordie's bequest. Eight Heriot's teachers were in Flanders by Christmas of 1914 and six more were in training. At pupil level the numbers donning the uniform of cadets rose sharply and all of the other senior pupils were also given military drill on a weekly basis. All pupils were affected by the latest battalion of the Royal Scots Regiment being granted access to the school's buildings other than the central one with its quadrangle. The death of a former English teacher in September 1915 was deeply felt. By the end of the following year there were eighteen women teachers at Heriot's.

The return to Loretto of a lieutenant-colonel poisoned by gas restored its first CO to the Corps. That released two teachers for service, and both were killed within months of arriving in France. There was much grief among those who had known the one – in particular – who had been in charge of the Nippers' house. At Fettes a housemaster responded to the deaths of six out of nine of his last peacetime prefects by considering himself a 'shirker' (though above military age) and going to drive an ambulance on the Italian front. Someone has computed that Fettesians served on twenty-five different fronts.

As against pre-war assumptions about the military value of games, Robert Philp observes: 'The bravest were often those who had not excelled at school or been the titans of the rugby field. The Anderson brothers had won no athletic distinction at Fettes, and two of them were so frail they were nicknamed "Crocky". Yet all four of them – the entire family – died in the field. William, the eldest, was the last to fall, but not before he had won the Victoria Cross.' At some distance from Fettes, Beith asked about 'the atmosphere of a great school in war time… How must boys have felt with such a prospect before them?' Philp supplies an unlooked-for answer: 'The fatalism of seniors who knew that to leave school was to go to likely death in the trenches produced a harshness that made this the unhappiest period in the school's history.'

With cadets under consideration it is natural to dwell on the youthfulness of many who died. One hundred and eight of the 246 Fettesians were under twenty-five. Especially poignant is the former Stewart's pupil who died of wounds before the award of his Leaving Certificate, which was presented to his brother at assembly. War poetry is associated with Wilfred Owen, who recovered from shell-shock at Craiglockhart War Hospital only to lose his life in the last week of the war. Owen had time and opportunity to develop his talent – not least in Edinburgh. A Watsonian poet, Hamish Mann, was only twenty at Arras on 10 April 1917. Written four days before his demise, 'The Great Dead' has recently been put to music by a girl pupil of George Watson's College. It starts:

> Some lie in graves beside the crowded dead
> In village churchyards; others shell holes keep,
> Their bodies gaping, all their splendour sped.
> Peace, O my soul… A Mother's part to weep.

After the Armistice school chroniclers took stock. One calculated that 62.5% of 3,102 Watsonians who served were volunteers, which is to say that they enlisted before the Military Service Act of 1916 introduced conscription as the only way into uniform; 62.4% of them were commissioned officers. One effect of the act was to create the category of Conscientious Objector; another was to slow the progress from OTC to commission. By the summer of 1917 there were no eighteen-year-olds at the Academy, as they were undergoing a more careful preparation for war than had been offered hitherto. Seven of the 1915–16 Loretto XV failed to survive the remaining period of hostilities, but no one who left the school after that session made the ultimate sacrifice. The crippled and often shortened lives of the wounded are scarcely recorded, although the High School numbered at least three hundred alongside 182 killed.

82. *Farewell to Edinburgh.*

Without making too much of what might seem a tasteless comparison, the war dead of Edinburgh boys' schools ranged from 17 to 23 per cent of all who served. Boarding institutions came closest to one in four, and Major Beith described the Fettes sacrifice of 246 out of 1,094 as, 'with sorrowful pride, second to none'. Watsonians died in far greater numbers, of course, but Fettes also came second in proportional terms to Loretto's 147 out of 628. Perhaps 177 Merchistonian deaths represents an even greater sacrifice, although the numbers who served are unknown. Record-keepers also listed decorations awarded – sometimes by the other services which have hardly been mentioned and sometimes, as with the *Croix de Guerre*, by other nations. A recent book by Alasdair Macintyre celebrates the granting of the Victoria Cross to *Nine Valiant Academicals* in all conflicts since the Indian Mutiny. Two were in the Great War. Two Fettesians also gained the VC then – one the oldest of four unathletic brothers, the other killed at twenty-one. That level of heroism is too rare to justify comparison among schools, but the awarding of 146 Military Crosses to Fettes officers up to the rank of captain (thus 'the distinctive award of the front-line soldier') is unmatched by any school of equivalent size.

The Fettes war memorial features the striking bronze image of a fallen officer, his hand waving the platoon forward. The words 'CARRY ON' are prominent on the sandstone plinth. Fettes boys who paraded in front of it

83. *Lest Fettesians forget.*

each November were expected to carry on in the same spirit. The pillared Watson's memorial was transferred from Archibald Place to Colinton Road, the Royal High School doorway (made over to a school-leaver's rite of passage) from Calton Hill to Barnton. The raising of an obelisk for 463 Herioters coincided with the three-hundredth anniversary of the founder's death, and two ceremonies were held that year. Loretto turned to the architect Sir Robert Lorimer who had redesigned much of the school after Almond's time. The result was a striking development in the chapel which already bore his mark – 'that collection of finely carved panels, enlivened by coloured armorial bearings and regimental crests, which became such a decorative feature of the building… There were also commemorative bronze or brass plaques inserted in the stone walls above them. The largest and, appropriately, the most impressive panel records the loss of Almond's three sons.' With such symbolism, varying from school to school but always bearing the message 'Lest We Forget', the cadet corps was there to stay.

However grand they were, these carved and inscribed memorials cost less than the sums donated by parents and classmates. The surplus was put to practical purposes, including help for widows and school fees for dependants. Merchiston wanted to erect a memorial hall, and refusal of planning permission on a crowded site was one reason for the move to Colinton. The Academy built a gymnasium for £10,000, the High School acquired Jock's Lodge. Loretto also opened a new playing field but the idea of adding a monumental archway was dropped on aesthetic grounds. Rising numbers at the Institution caused the Queen Street building to be abandoned after the war, so that a memorial entry hall became part of the new Melville Street premises. Stewart's cenotaph opposite the main entrance took the form of an obelisk with steps on four sides leading up to lion heads. Serpents gripped by them have the Earth's sphere in their mouths, 'the whole group symbolising the triumph of Right over Wrong.'

An ante-chapel was added to the interior of Stewart's, and the High School marble porch with its gateway was also conceived as an indoor structure. Watson's had an oak display cabinet (since replaced) which went from the stair head at Archibald Place to the Masonic Hall at Colinton Road. It displayed the pages, turned each day, of the *Watsonian War Record.* Once the names of the dead had been finalised it was natural to compile obituaries in book form. At the start of the third millennium, quarter of a century after the school moved for a third time, an *Edinburgh Institution and Melville College Roll of Honour* was published to put Melville and Stewart's on an equal footing.

'Military training should be an essential part of a school education,' according to the Academy Rector who welcomed the OTC. That principle held good in the inter-war period when the Corps went from strength to strength as a compulsory part of the school week. In 1930 another Academy Rector reported that all competitions for guard-mounting, band, team and individual dancing, and individual piping had been won by the 'the best contingent in camp'. When Britain's appeasement policy was at its height a record fifty-six Academy boys passed Cert. A. At the other classical day school the nearest thing to military activity had been a rifle club behind the bicycle shed, but High School Rector King Gillies brought in the OTC in 1926 for the sake of adding 'a certain tone to the discipline of the School'. Membership was voluntary, as for other day school pupils, but not at Melville Street where a chronically wounded headmaster provided the lead.

The peacetime Stewart's Corps functioned as an 'autonomous' body after losing the government grant of five shillings a head. OTC status was then granted in the Thirties with proper funding and better equipment. Rough battle-dress with webbing was already used for working purposes. Under OTC regulations it now replaced the scarlet doublet and 'the last Edinburgh example of the dress of the old Line was gone'. Pipe bands led schoolboys in khaki: 'Complaints kept reaching us that we were going too slow and the troops were going to sleep on their feet, or too fast, so that we should have reached Myreside before the last platoon had rounded Holy Corner.' These Watson's marchers might have caught a glimpse of Merchiston punishment drill on 'the path round the bowling green, traversed at the double, possibly with "Knees Up" and rifles at arms' length overhead.' PD was used for classroom and other offences. In a similar mixing of military and everyday worlds, an Accie wrongdoer recalls being forced to wear corps uniform all week, with fellow partners in drink deprived of their lance-corporal's stripes.

The Watson's contingent reached four hundred volunteers in time of war, but after the Kaiser was beaten numbers fell to seventy. Corps weariness apart, there were economy cuts and also alternative attractions. A less military alternative was provided when Cadet Scouts separated to become Boy Scouts – the Watson's troop balancing the fun of summer camps and treks with involvement in the Craigmillar Boys' Club for re-housed slum-dwellers. Scouting attracted school captains and rugby-players as well as boys in general. The troop had to be divided into four sections and then two troops were formed. But the Corps fought back to a high level of proficiency, and when the new Watson's College buildings were formally opened by Prince George in September 1932 there was an OTC guard of honour. The royal visitor stopped in front of 'the Goliath of the Guard', a youngster of six foot four, and asked if he was still growing. The cadet's untutored reply was 'Naw!' The Prince smiled and moved on. Ten years later, as Duke of Kent, he was to die in a plane crash which some have associated with his desire for peace with Germany.

Alexander Mackenzie was a Watsonian who taught Classics in his old school for forty years after serving in the Royal Engineers. He was involved in placing a pontoon bridge over the *Canal du Nord* when the last peacetime Dux was killed while advancing through machine-gun fire: 'The older men like ourselves who knew war was an overrated amusement, in spite of its camaraderie, could not show the same verve and enthusiasm as we had done a quarter of a century ago. In any case, the two wars were different in so many ways, and Horace's dictum that to die for one's country was a sweet and becoming thing had, of course, been debunked by those of us who had seen grand young fellows in the flower of youth doing so with neither sweetness nor decorum. Chamberlain announced on 26 April 1939 that military training was to be compulsory and the resulting methods of recruitment precluded one, however patriotic, from rushing to arms as Watsonians did in 1914.'

The effect of the Second World War on the boys' schools of Edinburgh may be dealt with briefly. The Academy was identified as a military objective on German maps – one of three *Kasernen* along with Redford Barracks and Leith Fort. Fire-watching became a night-time duty for teachers while pupils accustomed themselves to carrying gas masks which, mercifully, were never needed. At Stewart's and other schools the Corps lost their kilts. Fettes kept iron railings when all around were losing theirs. There was no serious attempt to evacuate boys' schools (partial for the Academy and Melville, rejected by the Merchant Company schools which went part-time and co-educational instead) although many girls moved to country houses with their teachers. OTC became JTC – Joint Training Corps – as the War Office looked for officer material beyond the private schools. With the Battle of Britain at its height, the ATC or Air Training Corps was founded. 'Sandy Mac' (of pontoon-laying) was adjutant to another Watsonian who presided over the Edinburgh Wing. It drew on many schools. Another set of initials characterised Local Defence Volunteers as the LDV – an armlet-wearing schoolboy version of Dad's Army.

Cadet corps acquired bren guns, and new arms for shouldering – 'Ross rifles which were much inferior. Only a dozen or so Lee-Enfields remained for the use of the VIII… Brass buttons bearing the Fettes crest were seen no more. Fags at least did not mourn their passing. Polishing buttons was a disagreeable chore and the technique of dismantling and reassembling the old pattern of webbing belt was hard to learn.' At Loretto (where Pinkie was dug up for potatoes) the customary run after Corps was triumphantly validated by official statistics: 'In 1942 the Army Council instituted physical tests for all candidates for Certificate "A"… Over ninety per cent of Lorettonians gained credits for passing standards in higher age groups, more than half of them qualifying for two years above their own group.' Almond was alive in spirit. Others were alive in body. When further thought was given to school memorials World War Two casualties usually came in at less than a third of the names already inscribed. Fewer served this time around, and of those who did the death rate was about half of that in 1914–18. Boarding schools no longer suffered more than others.

CCF for Combined Cadet Force soon replaced all previous initials as Air Units were united with Army ones. Some schools added Naval Units. The amalgamation of armed services at school level matched the three possibilities for eighteen-year-old males going on to National Service – a two-year period of conscription which engendered some negativity at cadet level. Ten years after the ending of hostilities, speaking in a school debate against the motion that 'this House deplores the Corps', an Academy pupil paid the contingent a back-handed compliment: 'There are some who are good at Latin, and some who are good at Games, and some who are good at Music, and some who are no good at anything. But even these, in fact anyone if he wants, can be good at the Corps.' At the other day school with compulsory corps 'The Mighty Melville War Machine' was a common target for magazine humour.

Having come late to the CCF, the Royal High School was first to abandon it when National Service ended. Other schools relaxed the element of compulsion. In 1964 government cutbacks reduced financial support to three years, and senior Academy boys were allowed to opt out in favour of community work. Loretto took the same path: 'About a dozen boys were formed into a social service group. Acting with the Musselburgh Welfare Committee they were regular visitors to the houses of old people in the district. Using their own initiative they did whatever was most needed for each particular person. This varied from digging gardens, washing dishes, and decorating rooms, to reading aloud, and buying canaries. Most of all, they kept the old people company and helped them feel less lonely.' The scheme was popular and numbers reached forty.

Watson's CCF numbers remained unexpectedly high. An Artillery section added interest to the military side of things, and at a Myreside fund-raising Wappenschaw for the Pipe Band imaginary 25-pound shells were fired off 'in the general direction of Heriot's'. Initiative training activities were also borrowed from the Duke of Edinburgh's Award scheme by several contingents. At the Academy, when retention of compulsory CCF was being explained to parents, emphasis was placed on the 'non-military character of this activity in its present form'. As time passed fewer teachers had service experience, however, and one year Watson's lost four officers with only a single replacement. Then in 1970, to

84. *Watson's Combined Cadet Force.*

the consternation of many, the Corps' existence was terminated on the argument of going out at 'with a bang' rather than facing slow decline. Sir Roger Young was later urged to reinstate the CCF but the merger with George Watson's Ladies' College intervened.

At Fettes during Ian McIntosh's time as headmaster compulsory corps became a target for the rebels. One school remained uniquely firm on compulsion from fourteen to eighteen, and Melville College debaters even voted for it. One dedicated CO succeeded another and keen lieutenants were recruited to the staff. As the school roll grew during the Sixties an additional house was acquired along Melville Street, but the Corps could only function by having senior members spend Friday afternoons in TA drill halls and the University pre-

85. *Melville CCF at camp.*

mises at Forrest Road. Artillery, REME and RAF sections went off after the dinner hour, leaving their juniors in school. Easter holidays saw adventure training by Loch Tay, four nights out of seven in the open; summer activities went far beyond familiar camps at Cultiebraggan near Comrie. In competition with other units, victory at safe-driving gave understandable satisfaction to senior NCOs who went to Dreghorn Barracks. Page upon page of the *Melville College Chronicle* was given over to all this, and at the merger with Stewart's in 1973 the truly Combined Cadet Corps was the largest in Britain, justifying a maths-teaching Lieutenant Colonel as CO.

School magazines now feature CCF as one activity among many. Even at Stewart's Melville numbers are much lower, and similar compact units are found elsewhere. Summer camps take place as far away as Wales, the latest Army one near Penrith: 'By the end of the week George Heriot's had become known as the "CCF to beat". After taking part in training exercises such as first aid, leadership, field craft and drill, we left the camp having won all six British titles.' Regular Army camouflage

fatigues are worn nowadays and – with the Royal Scots connection over – Glengarry bonnets have been replaced by the Tam o' Shanter of the Royal Regiment of Scotland. Fettes at Cultiebraggan – voluntary – was recently reported by a girl. Photographs of corps activities (Army, Air or Navy) regularly feature female cadets in one uniform or another. Except at Merchiston, where the CCF was 'at a low ebb' in the Seventies before recovering and adding a Naval section, all-male.

86. *Footsore in fatigues.*

When the Royal High boys handed in their uniforms an exception was made for the pipe band, and over the years other Edinburgh school pipers and drummers have become less corps-dependent. Despite the expense of uniforms, bagpipes, drums and the rest of it, bands are generally in more flourishing condition than the contingents they were formed to serve. Melville acquired a band after years of practice chanter work with boys too young for uniform. Latterly Stewart's Melville went a stage further by adding a bugle section. Girls were introduced, the Mary Erskine School adding a third component to merger, as drummers and pipers. A girls-only Highland dancing group now accompanies the band on tour. Before this progression began individual Melville pipers helped Watson's 'during the declining years of their CCF and took part in the Annual CCF Beating of Retreat at Edinburgh Castle.'

Watson's pipe band boasted fifty-three members in 1958. Seven years later, it was 'on the brink of extinction' and unable to muster enough bandsmen for the annual competition. It went down with the CCF and subsequent attempts at a fresh start came to nothing, but towards the end of the Eighties a new head gave strong encouragement. School chronicler Les Howie arrived from Craigmount High (a rare example of state school piping and drumming in Edinburgh, largely created by him) and played a leading part in creating a very successful staged set-up at Watson's with three bands. Ironically this best of pipe bands – who have been World Champions at their age stage – cannot compete against the other independent schools for lack of a Corps.

87. *Settling in at Colinton Road.*

88. *Caps to be worn.*

89. *Lorimer's Loretto.*

90. *Victory in Europe, Regent Road.*

91. *To school by tram.*

92. *The Academy Hall.*

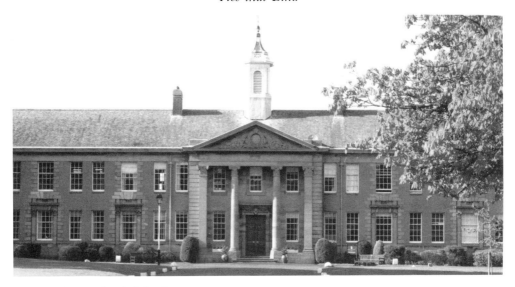

93. *Merchiston Castle School.*

94. *Corps day at Stewart's.*

95. *Scarlet blazers in the street.*

96. *Memorial Entrance Hall at Melville Street.*

97. *Daniel Stewart's and Melville College.*

98. *Hair Blair, basketball captain.*

99. *World-beating band from Watson's.*

100. *Make-up for a night op.*

101. *On top of the world.*

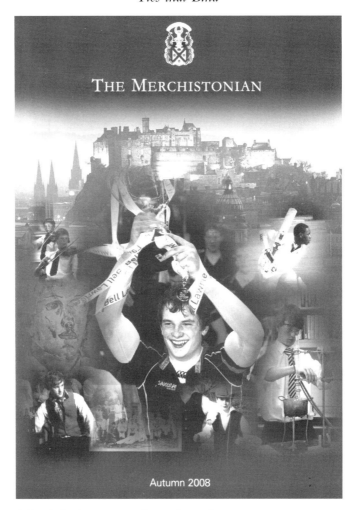

102. *School magazines have changed.*

103. *Merchiston ties that distinguish.*

Chapter 9

Beyond the Classroom

In these modern times independent schools make a point of offering choice – in classroom subjects of course, but also in a great range of 'extra-curricular activities'. Boarders have a special need to be occupied, but long hours of compulsory rugby, cricket and corps no longer dominate life 'beyond the classroom'. The phrase has a liberating feel to it. In the Sixties of last century when headmasters were keeping the lid on or bending to winds of change, the radical author R. F. Mackenzie (who came to grief while in charge of a Scottish Summerhill School in Aberdeen) entitled one of his books *Escape from the Classroom*. It described the pupils of a Fife mining town being challenged by a very different Highland environment, and responding positively as they rarely did to classroom teaching.

Almond of Loretto shared that spirit. Ordered to rest by doctors, he took to spending much of the spring and summer terms away from school. Moreover 'Almond frequently invited boys to stay with him in the Highlands both in term time and in the holidays. There were usually two at a time, and he selected them for different reasons. They were overgrown and needed a short rest from football; or they were delicate and would benefit from the Highland air; or they had personal problems which he wished to talk over with them; or they were simply boys in whom he was interested. But whatever the reasons, it is astonishing how many boys over the years paid a visit to Lochinver or Dunkeld or wherever he might be at the time, and who, without exception, remembered the relaxed atmosphere, the fishing, the long walks across the hills in all weathers, the endless discussions in the evenings on a multitude of subjects – and who felt much the better for it.'

School magazines of the present century provide an overview of what has developed from that outgoing spirit. *The Merchistonian*'s 2008 contents page lists Outdoor Pursuits, Trips and Tours and Exchanges as examples of activities which take pupils away from school as well as out of class. The first outdoor step at Colinton is a 'professional orienteering map of the school grounds'. Orienteering is an extension of cross-country running, beyond sport in the traditional sense. Music and Drama are also listed in the magazine's contents, and will feature here as areas of activity more out of class than in. When the Scottish Education Department ruled that Music must be taught in grant-aided secondary schools, a teacher at the relocated George Watson's lamented that 'there still survived two fatal prejudices – that boys as a whole had no use for Music, and in particular that when their voices broke they must not be allowed to sing.' At the time there was no senior school choir at Colinton Road, and the junior one had to be borrowed for closing functions.

Full-time music teachers did not replace part-timers until the Thirties, a contrast between 'skills and frills' in subjects being assumed quite generally by the teaching profession in Scotland. However that did not entirely exclude 'cultural activities'. At Fettes in the inter-war period tough rugger-playing 'Sparta' (as a former pupil recalled it) came to resemble cultured Athens under the leadership of a future Principal of the Royal Scottish Academy of Music, Henry Havergal. The contrast between a few motley instrumentalists held to together by staff, on his arrival, and the full orchestra mustered for later concerts spoke volumes. A visiting lecturer on musical appreciation 'found a large audience who listened, spellbound. The Fettes Choir sang the Brahms Requiem, the orchestra played the Bach Double Concerto with two Fettesians playing the solo violin parts… Double bass and bassoon players used to practise assiduously just because Mr Havergal wanted the part filled in the orchestra, and because the orchestra had become as much of a team as the XV.' As the school's modern chronicler puts it, 'Music became fashionable. Muscular rugby players who in the past had regarded flautists or singers as irretrievably unmanly were suddenly begging to join the choir.'

The past, then, was not altogether a cultural desert at Edinburgh boys' schools although, with *Crème de la Crème* in mind, it may be said that girls' schools in the music-and-dance 'accomplishments' tradition for young ladies gave a readier response to the performing arts. When hobbies, clubs and societies are added to the list of what goes on outside the classroom it becomes clear that the subject matter of this chapter is wide and varied. Where to start? Outdoor activities must take priority for their overlap with CCF camps and exercises.

The Duke of Edinburgh's Award Scheme for Boys (but only briefly limited to them) was set up on the lines of what Prince Philip had experienced as a pupil of Gordonstoun School in Moray. Headmaster Kurt Hahn's philosophy was centred on respect for adolescents and given practical expression through a broadly conceived 'expeditionary learning'. The Outward Bound movement followed and then the Scheme itself. By no means entirely outdoor in concept, it nevertheless culminates in a fifty-mile hike. Two years after the start the Duke himself visited Henderson Row and saw skills demonstrated by Academy pupils and visitors from Melville and Fettes. All the boarding-schools now enlist entire year groups at Bronze level for the sake of a grounding in outdoor skills under adult supervision. The extreme challenge of a sodden 2007 summer led to mountain rescue services coming to the aid of four Loretto girls in the shadow of Ben Nevis. Undaunted, they passed the 're-sit D of E' at Silver level and returned for more. The Duke's connection with Edinburgh makes the Scheme rewarding for participants from local schools, especially those who receive the Gold Award at Holyrood Palace in July.

The Duke of Edinburgh's Award is regularly pursued through youth organisations like the Scouts, Guides and – in certain schools – the CCF. At Watson's it was entirely a cadet activity until the tenth year of Roger Young's headship, when wider participation was achieved. By that time a Projects Week had been introduced during the summer term which took third year boys out of school while senior pupils sat exams. Then sixth year pupils were also introduced to 'projects'. The College's outdoor education has flourished at all levels since then, especially after the Merchant Company purchased Ardtrostan House on Lochearnside as a field centre for its four schools. Merger with the George Square girls (who were already following a similar programme) made that three. Ardtrostan was destroyed by fire, but other outdoor centres like Glenmore Lodge near Aviemore and the Kinlochiel Outward Bound Centre have also been called into play. There the voluntary efforts of teachers are supported by professional staff.

Large youth hostels are now taken over by parties of 250 and more. Having settled into their own merger, Stewart's and Melville looked back on Outdoor Education as it had developed from different approaches at Carbisdale Castle in Sutherland (for Stewart's) and Garve beside Fortingall – Melville leaning to physical activities whereas with Stewart's it was more a case of applying science to the environment. The Carbisdale

104. *Carbisdale Castle.*

Project over ten days is the common experience of all, now shared with Mary Erskine girls. Stewart's Melville has an Outdoor Education Store full of tents and rucksacks, and a fund of stories about 'canoes that sank, smelly wellies disappearing in the ooze, cagoule-clad figures glissading furiously out of control, orienteering markers that disappeared into thin air, burnt porridge, succulent fish suppers on the A9, frozen sleeping bags, surveying in thick fog, washing up a million greasy plates, blue skies and shining snow… Over the years an enlightened staff has by its initiative, enthusiasm and unstinting efforts provided a climate in which not only outdoor education but education out of doors has flourished.' Volunteer teachers going the extra mile without pay may be claimed as a feature of fee-paying schools.

The magazines of schools which now cater, in most cases, for both sexes show that girls are as keen as their brothers on 'boyish' pursuits. Loretto's Year 7s recently took over the Highland Adventure Centre near Blairgowrie for an Activity Camp; Heriot's third years claimed their share of Carbisdale; seventeen Watson's Projects groups spent a fortnight at locations between Orkney and Galloway; and dinghies were passed on by veterans 'who had sailed from the Geits' to young Academy pupils – all male for the last time. Stewart's Melville teenagers have an Adventure Club with Mountain Biking in its second season of 'mind-blowing stunt footage for the extreme sports film festival'. The club also offers camping in Glen Shee, beginners' kayaking at Cellardyke (then Canadian canoeing down Loch Shiel from Glenfinnan), hill-walking on An Socach and ice climbing at Kinlochleven.

Stewart's Melville's *The Collegian* also celebrated 'the 43rd time that for just short of two weeks the picturesque castle turned youth hostel was invaded by a group of fresh-faced, excited fourteen/fifteen year olds. "Carbisdale", as it is always referred to, is the one activity that all look forward to and all remember, and it is the last school trip that includes the entire year group.' Tribute indeed, but in all the accounts of adventurous times out of doors there is nothing to touch the Rua Fiola Island Exploration Centre between Luing and Lunga in Argyll. It lives up to its name with a choice of islands to explore, and parties of young Merchiston boys (in their own time, after school is over for the year) have responded to the careful preparation – safety always in mind – which leads up to the 'Robinson Crusoe' Survival Challenge. This amounts to being left adult-free on a deserted island and finding edible food and shelter for a night and a day. They have stories to tell and memories for a lifetime.

Teacher-organised overseas trips go back to the era of short trousers. Stewart's showed Edinburgh schools the way abroad with a 1923 journey to Amiens and Paris. It turned out to be the start of 'a succession of visits' to French, Belgian and Swiss destinations during the Easter holidays. Three years later a Heriot's head of modern languages led a five-week camping tour of France and northern Spain, and a month under canvas near Grenoble followed in what became an 'almost annual' excursion. During the Thirties school cruises were taken up by consider-able numbers of Her-iot's boys, and other schools were also in-volved in the *Neuralia*'s North Sea crossings from Leith to Scandin-avia. After peace return-ed to Europe kilted Watson's boys headed for Haarlem in Holland (where food was even

105. *Watson's to Holland.*

scarcer than at home) as part of an exchange organised by the World Friendship Association. For the remainder of the Forties it became possible to speak of an early 'trip bug' – to liberated Paris one year and the Normandy beaches another.

In the Fifties groups were taken regularly to Europe by stages no less arduous than the Channel crossing at Easter. A Melville boy reported the annual Swiss Trip in terms of mixed ordeal and wonder: 'From Calais to Basel was probably the least enjoyable. It lasted from six o'clock on the Saturday night to six o'clock the following morning. Since none of us managed to sleep on the wooden-slatted seats, you can imagine how we looked and felt. Here in the station we had our first continental breakfast which consisted of coffee, rolls, butter and cherry jam… On the Monday, our first full day in Switzerland, we went up the Rigi by mountain railway and words can hardly describe the wonderful scene which met our eyes at the top. An ordinary camera could hardly do justice to the snow-covered mountains glistening in the sun with the deep blue of the sky above. That was the most wonderful scene I have ever had the pleasure to set my eyes on.'

Merchiston Through the Sixties (as described in the *School Register*) saw 'a proliferation of holiday expeditions arranged by members of staff' but only a few of them involved foreign travel. Nor did Fettes or Loretto lay emphasis on it. For boarders, presumably, it was considered that long vacations with families would provide suffi-cient opportunities. That att-itude has changed. The long-est photo caption in *A Keen Wind Blows* captures the Eighties wanderlust of Fett-esians: 'In recent years the School has undertaken a series of expeditions to such far-flung places as Siberia, Mongolia, Ecuador, Kenya, Arctic Norway, Zanskar [in Indian Kashmir] and Switz-erland, the key elements of which have been activities such as mountaineering, raft-

106. *From Siberia into Mongolia.*

ing and canoeing, as well as geographical and botanical field work. Here a Fettes party tackles the glacial field of Aktum in the Altai region of Siberia near the Mongolian border.' Nowadays *The Fettesian* looks beyond school to gap year travel as reported by youngsters in far off places.

Modern Merchiston boys have been to St Petersburg, Moscow, Flanders, Auschwitz and Switzerland – for ski-ing, of course, but also a Physics trip to the European Organisation for Nuclear Research near peaceful Geneva. China 2008 was a new destination at record distance for Watson's parties – exotic compared with the Costa del Sol 'to learn lots of Spanish and have fun.' Air transport makes all things possible. Heriot's International Service project extended to kibbutz life in Israel, and an Art party took in the galleries of New York. *The Edinburgh Academy Chronicle 2007* reported one of the exchanges which schools organise, this time with 'German partners', and a music tour to Virginia and Washington DC. Seven Stewart's Melville seniors went climbing in Corsica – the high point of a 26-page section on Trips and Expeditions. Small groups for many destinations may give an exaggerated impression of foreign travel, but rugby tours of Australia, South America and Japan are large-scale enterprises. All that may change in future, of course, if parents reject a travel supplement to the annual fees bill.

Boarding-school life with added Forties austerity made Fettes boys content with little: 'It would be frivolous to suggest that it was because we were thinking so much about food that we failed to miss those societies and clubs, hobbies and interests that seem to have proliferated in post-war schools.' That mid-point of last century provides a possible baseline for the proliferation that followed, but it would be wrong to imply that there were no previous clubs. The Royal High School's Literary and Debating Society celebrated sixty years of continuous existence about then, and it cannot have been merely coincidental that the first BBC general knowledge quiz *Top of the Form* was won, round after round, by a confident and knowledgeable High School team. Debating societies date from the time of Gladstone and Disraeli, but no other school was able to follow up a 'media' triumph of this sort by having members shown round the Westminster Parliament. They went on to discuss their impressions on radio. Coming into this *Schola Regia* tradition, Robin Cook was well prepared for the floor of the House. Perhaps a future Foreign Secretary will emerge from the eight debating teams currently put out by Heriot's, two of whose latest sixth form members were recognised as world champions.

For clubs and hobbies to flourish, means must be provided. At post-war Fettes an hour between tea and prep was set aside for clubs or quiet reading, which led to 'the emergence, under the umbrella of "organised activities", of a remarkable variety of pursuits – so many, in fact, that "Reading" prep became a misnomer since it was always open to exchange the stern discipline of the printed word for the hospitable *milieux* of the Reel Society (which cast the sounds of its revelry far across the night) or the Model Railway Club.' Modernity at Watson's was marked by the Radio Club's frame aerial on the roof of the Geography Department – in contrast to the dark room efforts of the Photographic Society. Further depths were plumbed at Heriot's when a new building included club rooms two floors below playground level, mainly for storage of outdoor equipment but also introducing a subterranean weight-training facility.

The all-purpose Melville College gym had its usefulness widened still further beyond physical exercise in order to serve the needs of Brains Trusts and Hat Nights put on by the Literary and Debating society. Larger evening gatherings took place elsewhere for the Edinburgh Schools Citizenship Association, Film Society, and Scientific Society. These

107. *Melville's all purpose gym.*

brought contact with other schoolboys and – by far the greater attraction – school-girls. Scripture Union had camps as well as meetings. Charitable work has always engaged the attention of many, not least through 'Fet-Lor' or the Fettesian-Lorettonian Boys' Club. In addition to more than fifteen school societies supported by Academy boys in the Seventies, 'Pursuits' became established on Friday afternoons for staff-led hobby groups in everything from stone carving to bookbinding, fly-tying to public speaking. Fashions change, however. Our mid-century Stewart's observer is apparently wrong to have imagined (from a schoolboy point of view) that 'the stamp collectors are likely to be with us always.'

Interest in hobbies is generally strong among pre-adolescent boys, and nowhere more so than in Loretto's house for Nippers – almost a separate preparatory school on the further bank of Esk. One head's report was informal: 'Here then a term. Internationals have been visited, Saturday evening films have been shown, matches played; visits to Carberry [Tower, where Mary Queen of Scots surrendered] with a jumble of transport, and the evergreen thrill of fresh snow; a new time-table; over 600 books borrowed from the library; a new film projector, object of fascination to staff and boys alike; incessant play rehearsals; lectures and talks – one on reading the Scriptures, another, with self-provided illustrations, on Scottish Songs; the hotly-contested ping-pong tournament; leatherwork and carpentry, the mingling of wallets and tables, of gun belts and standard lamps; the newly formed Debating Society for the top two forms, a haven of lively, though often irrelevant discussions… These and all the other innumerable events which go to make up a normal School term are none the less enthralling for not being remembered.'

The quiet insertion of '600 books borrowed from the library' gives pause – and provokes a contrast with Watson's after World War Two when forty fewer books were lent from a stock ('not deficient by contemporary standards') of 2,384. The generosity of a Watsonian changed that when the first in what became a series of new libraries opened in 1950. Within three years, thanks to gifts from former pupils in several quarters of the globe – and a new custom of sixth year leavers donating a volume – the shelves were bulging. Borrowing increased nine-fold as a result. Headmaster Ian Andrew understood the importance of providing popular books as 'ground bait', with light reading as a way into literature. Roger Young introduced unsupervised library periods for the top two year groups, and then improved them by adding a separate Sixth Form library. Self-disciplined study was his aim, however, rather than reading as the most popular of hobbies.

The Herioter for 2008 provides an up-to-the-minute overview of groups which stay behind at the end of the day. The Camera Club is distinct from the Digital Photography Club, now in its second year. The older group advertises for members by exhibiting a pre-electronic masterpiece of German design. It is also a business operation, in sufficient profit from the sale of Christmas cards to buy a new enlarger for the dark room. S4-6 Film-Making is a new activity with forty members being led by three teachers into story-boarding, screen-writing, shooting, editing and performing in front of the moving camera. At the younger end of the senior school a Fashion and Textiles Club offers the chance to create make-up bags using different embroidery stitches on sewing machines. Also at S1 level, boys of the Robotics Club use programmable Lego bricks to make mobile structures with 'battering rams, scoops and firing devices so that we can have battles between robots.'

Outdoor theatres of Greek city states began the Western theatrical tradition. The Athens of the North lends itself more to indoor productions, however, and near the end of the nineteenth century the *Antigone* of Sophocles and the *Alkestis* of Euripides were performed inside the Edinburgh Academy Hall – in the original Greek. Rector Mackenzie was leading tenor in the Chorus and a classically-educated audience (it must be presumed) paid three shillings each for admission. On the second occasion the cast consisted of sixteen Academy boys, six Academicals, nine masters and seven ladies. The inclusion of the latter group – unthinkable in Athens

– was defended by the Rector on the grounds that the Academy was not a boarding institution: 'What could be more natural for a school where home life bulked largely than that it should, upon such occasions, invoke the aid of the sisters of the boys?' But the experiment was not repeated.

Daniel Stewart's made a similar gesture by co-opting black-stockinged Edwardian girls, but when the presentation of short pieces resumed after the Armistice it was with all male casts. History master John Thompson was there, well placed to record development: 'The hesitant first steps of 1924, when scenes from *Henry IV, As You Like It, The Merchant of Venice* and *Julius Caesar* were produced in the gymnasium, soon became confident and year after year the Literary Society produced a Shakespearian play – *Julius Caesar* in 1927, *Twelfth Night, Macbeth, Midsummer Night's Dream* … plays which gave a taste of acting to a large number of boys.' The senior boy who was 'memorable' as Lady Macbeth is not so well remembered as deep-voiced Tom Fleming, whose first speaking parts were at Stewart's.

'The 1939 war stopped dramatics – a glass-roofed gymnasium has drawbacks – and there had again to be a fumbling revival while acting ability was nursed. We began with one-act plays – *The Changeling, King Alfred and the Neat-herd* and like juvenilia. But by 1950 the society was confident enough of its powers to stage *Murder in the Cathedral* with the chapel as theatre and, more ambitiously, to offer *The Lady's Not for Burning* in the Cygnet Theatre and *Androcles and the Lion* in the Lauriston Hall… It was part of the charm of *Murder in the Cathedral* that it was a domestic production, the last in which we entertained parents and friends at home. It is most unfortunate that we should have to do these things in the hired houses of strangers.' Friday night 'domestic' meetings continued to host play-readings, however, with Irish accents attempted for *The Playboy of the Western World.*

When Loretto acquired a new gym, twice the size of the old at ninety feet long, it was for 'theatricals' as well as physical education. Members of the audience wore formal dress for the opening all-ticket performance, and a special train of first class carriages took them back to Edinburgh. Merchiston's move out to Colinton saw improvement on many fronts, but school drama was hampered by 'a primitive stage set-up and prehistoric lighting which made the presentation of anything but one-act plays impossible, and productions were confined to farces and thrillers.' However the Governors were persuaded to loosen purse-strings for 'a flexible switchboard and a set of battens, spotlights, flies and backcloth supports.' The school joiner's stage experience was put to good effect in creating scenery, and the Shakespeare play 'became an almost too well established custom. In spite of the difficulties entailed by clothes rationing and its attendant troubles, a substantial wardrobe of Renaissance costumes was built up… The performances derived much benefit from the costumes being made on the spot and not hired, and from all the later rehearsals being taken on the stage itself, as anyone with amateur theatrical experience will appreciate.'

The Royal High's dramatic society was formed after the stimulus of an address by Poet Laureate John Masefield. Even in the Twenties the annual alternation of Shakespeare with French and Classical theatre was occasionally varied with plays written by pupils. Every year the Gateway Theatre in Leith Walk was filled by the parents of boys whose black blazers were exchanged for colourful stage costume. Karl Miller, who went on to become a founding editor of the *London Review of Books*, was involved in adolescent play-writing – *The Authors of Mischief* telling the story of Bailie Macmoran who was shot by a High School boy. A notable High School teacher introduced the author of a 'play for voices' before it became *Under Milk Wood* on radio: 'That Dylan Thomas was a force among the more literary boys was due to Mr Hector MacIver.' In adult life Miller was confronted 'every few days' by review copies where the author wrote 'harrowingly of his sufferings at his English public school.' His own memories of Edinburgh school days – like those of Muriel Spark at Gillespie's – were stress-free. By the end of the Sixties young actors from what later became the first boys' school to go co-educational were sharing the stage with Gillespie's girls.

Although it involves music, and further development of drama lies ahead, the origins of Gilbert and Sullivan in Edinburgh schools deserves to be discussed here. Magnus Magnusson linked this with the arrival of E. R. Hempson at the Academy by way of Flanders and Cambridge who in July 1922 took the leading role in *Trial by Jury*. Much later a member of his form class recalled this 'tall thin man who leaned backwards when walking, his pelvis thrust forward, somehow giving the impression that unlike the rest of us he had no bottom. One of my young contemporaries informed me that this was because he had it shot away when crawling along a shallow trench.' However that may have been, Hempson began the tradition of operettas at the Academy. The still-flourishing Edinburgh Gilbert and Sullivan Society of Edinburgh was founded in the following year and other schools were influenced in turn. 'Hemp' was assisted by a former D'Oyly Carte principal singer, wife of a distinguished Accie cricketer and described by Magnusson as 'the delectable Aileen Davies'. The future *Mastermind* question-master, who left as Dux of School with many prizes including one for singing, admitted that his feelings for Mrs Davies were widely shared as 'every Academy boy who took part in these productions fell helplessly but secretly in love with her.'

The Edinburgh International Festival of Music and Drama came into being a year after the school-leaving age was raised to fifteen in Scotland. The 'elementary' status of most teenagers was ended by a policy of Secondary Education for All – no fees attached. Senior secondary schools, equivalent to England's grammar schools, began to measure themselves against the fee-paying sector. In response the boys' schools of Edinburgh made a point of providing value for money: small classes, old-fashioned discipline, good exam results – and all the extras including festive music and drama. The Academy's Dramatic Society put on Shakespeare in the main oval hall up to the end of the Fifties, when the Prep Hall came to be preferred for its larger stage and better facilities. Robert Kemp, whose plays regularly filled the Gateway and whose adaptation of *The Three Estates* made early Festival history, had sons who walked to the Academy from Warriston Road. Kemp praised a school production of *Macbeth* for its 'sense of communal enthusiasm and team-work which supplies the fundamental charm of these performances.' He also advised schoolboy actors not to get carried away by dreams of stardom.

The House play came to Fettes in wartime and continued as part of a lively drama scene when peace returned. Much of it stemmed from the school chaplain, 'an unconventional and provocative cleric with a flair for the stage, who from 1949 produced a series of serious classic plays ranging from Ibsen, Chekhov and Shaw through Fry to T. S. Eliot.' The Sixties saw Ben Jonson's *Volpone* produced as a school play. It was marked, unusually, by three magazine photographs (in black and white) of actors against a set which lay 'somewhere between sumptuousness and decadence, full of blues and reds and gold.' In a later term one of the house plays, *The Winslow Boy*, was put on over two nights by Kimmerghame. Their housemaster not only produced Terence Rattigan's drama about a boy expelled from Naval College but also provided a full account for *The Fettesian*. In it he drew attention to the less obvious aspects of school drama:

'I shall say little about production, rehearsal, make-up, set-building and painting, lighting; these involve a great deal of labour by many people, often over a very long period, but they eventually advertise themselves and the results can be seen when the curtain goes up... What about the pre-1914 gramophone, records, camera, telephone and other such vital properties? ...

How do you carpet a drawing-room measuring 30 feet by 20 feet of highly irregular shape? We have had tarpaulins, underfelt (not recommended as it rucks up), hired carpets. This time we were fortunate enough to have a number of spare carpets of our own, and there were no less than seven of various shapes and sizes on the stage… And then poor old Sound Effects! It is never an easy job and correct timing is difficult. On this occasion he simply could not get realistic rain; needless to say, no real rain fell for a fortnight before the production, and the substitutes all sounded exactly like what they really were. The final version was manufactured by having half the House hissing round a microphone in Study Area.

'Prompt is a man who is never seen and, with luck, never heard; and yet he has to concentrate on every word through every performance, managing to look both at the actors so that he can spot when pauses are deliberate and when not, and also at his copy so that he always has the exact place. No sinecure. Our Prompt was also Call-boy in the intervals, giving the count-down of time and marshalling the openers with great firmness. He was also responsible for the exact timing of the curtain-pulling. And finally the most important unseen backroom boy of all, Props. He has to see that every detail on the stage is correct for every scene before the curtain goes up; he must see that every actor goes on to the stage properly equipped, i.e. with the handkerchief, the bag, the pipe, the

stick that has to be used in the course of the scene; and at every exit he has to seize the same properties back, actors being notoriously forgetful and careless, and put them by carefully for the next time. It is a very busy and difficult job, and for it there is not even the reward of seeing the production even once.'

The start of the Seventies saw girls being admitted to Fettes at sixth form level, and *A Keen Wind Blows* illustrates the effect of that on school drama. The caption for a 1962 photograph of *Trial by Jury* draws attention to a male bridesmaid's reluctance to be photographed in 'her' outfit, in contrast to the mixed cast for *Antigone* (Anouilh out of Sophocles) ten years later. Once the idea of greater

108. *Trial by cross-dressing.*

naturalism came to be accepted single-sex schools began to share stage productions. Among the Merchant Company schools, the two George Watsons' Colleges might have been expected to enter into joint play-acting during years of preparation for the Colinton Road merger. In fact it was Daniel Stewart's which paid the first courtesies in 1968: 'The annual play goes on, the most recent production involving the girls of our sister school Mary Erskine, who successfully fulfilled the female parts in *The Caucasian Chalk Circle*' – hired house the Church Hill Theatre. Three years later *She Stoops to Conquer* was put on with a mixed cast in the Mary Erskine hall. Miss Harvey directed.

Drama did not falter when Melville joined Stewart's. Highlights of the first ten years of merger included Britten's *Noye's Fludde*, Priestley's *They Came to a City, Loot* by Joe Orton and – at the urging of a humorously military-minded head, *Oh What a Lovely War*: 'Dialogue, movement, song and dance were forged into a company of 1914 Pierrots on a seaside pier. It was worth all the sweat and tears to see these young people come alive on stage and even better was the reception they got. The tinsel and ragtime of the opening numbers, the comic parade-ground rifle drill and the girls' recruiting songs soon gave way to a sadness and desolation as we were transported to the Somme.' That year Heriot's combined with Cranley to put on *HMS Pinafore* in what turned out, with shocking suddenness, to be the last session for the girls' school at Spylaw Road. Heriot's then admitted the first batch of girls in the autumn term of 1979. Single-sex schools still co-operate: St George's comes to the aid of Merchiston (*Romeo and Juliet, Blood Wedding*) as well as the Academy, taking *The Beggar's Opera* to the Millennium Festival Fringe.

But Drama has since become, if not quite a classroom subject (studios as well as stages) a recognised part of the school curriculum. Staying with Stewart's Melville, *The Collegian* of 2007 bade farewell to a drama-teaching member of the English Department. In five years she had become head of a new and separate department, produced plays with all age groups including the appropriate one for *Adrian Mole* (the 'inaugural' S2/3 play) and acted as an external assessor for Higher Drama, before going on to at least equal things with the British School in Brussels. The same issue of the Stewart's Melville magazine reported *The Compleat Wrks of Wllm Shkspear* (in ninety minutes), *The Crucible* (video clips bringing seventeenth-century Salem into meaningful contact with McCarthyism) and *West Side Story*, 'Bernstein's score causing notable worry in the school's music department and the large number of dance sequences making this one of the more demanding musicals.'

Everything short of *High School Musical* has been staged in recent years, with music (and art) departments fully involved beyond the classroom. Music deserves more than there is space for, no doubt, but it is better heard – or performed – than described. School music has developed in the first place through singing and boys, whether broken-voiced or not, take part. Kilted Merchiston singers recently did so in large numbers for a joint concert with St George's in the McEwan Hall. An odder collaboration was between the Merchiston Close Harmony Group and the Pipe Band for a Canadian tour. Loretto's chapel offers a poignant setting for Remembrance Day hymns, ending with the Last Post by a girl trumpeter and the pipe major's 'Flowers of the Forest'. Inter-house Songfest is competitive and cheerier. Watson's Ex Corde Choir sing from the heart, sometimes with a rock band – as distinct from the classically-inclined Chamber Choir and College Chorus. As with the other large co-educational day school, Heriot's, girls audition more readily. This is a general phenomenon: only the Academy's choir photos still show boys in the ascendant.

Directors of Music (far different from the part-time instructors of old) now have charge of school auditoriums built with acoustics in mind. Rehearsal leads to performance on the bigger stage. When Heriot's went forth for their Queen's Hall Concert there were brass, flute and saxophone ensembles which reformed within Senior Concert Band and Second Orchestra. After the interval the Junior Concert Band, 'with shades on, got the audience going with "Born to be Wild".' Different tones were heard in the school's traditional Greyfriars Concert. The Erskine Stewart's Melville Big Band has resisted strong Glasgow competition to win the jazz section in successive years. ESMS's Wind Band is also a combined effort, so that it comes as a surprise to find SMC Strings all boys – that emphasis, surely justified for this comb-ination of schools – on gender again. Annual events involving orchestral and choral music regularly draw the parents of Edinburgh schools to the Usher Hall and similar venues which on other occasions charge Festival prices. Pride in performance is evident in the audience as well as on the platform.

Chapter 10

The FP Phenomenon

Former pupils or FPs (rarely 'old boys' in Scotland) have gathered themselves into associations linked with the Edinburgh schools in question, hence *Ties that Bind*. There is history in it. Towards the end of the eighteenth century 'past scholars of George Watson's Hospital' gathered at Fortune's Tavern in the High Street, but other hospitals were also represented so it was hardly the first Watsonian club. Earlier an association was formed for George Heriot's 'Auld Callants', meaning old boys. Their Decorating Club was inaugurated with the purpose of 'busking' the founder's statue for June Day, a nine-hour job carried out through the previous night. Caps and bells were handed out by club officials and passed down through members limited to eighteen at a time. The four-year membership ended at age twenty-three, by which time all were out of apprenticeship. This was a group of seasonal craftsmen whose skills were also applied to Charles II's equestrian statue and the roof of the old Parliament House.

109. *Decorating the statue.*

Baxter's Tavern served dinner on 4 June each year to these tradition-bearers, with favoured masters joining them at table. Ceremonies in the quadrangle included the game of bouncing and then punching a ball to 'douf' it on to the slates. Membership was allowed to grow (but only to forty-three) by nineteenth-century rules which threatened that drunkenness at any of the four annual meetings would lead to expulsion. Another rule read out was that any member who wounded or bruised another should be fined half a crown. Every May decisions were made about who would do what with ceremonial shield, horns, vases and flowers which included 350 dozen narcissi. In 1807, on grounds of cost and sobriety, the 'Old Herioters' were denied entry for nocturnal decorating purposes. They broke in anyway and recruited 'garrers' – institutionalised school bullies – to their aid, forcing juniors to toss their supper jugs in the air and run naked through the quad. Injuries were sustained.

Decorating duties then passed to boys – forbidden to steal flowers – under gardeners hired for the occasion. After a June meeting in Murray's Tavern, however, 'a general throwing of Sticks, Stones and Turfs took place which brought the Properties down a good dail sooner then they were put up.' The Decorating Club continued to meet, though barred from busking, and a Heriot's Benefit Society was also created. It had an entry fee and regular meetings of members who paid two shillings a quarter, in exchange for which they were supported in sickness. They had to be under forty years old, 'of sober and good character, and free from any maim or bruise or any secret bodily disease.' After years of exclusion the Club was once again permitted to decorate the courtyard of the Hospital for its 200th anniversary in 1859. 'The design was partly supplied from the recollection of auld callants and partly copied from a sketch in the possession of a truly aged callant, who was present at his 72nd anniversary celebration.'

The first association of High School former pupils took place a year after the Heriot's quadrangle riot, when fourteen of them commissioned a portrait of Rector Alexander Adam months before darkness fell upon his teaching. The painter was Henry Raeburn, a Heriot's orphan who gave his name to Raeburn Place. When the portrait was handed over to the Scottish National Gallery half a century later, reference was made to 'the surviving members (five in number) of the High School Club'. No doubt one of the non-survivors was Sir Walter Scott whose portrait had been painted in the same year as Adam's. The Rector who succeeded him, James Pillans, also sat for Raeburn.

110. *James Pillans.*

As already noted, masters kept a class for four years before handing it over to the Rector – hence the idea of group loyalty from a given era. The point is made by the title of a published work, *History of Dr Boyd's Fourth High School Class* – men who had studied together under him from 1841. The First Class members had earlier come together under James Boyd when he exchanged the post of Heriot's House-Governor for that of a master at High School Yards. The Fourth Class gave Boyd his customary parting gift in the form of a sofa and chairs, one of which was brought in and sat upon while the Dux made a speech. In his reply Dr Boyd warned against setting up a club too early, adding that they 'might never again all meet together on earth.' Eight years later a circular was sent to Class-Fellows with known addresses and fifteen met to agree a constitution, elect office-bearers and enact bye-laws which included a five shilling fee at entry – all according to precedent. Annual dinners kept clubs together, and this one's first was held at Greliche's Hotel Français in Princes Street. Later dinners were held in the Rainbow Hotel, North Bridge.

The report suggests a decorous occasion under the eye of a respected pedagogue, although there were twenty-three toasts. One was to deceased Class-Fellows – already seven in number out of a class attended by forty-nine. About half were present at Greliche's when 'many school reminiscences were recalled' under the chairmanship of the Infirmary's House-Physician. By the time they met again he had died of cholera at Scutari: two Boyd Clubs were represented in the Crimean War. Dr Boyd, whose prophecy was thus fulfilled, came to the end of his own life in the following year. Large families kept the Victorian population growing, but high levels of infection at home and abroad made this an age for the consolations of religion. Class clubs grew old together and in extremity two members met in the sick room of one: 'The Club did dine. They took affectionate leave of each other, and within a fortnight the Club, in the person of Mr Black, attended the Secretary's funeral.'

A Fifth Boyd Class was also commemorated. The diary of a fifteen-year-old member has him returning home to Scotland Street at two o'clock: 'I learned my lessons consisting of portions from the [Ruddiman's] Rudiments, Roman History and Geography.' However clubs of this kind ceased to be formed because of added school subjects and abandonment of the class-ical teaching structure: there were now many masters' classes to consider. A general High School former pupils' club was founded in 1849 with a membership of 247. It grew steadily to 829 by the end of the century and then rapidly to 1,569 under the en-couragement of William King Gillies as Rector. After bidding him farewell, leavers passed through the Memorial Door 'to be welcomed there by a rep-resentative of the Former Pupil's Club.' Membership at

111. *William King Gillies.*

that point cost half the normal guinea sub. Convivial dinners apart, Clause IV required the association 'to promote the interests of the High School, maintain a good understanding, and form a bond of union among the Former Pupils of that institution.' Prizes and medals out of funds collected at the AGM were one way of promoting school interests; lining the walls with engravings of distinguished alumni another. A particular intervention recalls the first Raeburn portrait. When Dr Adam's memorial stone in the Buccleuch parish churchyard fell into disrepair the FP Club paid to have it restored.

Class clubs were also a feature of the Edinburgh Academy. Dining members of Tamson's Class were greeted in verse by Robert Louis Stevenson – although his opening stanza does not give a true impression of D'Arcy Thomson's attitude to punishment:

> Whether we like it, or don't,
>   There's a sort of a bond in the fact
> That we all by one master were taught,
>   By one master were bullied and whack't.
> And now all the more when we see
>   Our class in so shrunken a state,
> And we, who were seventy-two,
>   Diminished to seven or eight.

More to the point is a cartoon (penned during his schooldays) of the less respected writing master rushing at the young RLS with a tawse, hence the reassurance to adult diners in another line of his verse: 'We shall never be strapped by Maclean.' Poetic licence also caused him to alter the number present for the sake of a rhyme: 'I was at the annual dinner of my old Academy schoolfellows last night. We sat down ten, out of seventy-two! The others are scattered all over the places of the earth, some in San Francisco, some in New Zealand, some in India, one in the backwoods – it gave one a wide look over the world to hear them talk so. I read them some verses. It is great fun; I always read verses, and in the vinous enthusiasm of the moment they always propose to have them printed.'

The Academy's 1841–6 Cumming Club began with twenty-two out of the ninety-seven who had studied under James Cumming before he left to become the Glasgow Academy's first rector. Four years had passed when the founders gathered in the Café Royal, Register Street. The wider Academical Club came into existence six years after the school opened but had little significance until Raeburn Place was acquired. An enthusiastic Secretary then found much to do as Treasurer of the Academical Cricket Club and President of the Academical Football Club. Sport offered a way for 'the Masters and the former Pupils to mix with those who are now studying at the School, and thereby create a friendly feeling…' The lease referred to 'ground for the game of Cricket and for other sports for the *pupils*' but there was never any doubt that Old Scholars would play there too. The first proper match was between 'eleven of the Academy pupils and eleven of the masters and former pupils'. Separate sports associations came together at the turn of the century under the Academical Club.

The Edinburgh Institution Club was formed after a Queen Street soirée in connection with the headmaster's wedding: 'It was perhaps the greatest

112. *Dr Robert Ferguson.*

quality in Dr Ferguson's character that he readily knit very close the ties that bound master and pupil together. The schoolmaster and friend were completely united in him, and through their common affection for Dr Ferguson former pupils founded the earliest of the FP Clubs.' Looking back from the Thirties of the following century that may have appeared so, but the year was 1865 and there were certainly others by then. Apart from the general awarding of school prizes, the Institution Club organised a special examination for the senior class, and the boy who came top was awarded a gold watch and chain. The first associated sports club took up boating on the canal during a ten-year period which overlapped with the Football Club of 1872. 'Stution rugby has been sufficiently acknowledged along with cricket at FP level, but there was also a Golf Club with over a hundred members.

The Institution looked set to share the fate of Collegiate, Craigmount and other proprietorial schools as numbers fell in the nineties. It rallied partly through the efforts of a Miss Tocher who drew in younger boys, but the outcome of that might have been merely another Cargilfield House, the prep school in Trinity which moved to Cramond. A strong FP network saved the day: 'Early in 1910 the question was seriously raised whether the continuation of the school was to be long-lived. Its traditions made its disappearance a tragedy, its central position made its continuance a desirability, its widespread former pupils seemed to indicate that it should not be allowed to die… The essence of the problem was one of finance, obviously, and the question of the existence of a privately owned school was at stake… A small group became interested in the idea of a school being owned by its own former pupils.' A company was formed and a new headmaster appointed. Despite the disruption of war, Walter Hardie soon found himself with more pupils of all ages than 8 Queen Street could conveniently hold. A flitting to the vacated premises of St George's in Melville Street provided the answer. The strength of old loyalties was made apparent just before the outbreak of the second war when the Edinburgh Institution London Club declined to accept the new name of Melville College.

'A fledgling Watsonian could quite easily be excused for taking his Parent Club for granted. One is apt thus to accept a parent, to accept the family tree, the parental wisdom. But even in these cynical days [Welfare State dependency was later implied] the fledgling must realise he has emerged from a very well feathered nest into a world made, in the Club sense, at least, very comfortable. The boy who goes to his first Watsonian Dinner on leaving School must warm, one would think, to the fact that thirty-five branch Clubs, some very far away, are on that day remembering George Watson, the School which he founded, the friends at home made within the shadow of his beneficence, all their links in an indefinable family.' Another witness put it more plainly, describing Watsonians as 'clubbable people'.

Despite the example set by Heriot's Auld Callants, those who left the neighbouring hospital showed no inclination to follow suit. Within six years of entering the day school era, however, football and cricket clubs were established. Cross-country running provided an alternative for those not drawn to team games. Rugby and cricket forces were united in a Watson's Athletic Club during the negotiations over New Myreside, but it was not until the last decade of the Victorian era that the Edinburgh Watsonian Club began to hold annual dinners in the hall at Archibald Place. In the following one the custom became established of sitting down at table on the third Friday of January wherever Watsonians assembled. The High School's first *Schola Regia* magazine appeared in 1904. That

113. *Dinner at Archibald Place.*

year print also began the process of uniting 'Sonian sporting clubs at home with dining groups everywhere:

'Each of these clubs, although owing allegiance to Watson's, was a largely independent growth. What, we may ask, was it that brought them together? The answer lies in two closely linked factors – *The Watsonian* magazine and "Henry John" Findlay. The magazine, of which Henry John was the first editor, circulated the fruits of the editor's voluminous and world-wide correspondence. This dedication to, and love for, Watson's and all it stands for, fired the enthusiasm of others both in Britain and overseas. Henry John Findlay was not only the first editor of *The Watsonian*, he was, in everything but name, the first secretary of the world-wide club.' Elgar's 'Land of Hope and Glory' had caught the public imagination and Watsonian school songs echoed its sentiments. Against that background it hardly signifies that the Watsonian Club was not formally constituted until 1928.

Day school Daniel Stewart's was soon being made use of by its old scholars on two evenings a week, much to the annoyance of the janitor. A room was fitted up, apparently at their own expense, with a vaulting-horse, bars, rings and other gymnastic equipment. Headmaster William Wallace Dunlop mistrusted the growing cult of games but consented to act as Honorary President of the Stewart's College Athletic Club in 1886 – the wider club following fifteen years later. Under its umbrella the usual sports clubs flourished with the addition of tennis and high-wheeled cycling. When an annual sports day was instituted five of the events were confined to FPs, who continued to organise the affair without seeking or receiving much help from masters. History teacher John Thompson (looking back on it from 1955) was nevertheless a keen supporter of the FP phenomenon:

'There is much to commend the idea of taking as a text "By their fruits shall ye know them"; and of writing the history of a school simply in terms of its former pupils; for no school is an end of itself; each school is judged not by the ephemeral results of schooldays – successes in bursary competitions or Leaving Certificate examinations – but by the kind of men it makes.' He exaggerated the insignificance of youth when coming to the subject of rugby, however: 'The college club is too much overshadowed by the FP Club for me to spend more time on it. Almost all the best of the school players join the FP Club and then they normally improve their playing so that the memory of the brilliant schoolboy footballer is forgotten in the present achievements of the FP. Presumably even the boys themselves think of their place in the Fifteen not as the fruition of an earthly crown but as a stepping stone to higher things.'

Circumstances supported this unnatural view. At a time in 1920-21 when Stewart's College could not obtain a fixture with Watson's, the FP XV shared second place in the senior competition known as the Unofficial Championship. Gym-honed fitness may have explained the greater success of adults: 'The Club had a reputation for good forwards... We met with varying fortunes, never being champions but always acquiring the name of "spoilers", a name we have never lost.' Dr Thompson's cricket memories went back to mighty sixes struck over Inverleith's long boundaries: a Heriot's batsman at the pitch's south end hit a ball which bounced on Ferry Road and was retrieved from the neighbouring school's ground. Much later at the merger, when Stewart's and Melville FPs laid aside their local rivalry, the loss – to building development – of Ferryfield's excellent cricket squares was much regretted in the East of Scotland League.

Boarding-school life has a greater tendency to be remembered, as expressed by the Harrow School Song:

> Forty years on, when afar and asunder
>   Parted are those who are singing today,
> When you look back, and forgetfully wonder
>   What you were like in your work and your play...

It is therefore curious to relate that two schools which rivalled each other in all possible competitions should form a Fettesian-Lorettonian Club, in contrast to the segregated day school equivalents of Edinburgh. And long before 'Fet-Lor' brightened the lives of youngsters in the Canongate, a Fettesian cricket tour of Yorkshire encountered a last-minute shortage of participants and appealed to Loretto for help. Almond himself had just stopped playing but he encouraged senior boys to go. In years to come it was mainly Fettesian-Lorettonian rugby men who came together for tours of England. They never played north of the border, locally based ones tending to join Edinburgh Wanderers.

When Merchiston Castle was a town school in the days of Dr Rogerson there existed a 'flourishing old boys' club' with the son of a previous headmaster as its secretary. Receiving letters made it possible for him to compile a register for publication in book form. The seventh edition of *Merchiston Castle School Register* appeared in 1993 reporting activities over the previous twenty years. No doubt there were English models when the first *Fettes College Register* came out as a slim volume in 1889. Thirty years later, as a cumulative record, it ran to 378 pages. Lorettonians, late on the scene, had just started their own register. In the fourth edition of 1964 it ran to 3,919 names plus 55 Nippers. Influenced by the ex-Loretto master who set about 'introducing into a town day-school the distinctive flavour of the Public School', J. R. S. Young's 443-page *Edinburgh Institution 1832-1932* provided a fine example: historical summary followed by names, addresses and achievements – at school and after – to the extent that these were known. A later Melville College register updated the record to the time of the merger with Stewart's.

The Fettes register produced at the end of Edward VII's reign (much richer in content than a later centennial one) serves as an example of what a gentleman might take down from his shelves as an alternative to raking through old copies of *The Fettesian*. The opening section lists governors past and present before going on – more interestingly – to two head masters and ninety-seven assistant masters. Most of these were scholars, mainly classical, but three sergeants teaching drill are named. Almost as affecting as the first head's deathbed farewell, as read by generations of pupils on a wall of the Chapel, is the entry on the pianoforte and organ teacher who died there mid-voluntary on a Sunday evening. The bulk of the work is a List of Boys, some well into middle age and many deceased, with abbreviations used for maximum information on careers. Although distinguished as a classical school Fettes sent many leavers into the army, Sandhurst and Woolwich featuring regularly. Good Latin was required of those who won their way into the Indian Civil Service by competitive examination. The volume ends with a proud record of post-school academic achievement, mainly at Oxford and Cambridge, offset by annual accounts of school sports, lists of captains and tabulated results of matches. No wonder OFs were inclined to write to the editor when these fell off a bit: the only adult sporting references are to varsity blues and international caps.

Founder's Day on the warmest one to be looked for in a Scottish summer gave 'homecoming' opportunities for Old Fettesians – each to his former house, and a wander round when the annual cricket match went through a less than gripping phase. Selling off ground (with running track) was naturally resisted by those who returned. In difficult times heads cultivated OFs for the sake of necessary fund-raising.

114. Fettes Founder's Day.

When girls were admitted in sufficient numbers to fill a house, care was taken to make it the newest one: fewer objections likely. As for the other Fet-Lor half, it was not until 1946 that 'a growing feeling crystallised among those connected with Loretto that an Old Boys' Club or Society should be formed... It is, perhaps, surprising that no such organisation had been formed earlier, for in almost every other school in the country an Old Boys' Club was a *sine qua non*. Possibly the existence of the Fettesian-Lorettonian Club had fulfilled the athletic need...'

The athletic need of day school FPs was linked to playing-fields and premises. Raeburn Place provides an example of changing-rooms and social facilities coming together under the same pavilion roof. Myreside is another place where 'sport has always been associated with enjoyment and participation and friendship rather than with the desire to win at all costs.

This attitude and the hospitality for which Myreside is justly famous are, to my mind, the vital ingredients of Watsonian sport.' Former pupils took responsibility for providing a new rugby pitch and grandstand after the move to Colinton Road, but quarter of a century later the accommodation was still unfinished – 'no credit to the School or the Club.' Things have improved since then, thanks to the generosity of the Watson's 'family'.

The stand had extra changing rooms created under the tiered seating and also an indoor cricket pitch, slow-surfaced for learners. A new pavilion arose in front of the squash courts. There was a mixed lounge for wives and girl friends and a bar for men and rugby songs: on international days, with Murrayfield a merry walk away, beer is served in jugs not glasses. Cricket occasions are calmer. The Myreside Tea Ladies were legendary in their day, but now there is a women's Watsonian cricket team. An upstairs veranda faces the field which presents itself 'extremely well in the second half of the summer once the ravages of the rugby season wear off, and the main square is highly rated by batsmen… Few who have had the chance to watch a match on a sunny Saturday from the pavilion balcony, pint in hand, forget the experience.'

Premises are important. Goldenacre's grandstand has a Tea Room, thanks to the Heriot's FP Rugby Club – who were 'Heriotonians' in the early days. Tea apart, there is a long bar and comfortable seating for a panoramic view of acres made golden by the afternoon sun. Stewart's College borrowed prestige from the fact that internationals had been played on the Union Field, but the 'Puggy' bar under the stand was where rival FP teams mingled after doing battle. Stewart's cricket pavilion did very long service. Across the road Melville College improved on corrugated iron and a farm house, with the cow byre for changing, by means of a new pavilion. A corrugated iron stand sheltered rugby spectators from northerly showers. The merger of two colleges led to a parallel challenge of merging two FP clubs. This was done with all due formality in the Colleges' dining hall towards the end of the first term. Delay followed over premises, but when Ferryfield was sold off (in two stages) the need to create a new social centre at Inverleith became urgent:

'The emphasis changed from broad concepts and alternative locations to the final furnishing and fitting out of the Bar and Committee Room. Countless evening meetings of the Inverleith Committee representing the Rugby Club and Cricket Club pored over the plans and drawings deciding on such vital details as the dimensions of the beer hoist, the allocation of space in the ladies' cloakroom, the temptation to our more gymnastically

115. *Merged premises, Inverleith.*

inclined members offered by low struts and beams in the bar, the placing of the cricket scoreboard, the wearing of stiletto heels, the security of the fruit machine and how many stars we could expect in the Michelin guide… Now, ten years after our foundation, the Daniel Stewart's and Melville College Club is arguably the strongest former pupils' (or old boys!) club in this country or any other…'

How might the strength of an FP club be measured in relation to others? It is by no means obvious that these will become more successful over time, even where school-leavers outnumber the declining and deceased. The Stewart's Melville claim is based on 'active membership', and numbers of affiliated and branch clubs. The playing clubs, in particular the Rugby Club, carry the name proudly…' The original Institution players of Victorian times were open about recruiting men who had not studied with them at Queen Street, but the modern version came to seem unusual as a 'closed' club. Open rugby clubs became the norm. A corps of Scottish international players led to strong Sevens performances as far as Twickenham but even Douglas Morgan, who captained Scotland, could not raise the team to top level competition in the new league structure with replaced the Unofficial Championship. The club is no longer closed and has a slight majority of outsiders playing for the 1st XV. As a result, Stewart's Melville FP achieved promotion to the first division for season 2009–10.

Staying with this FP association which has flourished in fresh circumstances, the two cricket clubs combined in the summer before the schools did – pitches on both sides of Ferry Road being used for eight years before a housing estate was developed. Out of the accumulated statistics, all-rounders may take inspiration from international cricketer Ronnie Chisholm who three times made a half century and took five wickets in the same match. Reports follow (in *Stewart's Melville: The First Ten Years*) of clubs devoted to a range of sports from swimming and sailing to badminton, curling and golf; also in London, Cambridge, the Borders, and Aberdeen. It would not be hard to name other FP clubs with more affiliated and branch clubs, but the enthusiasm of newly-weds should never be condemned.

A section in that ten-year assessment is headed 'Where Are They Now?' This is a key question at the heart of after-school life. At the most basic level it represents the plea of secretaries for word on changes of address. At the highest it becomes Where Did They Get To? in celebration of famous former pupils – as with one for the 175th anniversary in question, *175 Accies: A Collection of Biographical Sketches.* Somewhere in between come obituaries of the fairly well known. Then there is the challenge of saying something interesting about an inevitably random group of people as word comes in and space allows. *Crème de la Crème* showed that early magazines were started primarily for old girls, sometimes with hardly a word about the school attended. Over time the balance shifted towards the young, allowing less and less space for an FP Section at the end. The same is true of boys' school magazines.

The Watsonian (the golden jubilee of which was celebrated in book form) came into existence partly out of the correspondence generated by former pupils. It became customary for a slightly built Secretary to stand on his chair and read out telegrams at the annual dinner. Such was his knowledge of the senders that this became a star turn. Postage costs eventually reduced this journal of record (and much else) to annual appearances from three times a year, with consequent problems of space. Forty per cent of it was nevertheless devoted to former pupils when Gavin Hastings played for the school on Saturday mornings and Watsonians after lunch. A third of the contents for FPs remained normal in the Nineties, but since the advent of a more school-focused magazine the share has dropped to ten per cent. The only Watsonians listed now are dead ones, male then female. With a membership of thousands augmented by Women Watsonians (the Club has since become as mixed as the school) it was never going to be possible to provide much of a Friends Reunited service. Reunions by year group are reported instead.

The Academy, Fettes and Merchiston have gone some way to resolve the difficulty by publishing separate magazines for those who went before. The *Merchistonian Newsletter* was a slim affair in its first issue at the start of the third millennium but has since expanded greatly, and the *Old Fettesian Newsletter* has attained 148 pages, square-bound, unlike previous stapled versions. At A5 the page size of this production (as with the Academical one) is half that of the school magazine. The Merchiston equivalent matches the dimensions of what used to end with a 'Merchistonia' section. Like most school magazines nowadays *The Fettesian* is a multicoloured glossy, giving the impression that pupils and their parents (and potential parents) require stimulus.

Old boys were formerly expected to be content with a good read, but Newsletter No. 53 of July 2008 has many photographs and all are in colour. Perhaps the coloured advertisements pay for them. Widespread Fettesian membership is implied by the addresses of seven regional secretaries in Scotland, six in England and twenty-six overseas. Five of these are North American and there are four in Australia. While not necessarily implying groups which meet, even to dine, they offer points of contact. Two or three may gather – women as well as men nowadays – and more did so for sixteen OF Events reported in the latest issue. A return slip is included for information on the doings of readers and others known to them, which forms the basis of OF News arranged alphabetically (for some reason) 'by year of leaving post-1970 and by year of entry pre-1970'.

The Academical's current editor began by ringing the changes, with extracts from letters to him followed by items on Accies from the school weekly news sheet and ending with 'news from individual Academicals and via the media' – a watchful eye kept on *The Scotsman* and other outlets. Now the magazine publishes news of members by decades of leaving school. An increasing amount of information is taken from the Academy website. News of grad-uations celebrate early achievement. Marriages (also a male civil part-

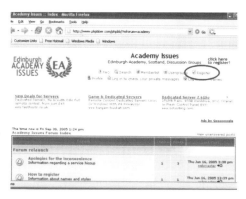

116. *Accies reunited.*

nership) are followed by births. Obituaries go well beyond lists, especially in the case of long-term members of staff. Generous space is also given to departing teachers though not, as in the Academy Chronicle, to new ones. In both these examples of 'newsletters' directed at former pupils, there is summarised school news and a range of other items – mainly nostalgic – for the sake of a good read.

The question 'Where Are They Now' was answered in light-hearted fashion for Stewart's Melville, it being relatively easy to make something of a ten-year period. After a predictable number of captains and duxes, the categories reported – or dreamed up – included Foreign Venturers, The Highly Strung (racquet sportsmen), Iron Men (golfers), Electrical Connections, More Lawyers, Economists and Accountants (no humour there either) to finish with those who had merely found occupation in Edinburgh: Home Sweet Home. Fifty years earlier High School historian William Ross felt constrained by the small book which was passed out to every leaver as a *vade mecum* by the *alma mater*:

'My predecessors have given lists of eminent former pupils. Limits of space preclude me from following their example… In the case of an old School like ours the list, could we make it complete, would inevitably be a long one… We know that in more recent times we can claim many Moderators of the Scottish Churches, an Archbishop of Canterbury, a Roman Catholic Archbishop of St Andrews and Edinburgh, three Lord Chancellors, many Lord Provosts of the City, Senators of the College of Justice, and Professors of the University, as well as sailors, soldiers, statesmen, poets, painters, inventors, and indeed men eminent in every walk of life.'

The Greyfriars' preacher for bicentennial celebrations which brought the Heriot's Decorating Club back into the fold provided a wider overview: 'No man can deny that an institution which, during 200 years, has fed, clothed, and educated more than 4,000 of the sons of our burgesses – which in the course of the last fifty years has turned out, to my knowledge, upwards of fifty members of the College of Justice, fifty medical practitioners, thirty clergymen, and forty teachers and professors, many of them bearing names of the highest note in their several professions… No man can deny that an institution which has done all this, and far more, has fulfilled the pious wish of its founder…' One hundred and fifty years later a great deal more could be claimed by way of achievement for what is now firmly established as a co-educational school, particularly since responsibility for feeding and clothing ended with the hospital era and – more recently – since rising fees have altered the nature of the intake.

It would be wrong to end a chapter on this subject without addressing Brian Lockhart's claim that, under inter-war headmaster William Gentle in particular, a preference for internal staff promotions was counter-productive. His deputy succeeded to the post but soon retired, and the Governors signalled a change of direction by interviewing four outsiders for the post. Dr Dewar's dispute with rugby-minded masters has been discussed but he managed to annoy others as well. Another provocation was to restrict FP attendance at the Buskin Ceremony – before he had experienced one. *The Herioter* responded: 'Now, as possibly never before, all of us who are proud to be connected with the school are united in defence of our traditions.' Dewar managed to face down his critics over a 23-year period by being an effective moderniser, but the impression from that now distant age is one of excessive loyalty: 'For former pupils the "burning question" was how to satisfy the widespread desire to continue the family tradition of having been schooled at Heriot's.'

On a lighter note, comment is due on the old school tie. Leaving aside FP blazers, badges and scarves, it took ten years for Watsonians to settle on one. Colours were agreed, then altered (narrow and broad Oxford and Cambridge blue stripes reversed) until the 'Heart-in-flame' became the necessary trademark just before the second war. Aitken & Niven and three other official outlets were finally able to sell what has since remained unchanged. When the Daniel Stewart's & Melville College Club agreed to have a new tie there was delay because of the lack of a combined school badge. Meanwhile 'the two existing ties were blended and reblended.' Old members insisted on wearing the familiar neckwear 'until it wore out,' but eventually a new tie with two historic badges prevailed – at least among the younger members.

Chapter 11

Bringing Back to Mind

The second last chapter of *Crème de la Crème* has the same title, and part of it may bear repeating: 'Memories are the making of a book like this: set them alongside facts and a story emerges. Some people can hardly remember anything about childhood, never mind school – they "put it behind them" – while others have what seems like total recall… Once the process of bringing back to mind is begun, memories increase.'

But men and women do not necessarily remember in the same ways. The former pupils who featured in the last chapter may not be as mindful of actual schooldays as they are enthusiastic about adult sport and social activity. Women might be thought more likely to recall their own childhoods because of spending more time with children. Furthermore those old girls who contributed stories to the last book had rarely thought of putting them into print. By contrast, no informal attempt has been made to tap into the memories of men because so much is already available. *A Hundred Years of Fettes: Memories of Old Fettesians 1870–1970* is a case in point, begun by a housemaster's collation of the first half century. As readers of *Ties that Bind* are being encouraged to bring things back to their own minds, however, only stories within living memory appear. There is a further emphasis on early schooldays (preparatory or junior) which are less readily recalled.

Some will have had similar experiences to David Daiches who started school just after the Great War, even though his family background was distinctly unusual. *More Memories of the South Side* (which includes those of Daiches) could be anyone's, but *Two Worlds: An Edinburgh Jewish Childhood* is by a Watsonian who, because of the Saturday Sabbath and his father being Edinburgh's highly distinguished Rabbi, had to ask the way to Myreside: no sport for him on the Jewish day of rest. Daiches, who knew the social difference between back greens (for flats, a block away) and back gardens, entered Watson's at six and a half. His journey to school was a short one across the Meadows and he and his older brother Lionel could make it running in four minutes. The bell of Sciennes School rang at ten to nine and provided a warning for the nine o'clock start at Watson's.

A pupil perspective emerges on Headmaster George Robertson's rules from England. Prior to his arrival Watson's boys were free to use the Meadows as their playground during the half-hour lunch interval. When Daiches started school, pupils ate their sandwiches on grass while noisy seagulls hovered, or went to Lauriston Place to exchange insults with Heriot's boys.

For David Daiches the unforgettable 'Miss Brodie' figure in the last year of junior school was his first male teacher, a bald man with a greying ginger moustache, W. W. Anderson was nicknamed 'Dub-Dub' after the sound of his initials. He never used corporal punishment but kept discipline by a combination of sternness and light-hearted sarcasm. There was much emphasis on memorisation in the classrooms of these days, and mnemonics humorous or otherwise eased the strain. Rules like 'i before e except after c' were embedded for life. Times-tables made the number bonds of modern primary maths automatic. Dub-Dub conducted the chanting rows of boys with his pointer. Watson's teachers all had one, and each held it in a distinctive way.

117. *W. W. 'Dub-Dub' Anderson.*

The same 'intense mental activity' which the visiting American Horace Mann had observed in Edinburgh many years before applied to Dub-Dub's classes. He was an extreme example (without the tawse) of a traditional Scottish dominie. Boys sat in order of attainment in whatever was being taught and tested, with the brightest in the back row and so on down to the front. At the start of lessons the top five boys at the end of the previous day were seated at the front, and rapid-fire questioning began as they tried to work their way back to the top of the class. The questions moved down the class, beginning by being directed at the new back row, which constantly changed in composition as the first boy to answer correctly forced demotion on all those above him. Surprisingly perhaps Daiches (who was one of the brightest) recalled that this master seemed to take pleasure in making fun of clever boys: perhaps it was some kind of reverse motivation. Weekly marks led to class places and prizes at the end of the year, with top of the class earning remission of fees for the following year. In senior school David Daiches was able to earn such a bursary, having become fully aware – through the formative influence of Dub-Dub – of how competitive Scottish education could be. It did not seem to do his love of all things literary any harm.

A few hundred yards from the Myreside ground which one Watson's boy hardly knew was Merchiston Castle School. Veteran master James Rainy Brown recently appealed for memories of the original Merchiston. He received them from a man who chose anonymity but who, from a reference to crystal wireless sets 'under the blankets in the dorm', appears to have been a contemporary of David Daiches: ' "Rise and shine" came from Old Bill with the bell at 7.00 a.m., then a run to the bowling green before breakfast at 7.30. Shoes were inspected at Assembly when passing the "Sixth" at the foot of the stair… It was mandatory to wait at a door if a prefect or member of the Sixth was approaching – however distant – unless "nodded on". Prefects' Gym for all newboys included push-ups and climbing a rope using arms only, and chastisement with a "twistie" if Not Trying Hard Enough…

'There was Leave-out on Sundays and some Wednesdays and Saturdays – cards to be signed by the hostess. Evening service was in the Assembly Hall conducted by the Head or by a visiting preacher. Anthems included "Jerusalem"… Newboys wore knickerbockers, then shorts. Blue and white ties were followed by blue knitted silk ones. The cardinal sin was "putting on side" in any of its forms. Compulsory skipping was at mid-morning in the playground. The grub cart came twice a week – queuing was in teams supervised by prefects. The bicycle inspection, brakes and bells, was midday on Saturdays before we could cycle out to the grub shop at Colinton.'

Schoolboys and food go together, as in a Thirties account of hearty Loretto eating: 'Breakfast was designed to withstand Musselburgh's weather even in mid-winter. I can remember the joy of returning from a "Links" run and sitting down expectantly in Hall where a large coal fire was blazing. Porridge, properly cooked, was on offer every morning except Sundays… This was followed by a cooked dish, usually something fried like sausages or an egg, or bacon, white pudding or black pudding, and occasionally a herring in oatmeal or a kipper. Best of all were the baps, warm from Hunter's bakery in the town and spread lavishly with butter and syrup ("squish") or, twice a week, marmalade. To drink there was either tea or milk though the great majority of us drank milk.'

Loretto boys averaged a quart of milk a day. School dinner consisted of soup or dessert along with a fish or meat course – the latter sometimes carved at table by a sergeant-major drill instructor. Much interest surrounded puddings which 'varied considerably in texture and popularity', this

Lorettonian making clear his distaste for rice pudding and 'the bread and butter concoction with the pale yellow liquid in which a few currants floated disconsolately under a covering of soggy crust.' A snack followed the inevitable afternoon games, but Scottish high tea (with a cooked course) was only available three days a week. 'On the other days you could produce your own egg, write your name clearly on the shell, and leave it in a special rack in the Hall after games. At tea-time it was returned to you, hot and boiled.'

Paul Henderson Scott's diplomatic career encompassed the Cuban missile crisis before he retired to leadership roles in the Scottish National Party. The Regent Road building was to become a 'shibboleth of independence' in the discussion of a Scottish Parliament: 'I was fortunate in my school, the Royal High School of Edinburgh, which I attended from the age of five to eighteen. At first the entire school was housed in Hamilton's splendid

118. *Hamilton's splendid building.*

building, an early nineteenth century reinterpretation of classical Greece, below the Calton Hill. It is a building which echoes the intellectual self-confidence of Scotland in the age of the Enlightenment... After I had been at school in this inspiring place from my first few years the Preparatory and Junior classes, as they were then called, we were moved to a new building beside the school playing field of Jock's Lodge. We returned with relief two or three years later when we reached the dignity of the senior school.'

'Gytes' confronted by schoolmasters in 'dark suits and academic robes' may be ignored here for the sake of more elusive memories. On these the poet Norman MacCaig is a good witness in a contribution to *Schola Regia*: 'The old Grubby was at the East entrance and is memorable to me for the gruesome cocoa it sold, half a cup of cocoa floating on half a cup of white slime. The playground was covered with gravel, which was asking for trouble so that most High School boys wore a badge on their knee bones as well as on their blazers. There we amused ourselves with cuddy-loups, relieve-oh, hopping-dig, a lethal form of football and even cricket… I keep reading books in which men write horrifically about their schooldays: sadistic masters, torture in the bogs, the lot. It wasn't so with me. Even fights were rare, though occasionally a blue eye would go down to the Dungeons and come out black. My life at the High School was a happy one.'

This echoes Karl Miller, whose time there extended into the post-war period: 'My own bent was literary. I belonged to the category succinctly described by Dylan Thomas – "thirty-third in trigonometry and, as might be expected, edited the school magazine." There were boys who weren't drawn to any part of the curriculum. Such a one was Sandy Brown, now a well known jazz musician who, viewed from a couple of forms below, seemed very precocious with his clarinet and his yellow bow tie flapping at his throat like some exhausted tropical bird.' Ronnie Corbett was another High School boy who went into the entertainment business and his autobiography makes clear that he was never bullied or even teased about his small size. This applied equally to his primary school years at James Gillespie's School for Boys (as distinct from Muriel Spark's newly separated girls' school) where he modestly reported no prime.

Although Ronnie Corbett did not remember being called names, a member of the class answered to 'Stinky' because his father was a fishmonger. Nicknames are interesting as an aspect of boys' school life since girls, generally speaking, did not use them. No doubt that difference is explained by the fact that teachers used to address even quite small boys by their surnames. This impersonal style reflected the fact that upper-class adults also called each other Smith or Jones – or Smith-Jones. Brothers attending public school together were major and minor, and the written version added initials – to the right of the surname after a one-inch margin. The avoidance of forenames is at an end in those boys' schools which have admitted girls, since it proved humanly impossible to maintain two modes in one classroom. Even at all-boy Merchiston, however, masters made the same change to informality. According to James Rainy Brown, who started teaching there in the Sixties, Merchie boys still use surnames or versions of them like 'Smithy'.

JRB testifies to a reduced tension of authority between teacher and taught and (perhaps as a result) less identifying of masters by nicknames. Daiches's 'Dub-Dub' was W. W. Anderson, unofficial games master at

Watson's during the last fifteen years of Victoria's reign. As with 'Dubya' for George W. Bush, the sound of initials explained it. One surname shared by two teachers required it: an Anderson who taught PE at Watson's was 'Gym Andy'. There is interest in the fact that Magnus Magnusson identified teachers coming to the Academy after his own time by initials and surnames while presenting those known to him when young as 'Beanie', 'Billy', 'Boab', 'Bob Begg', 'Fergie', 'Fushy', 'Hemp', 'Ike', 'Pop', 'Ronnie Daw', 'Scabby', 'Teddy', 'The Moot' and 'Tony'. Not all masters were given nicknames, but one had several. B. G. W. Atkinson was a renowned cricketer who had once hit a loose ball – with an improvised overarm stroke – high above the boundary at Lords to smash the pavilion clock. As a teacher of Latin and English 'Bagwash', otherwise 'The Bag', 'Atco' or 'Atty', rarely had to ask for the tawse to be brought from its corner cupboard.

One Loretto headmaster who rejoiced in a nickname was A. R. 'Sconnie' Smith. He had been at the school and became an international rugby player after leaving. An anonymous article in *The Lorettonian* discussed 'the cult of nick-nomenclature', lamenting the fate of such Nippers as would never progress beyond their surnames. After considering obvious examples the author continued: 'But good as many of the foregoing are they do not attain the level of genius. We now come to a class of nick-names which are inspired, are absolutely new creations and, for the most part, have no meaning except in so far as they describe the personality of the man… What is one to say of "Stotter"? One does not know whether to wonder more at the exquisite simplicity of "Wooks", the descriptive power of "Plum", or the pictorial force of "Swob"… Will anyone ever throw light on the origin of "Sconnie"?'

In the autobiographical *Life is Too Short* Nicholas Fairbairn maintains the focus on younger boys at school, since his five years in Loretto's Nippers outshone the ones which followed. They began with him three months short of his eighth birthday and self-consciously small. Almond had begun the practice of weighing and measuring each boy at the start and finish of each term, so that there was evidence of his three stone five pounds and four foot one and a quarter. He was light enough for seniors to pick up by the neck, and to be called 'Henry' after a cartoon figure of the time – although by no means as small as Ronnie Corbett. In most un-Lorettonian fashion Fairbairn Minor (who also had older cousins at school) took an early dislike to rugby and gym, but in his last year as a Nipper he captained the hockey and cricket

119. *Nipper starting out.*

elevens and was made Head of School. Fifty boys looked up to him.

Margaret Thatcher's Solicitor-General for Scotland never lost touch with his inner *enfant terrible*, but the impression emerges of modelling on masters. The schooldays of Fairbairn, N. H. began under Nippers Head-master C. S. 'Tim' Colman. He always sport-ed a Cambridge tie and wore trousers suited to the golf links rather than dark suit and gown. The boys respected him fully without any fear, and through his languorous manner it was obvious that Tim was concerned to further the progress of each one of them. S. T. Hutchinson, otherwise 'Hutchie', who taught Latin was scarcely less revered than the Head. Son of an Anglican clergyman, he had tremendous presence – centre-parting, hooked nose and a deep voice which was used to tease and dominate by turns. To be beaten by his flat puddex was an experience which paled beside Hutchie's use of a cane called 'Long John'.

A triumvirate of memorable teachers encountered early was completed by the brother of James Mason the actor, who sounded like him and imparted an element of glamour to the French language which he taught. At the same time there was a certain boyishness which contributed to his popularity with young Lorettonians. The common element which made all three of them good teachers as well as memorable ones was an evident respect for scholarship above the constraints of classroom and curriculum, and Nicholas Fairbairn was duly uplifted. The impression of a masculine society is strengthened by the school doctor who, recognising the future woman's man and his pleasures to come, gave priority to checking the descent of the small boy's testicles. Young Nicky took delight in the blonde matron's legs, skin and sex appeal, an interest he was conscious of sharing with the Head of Nippers. Other boys spotted the undeveloped bond between pupil and matron in the fact that he was never sent back to brush his hair before breakfast – however much they ruffled it up.

There was at least one inspiring teacher in the upper school – an artist who confirmed the judgement reached in early years that Fairbairn's remarkable imagination was capable of being expressed through colour. After studying Classics at Edinburgh University (he sold his first painting as an undergraduate) the advocate's 'devil' solved the problem of his idle year – without income from the law – by earning £2,000 for a one-man exhibition. His verdict on Loretto was ambivalent. Almond's encouragement of independent thinking was admired, but Fairbairn felt that the cult of team games had been taken too far and the intellectual freedom which Almond had also sought to encourage had fallen off. On the positive side, however, Loretto was a good preparation for adult life in the sense of an easy-going respect for other people, thanks to community values which had been retained. Anti-intellectualism represented the reverse side of the coin, but it would be fair to say that academic standards were rising – under exam pressure – by the time Fairbairn left.

120. *Loretto working harder.*

A link may be made with Edinburgh's cultural elite through the young lawyer's enthusiasm for avant-garde productions at the Festival. After a Sixties 'happening' which featured a nude model being pushed across stage in a trolley, the Procurator-Fiscal brought charges against the perpetrators and Fairbairn successfully defended them. Three of the rising literary men who contributed essays on their Fifties childhoods for *Jock Tamson's Bairns* attended public schools. None remembered his schooldays with much affection, and the common charge (encouraged by the context) was that their education had not been Scottish enough. The senior man was Allan Massie, novelist, critic and journalist, whose commitment to the United Kingdom was encouraged by being sent to Glenalmond. Massie has not altered that view but it has become his considered one. As a budding seditious writer he felt himself a misfit – not really officer material.

John Herdman's 'dark exploration of ambiguous worlds' (from his website) was to be developed in novellas and short stories. He chose not to name his Edinburgh place of education but it was Merchiston, where prefects championed a system of graded rewards. These were often trivial – on the level of how many blazer buttons were to be fastened from one year to the next – but Herdman who became a prefect himself in due course acknowledged that many of his school memories were positive. The education he received may have little about it that was Scottish in character, but it certainly broadened the mind.

The Academy was viewed less favourably by Giles Gordon, London gossip and literary agent, who professed to being deeply affected whenever he saw someone wearing an Accie tie in Piccadilly. Part of his response was one of disdain for those adults whose narrow lives led them to shelter behind such conformist dress, but it was mixed – he claimed – with guilt for not showing an equivalent loyalty to the school in Henderson Row. As for Scottish literature being taught at his old school, Gordon regarded it as an impossibility because so many of the staff were English. To be fair to the Academy staff, wherever they happened to be born, the same failure to teach Scottish literature beyond 'Tam o' Shanter' could have been laid at the door of all Edinburgh schools of that age.

Arnold Kemp (son of the playwright) had similar things to say in *The Hollow Drum* – 'Agonised Deference' the relevant chapter. The deferential agony stemmed from the fact that the Academy was trying to match the English-style 'public' schools and their system of putting the brightest boys forward – through A Levels – for admission to Oxford and Cambridge. And yet the Academy was at the same time very Scottish, very Edinburgh. Most boys sat their Highers (heading for careers in Scots Law, perhaps) and applauded even higher-fliers at year's end. Arnold Kemp's older brother David fell upon a middle course, that he would enter for the Bursary Competition for entry to Edinburgh University. Schools like the Royal High put their best pupils in for it as a matter of course, clear financial benefits being available. David Kemp found no Academy master who could help, so made his own way to the Old Quad for the sake of finding a syllabus.

Some of this stemmed from a local influence – that of Fettes College which provided a target for rivalry on all fronts. Fettes had many Scottish pupils, including not few from the Glasgow area, but it was as much a public school as any in England. The Academy, in Arnold Kemp's opinion, fell between two schools. Meanwhile the neighbourhood day school was merely another fixture to Fettesians whose minds were on other things than Scottishness: 'The act of recollection soon brings competing impressions crowding in upon the memory. What for instance of lunch, that greatest social occasion when we might discuss the Test match with the soup, Roman poetry with the stew, and Cliff Richard with the pink blancmange?'

Arnold Kemp left school after the Highers year and followed his brother to the local university. Both lived at home and frequented the town, like most Scots students of the day. Massie, Herdman and Gordon took the Oxbridge route but Kemp, having opted for a career in journalism, made a more remarkable relocation – for one brought up in Edinburgh – by moving to Glasgow. There he became editor of *The Herald.* These large cultural questions (now on the agenda of a Scottish Parliament at Holyrood) may be put aside as we follow Arnold back to early childhood. With the school a part of his neighbourhood, the Academy Yards were merely another place to play. A more accessible and interesting one lay close by in the district known as Puddocky. The Water of Leith ran past the back gardens of Warriston Terrace where the Kemp family lived and, it offered a paddling paradise for young children.

Kemp's story in *A Scottish Childhood* concerns a pet duck which neighbours thought would benefit from access to the river – somewhat on the lines of a cat-flap. Arnold responded to the invitation along with other boys of the neighbourhood – 'urchins' in spirit if not in social fact – by levering out stones to create a way through for the duck. The hole in the wall felt like a fine achievement for an evening's labour with whatever tools came to hand.

That summer the family holiday cottage was high up an Angus glen. Arnold Kemp's future as a pressman is evident in the observation that in these days newspapers did not reach that remote spot until the following day, by which time a telegram had been sent by his grandmother. The message was that firemen had pumped out the Kemp house so no great cause for concern. The river in spate had burst into the gardens of Warriston Terrace. Knocking down the Lord Provost's dividing wall and the ruin of his garden was only the most spectacular part of it.

With younger boys under discussion it is worth pointing out that the Academy opened a junior department for beginners at Denham Green in Trinity just after the war, and a Prep School followed close to New Field. Playground games flourished at all levels. The Yo-Yo returned to Daniel Stewart's, as recorded by a history teacher with an eye for these things and their curious origins: 'The Victorian bandalore made its silly reappearance in the thirties, to go underground and reappear in 1954. But these were passing crazes. More firmly rooted have been conkers and bools, cockie-rosie and cuddy-wechts. The last is temporarily in eclipse – clothes rationing may have caused it to be frowned on – but cockie-rosie still returns to the junior school with the swallow and raises its little song to say that summer has come back again.'

Children's language of games was confined to the playground. No teacher permitted it in class but there was one adult who spoke broad

Scots – the Janny or janitor. On frosty winter nights in Victorian times it was customary for him to pour water in front of his lodge at the Academy, and Stevenson was one who rejoiced in 'the slide at the Janitor's gate'. His wife sold biscuits, buns and other forms of sustenance at break-time. A successor held the post for thirty-six years. When he retired at eighty his testimonial came from a rector who had taken many a pipe in the lodge, with praise for his calming influence on 'the effervescence of Geits.' Perkin, the Stewart's janitor of Edwardian times, was honoured with a caricature and a nickname:

> On the highroad to Queensferry
>   There dominates a very
> Handsome building, tall majestic and sedate,
>   Where the fussiest of freaks
> Who is nominated Peaks
>   With a dog and wife and slavey guards the gate.

Guarding the gate to keep tramps out and boys in was one of the janitor's principal duties at George Watson's Hospital, which extended to swabbing schoolrooms and carrying coal. The Janitor's Lodge is the only part of the original Hospital to survive. In day school times a charming portrait caught 'Davie' in his top-hatted glory – and also something of the affection felt by pupils. David Daiches paid tribute to a successor, having been directed to the headmaster's room by a cheerful gentleman of the playground who turned out to be Willie, the senior janitor. His deputy Fairlie was often ill-tempered and his first name never featured. While Daiches was still wearing the maroon blazer Willie retired and was often to be seen with his 'cleek', or all-purpose golf club, on the nine-hole course at Bruntsfield Links – more pitch and put than golf. It may be added – balancing the Academy's bun-dispenser – that the last Watson's janny

121. *The Jannie: Stewart's Perkin ...*

122. *... and Watson's Davie.*

before the girls arrived from George Square had a wife as influential as himself. Corridors were never cleaner.

Class reunions provide opportunities for sharing memories. George Heriot's hosted such an event for those who left half a century ago – fifth and sixth year pupils in 1957–58 – as reported in the alumni-focused *Quadrangle*: 'School dinner over, we drifted off reminiscing on the way. Did we dilate reverentially on these history-haunted precincts? No, we recalled the delinquents who tried to blow up trams with charges on the line on Lauriston Place. Did we nostalgically ponder our chapel in the moonlight? No, we recalled Greyfriar's services where someone ran a book on how long the chaplain's sermon would last.' An apology from Canada appeared in the newsletter. John G. Gibson lives in Nova Scotia, an acknowledged expert on the old styles of piping and dancing which crossed the Atlantic in emigrant ships – leaving these matters to military bands and the Royal Scottish Country Dance Society. His love for all things Gaelic began at a one-teacher primary school in Glenfinnan. As a variation on Kemp and the others concerned about excessive English influence, Gibson feels that his later education was wrong to ignore Highland and Celtic values. But Lowland Scotland is to blame, not Heriot's. This former pupil merely paid tribute to 'Abers' Abercrombie who got him through Higher French in a year.

Also in *Quadrangle* there appeared a letter from the USA by someone who left the Class of 1958 early: 'No one enjoys more hearing of academic or sporting or business success than myself. Most of the boys who left Heriot's with me did not hit the headlines in any of these categories, but that did not label them as failures… I left because I was no longer interested in the kind of education I was going to receive. I felt that the two years would be better spent learning a useful trade. My parents who scrimped and saved for the fees were expecting more – perhaps a lawyer, a doctor – but I was hell-bent on leaving. I applied for an apprenticeship as a compositor in the printing trade. The careers master sent me along with another boy and I was the successful applicant. My employer was an FP. I served six years before reaching journeyman status, attending day release and evening classes at the Heriot-Watt. Mixing with those from other schools, I realised what a wonderful education I had received. Now, as a journeyman with a Heriot's background, I was able to seek employment anywhere in the world.' Jinglin' Geordie would have applauded.

Mention of tram lines in Lauriston Place recalls a transport system on tracks (including the suburban railway line) which made it possible for fee-paying schools to flourish. A Melville boy at the end of that first tramcar era illustrates the point: 'The school I attended had the benefit of being in the West End which meant that many pupils, by travelling each day into town from the country and suburbs, became part of the hustle and bustle of a city. It broadened perspective from an early age… My own experience centred round the use of trams to and from Colinton, the city centre and Ferryfield. Particularly memorable was the 8.12 a.m. It was a part-route tram to Princes Street catering mainly for school children. There was a rainbow of uniforms from Cranley, Watson's, St Denis, Gillespie's, George Square, Heriot's, Stewart's, Queen Street and the Royal High. Some mornings there were fifteen boys and girls in the back part of the upper deck on bench-seating made for five.'

A fellow pupil recalled the rambling interior of what had been built as separate terraced houses in Melville Street: 'There was a compact unity about the place which helps the mind to re-explore it. The front door with its porch and flagpole was for pupils of all ages. So was the panelled hall with its war memorial above the fireplace (caps off) and then, through the central arch, those mica-sparkling steps down to the Gym and basement. There was diversity too, with three areas approached by stairs from street level: Prep classes to the left, with infant classrooms on the ground floor; Junior classes at the rear of the Hall; and Upper School on the right, past the Prefects' Room… "Progress" was the great object, judging by reports which went home every term, and we did progress – up and down these stairways, day by day and year by year. The walls gave a dark impression of bygone sporting heroes, carefully posed, but the modern uniform was bright: scarlet blazers as resplendent as Hussars' tunics lightened the gloomiest recess. White shirts and shorts for

123. *Terraced houses in Melville Street.*

summer days added to the cheerful effect. It is easy to feel nostalgic for that small school in Edinburgh.'

An Academy boarder of the same era developed a similar awareness on the edge of the school's playing-field: 'When I arrived at Mackenzie House it turned out to be the first step in what has become a lifelong interest in buildings and the built environment. To a nine year old, the first impression was one of scale. The tall building could indeed, from some angles, resemble a castle, but it also had nooks and corners which appealed to the imagination. It was obviously different from all the other buildings on the Academy estate. Whereas the main school's simple classical lines were a reflection of the New Town, Mackenzie House was

124. *Mackenzie House.*

rugged and bold. From the lowest depths of its cavernous cellar and boiler room to the "sick dorm" high up in the roof, with a magnificent panoramic view of the city, this was a special place. The details were fascinating too: the wooden carved dog and the motto "Cave Canem" on the newel post of the house master's stairs, the teak and brass fittings in the kitchen...'

Finally Fettes. Although 'one actually lived' for fourteen hours a day in House, David Bryce's building was central: 'The first impression a visitor has of Fettes is gravel. It is certainly one of the most striking features of the place to a "new man". If he is posted to one of the "outhouses", he soon becomes familiar with the treacherous stuff as he struggles up to College with a load of books, or races down to House after breakfast to complete some chore or ill-prepared piece of prep. Those in the College Houses are spared such daily perambulations, but learn instead to detect from the roaring engine and slithering wheels the identity of each passing car and its owner. College itself is impressive to a small boy, especially the contrast between the rabbit warren of corridors on the ground floor where the plebeian throng hurry to and fro and the spacious quiet of the "quarterdeck"... Here masters and School Prefects walk undisturbed, along with Sixth Formers visiting the Library.' From premises it is but a step to ethos and atmosphere, these being classic images of a boys' boarding-school. It was soon to be altered for ever by the arrival of girls.

Chapter 12

Boys and Girls at School

The separation of boys and girls was more or less taken for granted in Edinburgh fee-paying schools, yet there was an example of something different to hand in John Watson's School. The austere grandeur of the Hospital building has been celebrated, and its development into a boarding 'Institution' may be briefly conveyed. Tidying-up proposals were made for turning John Watson's either into a boys' school or a girls' one at the time of the Colebrooke Commission, but children of both sexes continued in residence. As with other schools founded on charitable principles, the social level crept upwards. Writers to the Signet presided over the board of directors, and at a time when the roll had yet to rise above double figures twenty-five pupils were the children of lawyers. Almost as many came from the homes of medical doctors and ministers of religion. By no means all fathers of foundationers were deceased, although hardship cases – from the middle classes – were given priority. Boys regularly completed their education elsewhere and there were Fettes Foundation scholarships for some. Newspapers praised a George Square girl who won a scholarship to Oxford but failed to mention that nearly all her schooling had been at John Watson's.

Brothers and sisters attending together did not create much of a family atmosphere in the early days. Up to the last war they were only allowed an hour together each week, on Sunday afternoons in the entrance hall. There were boys' and girls' 'sides' in classrooms as well as dormitories, and also distinct roles – even in common enterprises: 'The main task of the Scouts was to bring order out of chaos in the Kiddern, a stretch of

125. *Clearing the Kiddern, or Kidron.*

woodland sloping down behind the playgrounds to the Water of Leith. That monumental project continued on and off for years, during which time the Scouts shifted tons of earth and stones… The Guides kept tidy the paths.' Boys also laboured to create rugby and hockey pitches in front of the school, and they alone were subjected to a cold plunge after an early morning run round them. Even drama (elsewhere due to become a unifying activity for the sexes) was divided between 'the presentation of burlesque or farce by the boys and pantomime by the girls.'

A break with the past was provided by seven years at Marchmont House near Duns during the Second World War, the Belford Road premises having been taken over by military personnel who were slow to leave. Reminiscences are of a freer time: 'Mixed team competitions became popular. We boys joined in hockey practice and, come the summer, some girls showed considerable aptitude at batting and bowling.' But rugby matches against Borders teams, coached by a Welsh teacher surnamed John, were taken more seriously. On returning to Edinburgh John Watson's was undefeated for two years against equivalent teams from boarding schools like Merchiston and day schools like George Watson's. 'Equivalent' meant up to age fifteen, although older pupils soon joined the school.

What follows in this final chapter is only partly about the retreat from single-sex education. John Watson's also serves as an introduction to the parallel theme of non-state schools struggling to survive in difficult times. The post-war mood, however, was one of optimism. In the Fifties foundationers were joined by fee-paying boarders at Belford Road, and a steadily increasing number of day boys and girls were added. A roll of 125 at the start of the decade neared the four hundred mark by its end, with JWS presenting pupils for Highers as a senior secondary school. Meanwhile the starting age of nine had been lowered to five. In contrast to earlier staff-turnover, good teachers came and stayed. Expansion brought problems of accommodation and costly building, with science laboratories required, but it was the return of a Labour government in 1974 which led to closure. In March of the following year the Secretary of State for Scotland announced the end of financial support for grant-aided schools. The school's directors made their decision three weeks before the summer holidays, and it came as a great shock to pupils, teachers and parents. *The Scotsman*'s main headline for 17 June 1975 was 'Closure Blow for John Watson's.'

Other Edinburgh fee-paying schools had also been facing a discouraging financial situation linked to politics, but the first great change to affect the Royal High School had nothing to do with it. A decision to abandon Thomas Hamilton's classical building below the Calton Hill (where overcrowding had become 'chronic' despite various makeshifts) was made on educational grounds in 1962. At least thirty-four more classrooms were needed when the Council's Education Committee agreed on a move to the suburb of Barnton. Five years later the new building was ready with its many improvements for teaching and learning, although an article in *Schola Regia* expressed the view that it was 'modelled on the celebrated Swan Vestas matchbox'. Architecture and aesthetics apart, a second great change was imminent: the High School was on course to leave the fee-paying sector.

There were seven local authority fee-paying schools in Edinburgh, with the same number in Glasgow and others elsewhere in Scotland. Trinity Academy which charged nominal fees of £15 a year was co-educational at primary and secondary levels. The others (including James Gillespie's Boys' School – no significant connection with the better known girls' school) were for primary pupils. Before the move to Barnton sixty boys were admitted annually to the High School's Preparatory Department at Jock's Lodge out of about 240 who were presented for testing at age five. They usually progressed to the senior school on the basis of their normal class work. A similar proportion of one in four had hitherto gained places for entry to the first year of secondary education at Regent Road. Fees of £41 to £44 per session were about half those charged for the Merchant Company schools.

Politics came in through the unpopularity of England's Eleven Plus and Scotland's primary seven Qualifying test. Consigning the great majority of pupils to secondary modern schools rather than grammar schools (in England) and to junior secondaries in Scotland, had increasingly come into question. Harold Wilson's Labour government took office in November 1964 and local authorities were soon being required to draw up plans for ending selection. 'Comprehensive' schools were created out of Edinburgh's junior secondaries, for the most part, and attention turned to the Royal High as the representative of a highly selective form of education for boys.

During the lead-up to the Education (Scotland) Act of 1970 which ended fee-paying in local authority schools there was resistance by parents, former pupils and also by the Tory group which had a narrow majority on Edinburgh District Council – all to no avail. With fees no longer being paid there was an end to selection as well. The High School's relation to Jock's Lodge was now a remote one although visiting PE and RE teachers from Barnton took classes. After a transitional year in which all parents who requested secondary places for their sons were accommodated, the Preparatory Department became a local primary school. The Royal High at Barnton settled into its new role as a neighbourhood comprehensive in a notably middle-class neighbourhood. The final great change, after a delay for necessary building work, was when girls were admitted into first year classes at the start of the 1973–4 session. Six years later the school was fully co-educational.

When the government decided to freeze the level of financial support to schools outside the state sector there were twenty-nine grant-aided schools in Scotland, equivalent to England's direct grant schools. That meant no improvement was to be expected (despite rising costs) on the forty per cent of total expenditure met for Merchant Company schools. The figure varied (depending on endowments) for Heriot's, John Watson's, Melville and St Mary's Cathedral Choir School. The last of these was able to come to an agreement as a special case and it is now St Mary's Music School. Temporary relief was obtained after Edward Heath's Conservative Party formed a government in June 1970, with a rise in grant promised for the following session, but schools were already consulting together about an uncertain future and the possibilities of working along with local authorities. The two elections of 1974 returned Labour to power, more firmly after the second, and the announcement that grant aid would be withdrawn altogether by stages had the effect of closing John Watson's School.

Before any more of the grant-aided schools come under consideration, it is worth pausing to consider the effect of very high post-war birth rate known as the 'bulge'. From the early Fifties until the end of the following decade and beyond, large classes and teacher shortages encouraged parents to look for better education in fee-paying schools. John Highet's *A School of One's Choice*, published in 1969, showed that the pressure of demand on these was much higher than in the inter-war period, with rising rolls and tighter selection. Highet's interviews with parents revealed high levels of tension: 'One woman didn't speak to me for years because her son didn't get in and mine did.' (Stewart's mother) 'There was a lot of neighbourhood ill-feeling and resentment when we got in. People previously friendly scarcely even nod to us now.' (Royal High mother) 'There's real nail-biting tension. People regard it as a matter of life and death.' (Heriot's mother).

For their part the schools struggled to cope with demand in different circumstances. The admission of day pupils by John Watson's has been noted. Heriot's spent much of the Sixties seeking permission to create extra accommodation while satisfying the Royal Fine Art Commission that the 'wark' was fully visible from all directions including the Castle esplanade. Melville might have taken over the Academy building (when a move from Henderson Row to Inverleith was under consideration) or the vacated High School one at Regent Road. Both offered more space but not many more places, and it was decided not to move. Another house was added to the Melville Street premises and the roll rose by forty per cent in a decade to 563. At the start of the Seventies, however, it was a drop in Melville's primary one intake which led to negotiations with the Merchant Company over merger with Stewart's on the Queensferry Road site.

In the case of George Watson's, Edinburgh University's planned expansion into George Square prompted a different kind of merger. The decision to move out was taken before there was any political or financial pressure, but at first it was assumed that a new girls' school would be built on the University playing-field at Craiglockhart. Hilda Fleming (the last head-mistress at the Square) made the case early for a more straightforward – but radical – solution, that of joining the boys at Colinton Road. During the first year of the war part-time education had been provided there for boys and girls of the two South Side Merchant Company schools. (A similar arrangement was made at Stewart's.) By the time the threat of 'comprehensivisation' began make itself felt at the two Watson's colleges, with grant aid likely to be withdrawn, the Company's Education Board announced its intention 'within the foreseeable future to make provision for co-education.' *The Scotsman* of 4 July 1967 welcomed the 'recognition that fee-paying schools should adapt themselves to changing social conditions, even if it means becoming more like local authority schools.' It was thought that a co-educational George Watson's College would be more acceptable to government, and six years later parents of both schools

were told that the Scottish Education
Department had accepted the proposal.

Much remained to be done, in particular
the creation of a Home Economics Department at Colinton Road. It was to serve first
and second year boys as well as girls, with
cookery, fabrics and technical subjects taught
to both sexes as in comprehensive schools. At
the start of session 1974–75 senior girls
attended the first joint school assembly and
joined in singing the new hymn *Ex Corde
Caritas.* Their final year was spent at George
Square under Miss Fleming, now Associate
Principal of George Watson's College. Mean-

126. *Martha Kearney, GWC
Founder's Day speaker.*

while Principal Roger Young was seeing to the preparation of Colinton Road
for 'the amalgamation'. That summer the Founder's Day address was given
by Lady Tweedsmuir, to the amazement of some diehard Watsonians since
she was the first ever female speaker for the occasion.

A new block for primaries one to three was completed in time to house
the youngest pupils in Scotland's largest co-educational school: 450 Lower
Primary in thirteen classes, 600 Upper Primary and 1,400 in the Senior
School. It opened at the start of session 1975–76. Watson's went on to
become Britain's largest independent school when the grant money ceased
to be paid. Several years later children were still being turned away, despite
rising fees. Co-education advanced under different aspects. The former
boys' and girls' houses were joined under hyphenated names, as Cockburn-
Greyfriars. According to a press report, in their first term together the boys
were 'quieter, more polite – the girls less giggly and silly'. Staff had more
adjusting to do than pupils in implementing a complex timetable. With
mixed classes the decision was taken to end corporal punishment, but not
before a senior boy was given six of the best by the deputy head for riding
his motor bike across the grass in front of the main school. It is now a girls'
hockey pitch. A first group photograph of the Hockey XI appeared in *The
Watsonian*, albeit at half the size of the Rugby XV and Cricket XI.

Meanwhile pressure had been growing on the two Merchant Company
schools on the other side of town: Stewart's (strengthened by Melville) and

Mary Erskine – the former Queen Street school now in spacious grounds at Ravelston. The Company assured parents that both would continue as single-sex schools, guaranteeing a choice between that tradition and co-educational George Watson's, but there were difficulties. Comprehensive schools (because of their size and range of courses) had just been given a new promotion structure for teachers by the Scottish Education Department, with career/guidance posts in addition to subject ones. Stewart's Melville was big enough to do the same but Mary Erskine only just managed to achieve the necessary six hundred pupils (primary and secondary) in the summer of 1973. A substantial pay rise for Scottish teachers then had to be passed on to Merchant Company parents. Labour victories in the elections of the following year left these two schools facing a stark choice.

In February 1975 a remarkable two thousand parents and teachers gathered in the hall at Stewart's Melville to hear about projected fee rises which would take the school into full independence, set against the possibility of integrating one or both schools with the Lothian Region's educational system. Six days later a Merchant Company Schools Parents' Association was formed at an Assembly Hall meeting in George Street. A newsletter then explained the problem: 'The Merchant Company's total income represents a very small percentage of the budget required to finance the running of the three Schools… Annual expenditure is in the order of £2.14 million, of which 24% is the government grant, now frozen at its 1973 level at which time it represented 40% of the then annual costs.'

The Company's Education Board then consulted with local MPs and education leaders before announcing its intention (near the end of the first merged session at Watson's) to open a second co-educational school at Stewart's Melville. The Mary Erskine buildings and site, valued at £2.75 million, would be offered for sale to the local authority. Headmistress Jean Thow's annual report revealed a state of confusion: 'During the summer term there has been continuous manoeuvring of parents with children in Senior II at Ravelston to transfer their daughters to join brothers at Watson's and of parents at Colinton Road to quit the larger school for Ravelston.' Mary Erskine staff were told they need not fear for their jobs. Parents were told that the school's name and uniform and single-sex status would be retained during the first six years of Region control, but it looked as if Mary Erskine would be the second grant-aided Edinburgh school to fall after John Watson's.

The greatest of the grant-aided schools was Heriot's which had 1,544 boys in 1970, the year when Dr Dewar reached retiring age and was succeeded by his deputy head. Led by Allan MacDonald, Heriot's joined the Merchant Company schools in a fight for survival. Parental support, taken

for granted down all the years of low fees, now had to be cultivated. The level of support was already high among Heriot's parents, as Dewar had demonstrated to Professor David Donnison and his Public Schools' Commissioners (visiting Scotland) through a positive 92 per cent questionnaire response from mainly middle class households. Fees rose twice more but the roll reached 1,590 in 1975. By then a parents' association had been formed, giving the governors confidence to announce that if grant aid was withdrawn 'every endeavour would be made for the school to continue, even to the extent of going independent.'

127. *Dr Dewar of Heriot's.*

Heriot's parents attended public protest meetings along with those of other schools, but when talks were held with representatives of the Merchant Company it became evident that any sort of 'consortium' arrangement – with Watson's for example – was impractical. Heriot's would have to go it alone. The situation was complicated by the school's links with the local authority (Edinburgh's Lord Provost had always chaired the board of governors) and Labour members – under one of their own as chairman – made a sustained attempt to take control. A 'Hands Off Heriot's' campaign built up (former rugby internationalists prominent) as FPs' and parents' representatives made their views known to central and local government. Out of his Olympian retirement Dr Dewar wrote to *The Scotsman* on 9 February 1979 on the question of the Founder's intentions:

'Heriot had in mind the less fortunate members of his own merchant class in Edinburgh… When the hospital system was ended in 1886 and the hospital became a day-school, the elaborate provision for "fatherless bairnes" was continued and given an absolute priority in the endowment. At the same time a full secondary division was created complete with science laboratories and technical workshops; bursaries, both entrance and free-place, were provided on the basis of need… Until very recently

… one boy in every five at the top of the school was being educated free…
If today school fees are increasingly beyond the means of a growing
number of homes, this is in no way due to any change in policy on the part
of the governors. It stems directly – and inexorably – from the action of
Government in 1975 in freezing and phasing out the grant-in-aid.'

Within a few months help was at hand following Margaret Thatcher's
first election victory at the head of the Conservative party, although there
was still a local battle to be fought before Heriot-minded governors
regained their numerical advantage over regional councillors. Instead of
restoring grant aid the government introduced an assisted-places scheme
in 1981 for parents on low income. Aimed at pupils of secondary age, the
scheme was taken up by all Scotland's former grant-aided schools including the Merchant Company ones of Edinburgh, but it was particularly
suited to the traditions of George Heriot's school. Numbers there had
been falling during the Seventies so that (encouraged by the example of
co-educational George Watson's) 112 girls were admitted at the start
of the 1979–80 session. They have since achieved parity in all areas of
school life.

To complete the Merchant Company story, for Mary Erskine parents the
1975 decision to integrate with local authority schools appeared to mean
six years of Merchant Company education without fees. Also positive in
the short run, there was a boost to the rolls of both north side schools
through the enrolment of John Watson's pupils – an event referred to in
the annals of Stewart's Melville as 'that other lesser merger'. Ninety-four
new boys moved from Belford Road to Queensferry Road and a similar
number of girls to Ravelston. At the level of rumour it was said that
Lothian would rather have been offered George Watson's – the Royal
High School at Barnton already provided many places for the north-west
suburbs – but it was in the nature of a bombshell when the Secretary of
State blocked the purchase of Mary Erskine (cost thought likely to
outweigh the benefits) in a letter of 10 December 1975. A further Lothian
Region attempt failed in January of the following year.

The girls' school was now forced to follow the boys into a state of
'endowed independence' at a time when the roll had begun to decline.
Meanwhile Stewart's Melville experienced an eighteen-month period of
uncertainty under an acting head. Then in January 1976 Robin Morgan

was appointed Principal of Stewart's Melville College. Once a history teacher at George Watson's, he had been persuaded to exchange a secure post in charge of Campbell College, Belfast, for an uncertain future in Edinburgh. A 'twinning' arrangement with Mary Erskine, some way short of what had originally been planned by way of merger, was entered into at the start of his third session: 'On the 2nd October 1978, my 48th birthday as it happened, I became Principal of The Mary Erskine School and one of the few men in history to receive 800 girls as a birthday present.' Apart from joint activities in drama, music and outdoor education, the structure began (and still does) with a nursery and infant department for boys and girls at Ravelston leading on to a Combined Junior School at Queensferry Road: co-education for younger children on two sites. Secondary classes for boys and girls are taught separately on the two campuses, maintaining the tradition of single-sex education for adolescents, but the sixth form is mixed (again making use of both campuses) as a preparation for the college life which lies ahead.

At first Robin Morgan's manner did not go down well with the Mary Erskine staff on the two days a week he spent at Ravelston sending them memos, and the position of Principal Jean Thow became untenable. She

128. *Patrick Tobin, Jean Thow and Robin Morgan.*

retired, to be succeeded by a deputy headmistress. Morgan was old-fashioned in his enthusiasm for CCF activities (including shooting at Bisley) but even girls were persuaded to enlist. His attitude towards them might have been thought patronising or even chauvinist, but it seems to have worked: 'When I took over the Mary Erskine School I had my fair share of misconceptions about girls and girls' schools. I have jettisoned them all. I am a complete convert to the Mary Erskine brand of feminism, that is a blend of quite militant sex egalitarianism with a gracious femininity. My girls are all perfect ladies until you suggest that they are in any way inferior to the boys. I am so proud of my girls. They have never fallen short of my increasing expectations of them. They have never let me down.' In 1989 Morgan was followed as Principal of the two schools by Patrick Tobin, who later advanced a justification of the combined approach in his memoirs.

So far the focus has been all on schools in receipt of government money. Soon after coming to power the Wilson government set up a Public Schools Commission to look at ways of bringing independent schools into the national system. However the Donnison Report of 1970 made no difference. Having survived a difficult decade of challenge to authority the three boarding-schools and the Academy were if anything less stressed than before. The move towards co-education began at the least likely one, it might be thought – given the manly Spartan traditions of Fettes. It began inconspicuously with three Lansdowne House girls joining Upper Sixth science classes and leaving when the teacher did. The following year a governor's daughter was accepted as a day pupil for her final year, creating a male : female ratio of 440 : 1 – although she was joined by a friend at half-term. The example of accepting girls into sixth form begun at Marlborough at the end of the Sixties was then followed by other schools as a matter of policy. With nearly seventy applicants for the seventeen places allotted to them by 1974, the early female Fettesians were clever enough to improve the Oxford and Cambridge results. They also had self-assurance and good looks – loutishness readily repelled – and their sixth form presence reached forty by the end of the decade:

'Some of the cruel or philistine features of traditional school life had gone into retreat before the relentless questionings of the 1960s. As girls came in with greater maturity and found boys behaving like bullies or tyrants, they tended to point this out, and it all helped to stop the barbarities of the past reappearing… There was, of course, the danger that masters unused to teaching girls would over-indulge them. Many were quite unsure how to treat them, especially if they were out of line… Boy-girl problems never ran ostentatiously out of control, and no couples were found *flagrante delicto*, although methods of detection were probably far from perfect… The first girls were attached to Glencorse House, then to Carrington and then, as numbers grew, to other houses. But since the School had started with one girl, no one had really got down to dictating their life-style by any formal structure, and some boys resented the way they dressed as they liked…'

A well-attended debate having rejected by a massive majority the motion that 'This House believes that the introduction of girls has been a disaster,' it was no surprise when a December 1978 poll returned a 56 per cent

129. *Fourteen sixth form girls at Fettes.*

majority in favour of all-through co-education – and this despite the fact that only 25 per cent of the girls were for it. As one of them later told a journalist, 'For me Fettes was bliss from start to finish. I felt desperately special.' Opinions of pupils apart, it was a dip – quite widespread – in boarding numbers which lay behind the support of incoming headmaster Cameron Cochrane for co-education.

Nine months' notice was given for the admission of day girls into all levels of the Junior School in 1981–82, with the Senior School welcoming teenage boarders in the following session. Sixties-built Arniston House was earmarked for conversion to study-bedrooms, and when the level of applications proved higher than expected School House was also partly (and later fully) made over to the use of girls. Housemistresses were appointed. By 1988 girls made up 43 per cent of a school population which was as high as it had ever been. Exam results improved and the cultural life of Fettes was in fine condition. Corporal punishment was abandoned by masters as well as boys and 'muddied oafs' marvelled at the new Astroturf pitch for girls' hockey. *Floreas Fettesia* can still be sung for the school which opened a co-ed upper sixth form house in 2007:

'The work ethic remains strong. Excessive intimacy between the sexes has not, on the face of it, been a problem. The number of identifiable "couples" seems actually to have declined. Proximity, it seems, can take the heat out of some relationships… Entrants into the House bring with them seven different sets of house rules and conventions, which then have to be tactfully merged into some kind of common practice. In one girls' house, for example, girls had tended to relax during the evenings in pyjamas or wrapped in duvets. This was deemed inappropriate for a mixed house. After an initial period, discipline has been subtly relaxed in small ways, to provide "sensible freedoms".'

For the rest it may be enough to say that Merchiston has also opened an upper sixth house for its boys with magnificent views and circulating doors fit for a department store. The premises are made secure by key codes and en suite quarters are of such quality as to ensure discontent when exchanged for a university hall. Loretto admitted its first girls in 1986 at sixth form level and then throughout over a ten-year period. The closure of Oxenfoord Castle School for Girls' in East Lothian was followed by the arrival of girls of all ages. The 'Nippers' House is now for boys and girls aged three to twelve, and above that level there are two girls' boarding houses (younger and older) and two boys' ones. For some time now the Academy has admitted girls at the top of the school without the proportion ever reaching one in four. Music and drama have benefited considerably, sports hardly at all though one girl fought her way into the hockey team. By chance I was in the lunch hall at the start of session 2008–9 when girls were first admitted at all levels. Their numbers were quite meagre but will surely grow.

On 16 February 2009 (as economic downturn threatened to become re-cession) *The Scotsman* offered an 'exclusive' to its readers. According to Education Correspondent Fiona MacLeod, 'Independent schools in Scot-land are cutting staff and delaying building projects as they brace them-selves for cash-strapped parents removing their children in droves … Headteachers fear that job losses in well-paid industries, such as banking, will force parents to withdraw pupils as school fees put too much pressure on household budgets. With Edinburgh having a high proportion of children at fee-paying schools – about 25 per cent of secondary pupils – and many parents working in the beleaguered finance sector, the city's schools are expected to be hit hard.' Local heads who had been asked to comment agreed that this was no time for large expenditure on buildings. Watson's Gareth Edwards was content that the swimming pool which had been such a feature of modern school architecture at Colinton Road could still serve a while longer. David Gray, for Stewart's Melville, reported that the College's senior and junior departments were both full and added: 'We have no borrowings and therefore we are in a robust position.'

Frank Gerstenberg, whose sixteen years in charge of George Watson's ended in 2001, is a regular contributor to *The Scotsman*. Good on detail, he drew attention to the difficulty facing schools which had to budget and set fee levels ahead of session while taking precautions against a reduction in numbers: 'The withdrawal of one or two pupils from different years and different classes does not permit a school to dispense with the services of any teachers – and staffing represents a school's largest cost.' However Gerstenberg stressed that parents would be very reluctant to withdraw their children. Lower mortgage payments were liable to help, and grandparents might well choose to pay school fees rather than invest their capital at 'derisory rates of interest'. Edwards, his successor at Watson's, was ready to wait and see: 'The proof of the pudding will come in the beginning of a school year in September and actually how many children we have.'

As this book goes to press there has been nothing more of an exclusive nature to report. *The Scotsman*'s investigation has not been resumed – either that or there is no story. Rising numbers in the private sector have featured regularly in recent years at a time of falling school rolls in Scotland as a whole. A reduction, as forecast in February, would make headlines. Instead the front page on 29 August carried PRIVATE SCHOOLS SET NEW EXAMS RECORD. This amounted to an update of the evidence discussed at the end of Chapter 5, with comparisons made at the top levels of performance. Half of the A-grade passes in the Higher Leaving Certificate were gained by pupils from fee-paying schools. In a second form of comparison (A–C grades) 'George Heriot's School in Edinburgh topped the league table with 95.6 per cent of candidates passing their Highers'. In consideration of those days when only a few Heriot's 'hopeful scholars' aimed at university – and it was recommended that they should do so via the High School – no greater transformation can have taken place.

The change most obvious to the passer-by in Lauriston Place is that half the pupils are kilt-wearing Heriot's girls, and it would not be surprising to find that their exam successes have nudged even higher than the boys'. At any rate there can be no doubt about the success of co-education in Edinburgh's private sector. Parental choice having come into fashion even for state schools, however, it would be wrong to understate the importance of Merchiston – now a boys-only day school as well as a boarding institution. There is still a niche market for what is on offer there.

But it must be acknowledged that most parents no longer care deeply about single-sex education. A headmistress drew attention (after that other book had been finished) to a significant factor: 'dropping-off' arrangements, whereby it is simply more convenient to deliver sons and daughters to the same school. Changed days from my childhood when even the youngest primary school pupils crossed town by tram or bus with only the conductor for protection. Perhaps the new tram system, and the continuing preference given to public transport, will benefit private schools in years to come.

Edinburgh's fee-paying schools will survive the credit crunch, as it appears. With public spending cuts high on the agenda, they may also be allowed to avoid the front line of debate – out of the firing line, in other words. At a personal level, however, it is to be hoped that those who have read thus far will in future rise above social labelling in response to that old question, 'Which school did you go to?'

Index